SPEEDWAY
IN BRISTOL
1928-1949

SPEEDWAY
IN BRISTOL
1928-1949

ROBERT BAMFORD & JOHN JARVIS

TEMPUS

First published 2006

Tempus Publishing Limited
The Mill, Brimscombe Port,
Stroud, Gloucestershire, GL5 2QG
www.tempus-publishing.com

British Library Cataloguing in Publication Data.
A catalogue record for this book is available from the British Library.

ISBN 0 7524 3788 7

Typesetting and origination by Tempus Publishing Limited
Printed in Great Britain

CONTENTS

Acknowledgements   6

The Douglas Connection   7

Knowle Stadium   10

1928   12

1929   21

1930   36

1936   55

1937   71

1938   98

1939   124

1946   146

1947   160

1948   190

1949   224

ACKNOWLEDGEMENTS

The authors wish to express their grateful thanks to Billy Douglas, great grandson of William, for all his help in compiling the story of his wonderful family. Without his invaluable assistance, it would have been impossible to complete what is an integral part of the history of dirt-track racing in Bristol. Grateful thanks are also due to Glynn Shailes, Trevor Davies and Hugh Vass for their invaluable help in the compilation of this book. Acknowledgement is made to the photographers whose images help to complete the story of speedway in Bristol. These are: the Wright Wood archive, courtesy of John Somerville; Ralph Jackson; T.H. Everitt; J.P.B. Shelley; C.F. Wallace; F. Fowler; Stan Vicars. Acknowledgement is also made to *Speedway Star* magazine and the various speedway year-books.

THE DOUGLAS CONNECTION

John Douglas was the first member of the family to settle in Bristol. Born in 1833, probably in the Greenock area of Scotland, it is believed that he had an elder brother (William Douglas, born 1816), a sister (Jane Douglas, born 1815) and possibly a younger sister or cousin (Catherine), whose children married into the Williamson family in Scotland. The Williamson family appears to have been connected with the motorcycle of the same name, produced around 1912. John Douglas was an engineer and learned his foundry skills in Scotland, but moved to Newcastle-upon-Tyne in order to seek more opportunities. He married a girl from Northumbria and they had two children (Jane and William). The family moved to Barrow-in-Furness for a short time, prior to a permanent move down to Bristol. There they stayed at 22 Redcross Street together with a shoe manufacturer by the name of William Isaac Groom Davis. Mr Davis suggested the need in Bristol for a machine maker to the boot trade and John thus opened his business as 'John Douglas, Boot Maker's Machine Maker' in 1867 at Asher House, 5 Redcross Street. In 1871 the business was described as 'machinist', which indicated a broadening base of the type of work handled. By then there were six children in the family: Jane, William, John Percy, Edwin, Arthur and Catherine. In 1878, John took in a partner and the business became known as Douglas & Williams, Machinists. However, at about the same time, John's health began to fail and he died before the end of the year.

John's eldest son, William, had been born at Newcastle-upon-Tyne in 1859 and he followed in his father's footsteps, entering into the foundry business. When the Redcross Street business failed, he set up a new venture at Two Mile Hill, between St George and Kingswood. Along with his brothers John Percy and Edwin, they rented a workshop for £16 a year and, with a loan of £10, bought a small forge, vice and grindstone. The new business flourished and they were able to repay the loan within three months. William was then living at a place known simply as 'Batch', which was situated at the top of Old Market Street. On 24 December 1875, William married Eliza (later known as Elizabeth) Davis, the eldest daughter of his father's friend William Isaac Groom Davis. The census for 1881 reported William as a 'master engineer, employing five men and two boys' and that he was then living at 27A Old Market Street. By 1882, the business was called 'Douglas Brothers – Mechanical Engineers, Brass and Iron Founders'. Among other things, the company produced street gas lampposts and manhole covers. The company needed room to expand, but had run out of space at the Two Mile Hill premises, so William found a new site off the main road in Kingswood, in what was then Hanham Lane. They then built a new and larger factory on the east side of the road, while still operating at the Two Mile Hill works. The year was 1897 and the company was then known as 'Douglas Brothers – Boot and Shoe Machinery Manufacturers at Kingswood'.

In 1902, a brick factory was built on the west side of Hanham Lane (later renamed Hanham Road) and this included workshops, offices and a sports ground for the future use of exhibiting motorcycles. Eventually, the 1897 foundry on the east side of Hanham Road was closed down and houses were built in its place. Following the failure of 'Light Motors Limited', William was persuaded by his eldest son William Wilson Douglas to build motorcycles. William Wilson Douglas (born 21 December 1880 and known as Willie) was the first to investigate and follow the progress of Joe Barter with the 'Fairy' motorcycle in Bristol. Initially, William was unwilling to hear about motorcycles, but his enthusiastic son won the day and Joe Barter was engaged to design machines for Douglas at Kingswood. In 1907, the first Douglas motorcycle was produced. The new machine was loosely based on the Fairy, which had been produced by the Light Motors company. Willie took part in trials and in 1911 he was the first Douglas entry in the Isle of Man TT races. It was the beginning of an era. Douglas motorcycles obviously made an impression for, at the outbreak of the First World War in 1914, the firm were summoned by the War Office to supply 300 machines a week! They then set about building a factory in which volume motorcycle production could be achieved.

After the First World War, the Douglas twin led the way in terms of speed and boasted numerous victories in competitive events throughout the world. Indeed, 1923 saw 'Dougies' win the Senior and Sidecar TT races in the Isle of Man. Soon a dirt-track model was developed and these became very popular within the sport, due to the machine being far superior to previous motorcycles, which were not at the Douglas pitch of excellence. On greasy roads, the single cylinders and V-twins were hopelessly left behind by Douglases, for the simple reason that the Bristol-built steed refused to skid. Meanwhile, with cinder tracks booming, it had been found that these non-skidding qualities were the difference between success and failure. A Douglas promotional brochure of the 1920s claimed that theirs was 'the machine that made dirt-track racing popular'. It went on to pose the question of which was most important – the machine, or the rider? Continuing from the brochure, it stated that, 'obviously both do their share, the machine by its power of acceleration, ability to withstand acute banking on corners without turning over etc, and the rider by his knowledge of just how and when to make the most of the slightest opportunity for forging ahead. But there is one thing very certain. The most brilliant dirt-track champion is lost on an indifferent machine, and conversely, the rider who is just "average", quickly finds winning form when he has a mount that can, and will, back up his own efforts. The Douglas dirt-track machine belongs to the latter category.' Later the brochure states, 'due to its low centre of gravity, even weight distribution and perfect balance, it can be "broadsided" at angles that would mean a spill with the single-cylindered mount. The horizontally opposed twin engine develops amazing power – power as silky sweet as that of a turbine. It accelerates with a snap and a surge. Speaking of this acceleration, one well-known rider said that it was akin to being sucked up by a gigantic vacuum cleaner. Above all, it is reliable – it gets off the mark, while the others are still pushing – and it keeps going till the "finish" flag is dropped.' The brochure also contained two letters praising the Douglas dirt-track machine; one was from Stewie St George and the other from Sig Schlam, both, of course, very famous riders of the time. A list of Douglas riders was also included, which featured the likes of Ivor Creek, Larry Coffey, Sprouts Elder, brothers Roger and Buster Frogley, Billy Galloway, Vic Huxley, Syd Jackson, Keith McKay, Drew McQueen, George McKenzie, Len Parker, Arthur Sherlock, Skid Skinner and Fay Taylour. William Douglas, the founder of Douglas Brothers Engineering, a greatly respected man, known affectionately as 'the Guv'nor', died on 22 April 1937. Four members of the Douglas family rode at Knowle in the 1928-1930 period, these being Edwin (known as Teddie) and William (known as Billy), who were the sons of Willie (1880-1923) and John (known as Jack) and his brother James (known as Jim), who were the sons of Willie's brother John (1885-1937).

KNOWLE STADIUM

Knowle Stadium was described as a superb walled sports arena, ahead of its time and situated in the glorious surrounds of the local landscape. The remarkable story of the construction of Knowle Stadium, in just eleven weeks, was headlined as an exemplary achievement. With the removal of 100,000 tons of soil and stone from the fifteen acres of land, one of the best greyhound tracks in the West gradually took shape. The one-and-a-half miles of fencing and the all-surveying grandstand created employment for local workmen. A palatial car park, big enough to accommodate 1,500 cars, added to the magnificent spectacle. The total cost of it all amounted to £30,000 in the non-inflated currency of the pre-Second World War days. A large and enthusiastic crowd from all parts of Bristol and the West gathered for the grand opening on 23 July 1927, when congratulations were in order to Mr Albert Ford, whose dog Plunger came in at 4-1 to win the first race. Dirt-track meetings of an exploratory nature had already been staged earlier that year in Britain. At Camberley, Surrey, on heath land overlooked by the military college, the local motor club staged what was then billed as the 'First British dirt-track meeting' on 7 May. Then, on 25 June, under the organisation of Harrison Gill, the South Manchester Motor Club staged a meeting on a 600-yard cinder track at Dodd's Farm, Droylsden. That same year, a crude form of cinder-track racing took place on a quarter-mile track at the rear of a public house on the Wellingborough to Kettering road, The Half Way House. An attempt to stage a meeting at High Beech in Epping Forest on 9 November 1927 was thwarted by the ACU ruling body, as it contravened the Lord's Day Observance Society regulations concerning meetings on the Sabbath other than purely club functions. That proved to only be a temporary setback, however, as ACU approval was granted for the Ilford Motorcycle and Light Car Club to stage a meeting at High Beech, for club members only, on 19 February 1928. This has since been widely regarded as the first 'official' dirt-track meeting in Britain. Tracks sprang up everywhere after that and it was no surprise when the local newspapers announced, on 16 July, that the Knowle greyhound course was to be adapted for motorcycle racing. Bristol had been on the cinder-track list for some time, but nothing definite had previously been announced. Once it had been decided the sport was Bristol-bound, the promoters didn't have long to get ready for the new thrill, which had already been exploited at the likes of Audenshaw, Greenford, Post Hill (Leeds), Nelson (Glasgow), Bradford (Shelf Moor), Blackpool, Celtic Park (Glasgow), Halifax, Stamford Bridge, Marine Gardens (Edinburgh), Crystal Palace, White City (London), Mansfield, Wimbledon, Harringay, Barnsley, Wolverhampton and White City (Manchester) to name but a few of many venues. Mr W.H.E. Millman, editor of *Conrod*, the Douglas magazine, was very keen on the new sport, and the company's journal for the month of July was indeed devoted to dirt-track racing. This entertaining journal had many articles, for instance 'Dusting the dirt' and 'Cinder sifting' and there was a wonderful assertion of the new cinder-track enterprise, making it a must for those interested in the sport. The magazine also gave dates and details of forthcoming meetings and many superb portrait and action photographs. On 20 July 1928, it was announced by Mr T.H. Dickinson that dirt-track motorcycle racing would be in full swing at Knowle in August. He duly arrived in Bristol to take charge of the construction and general arrangements at the stadium. Mr Dickinson represented the British Dirt-Track Racing Association (BDTRA), and informed a *Bristol Evening News* representative that the dirt-track would be situated inside the greyhound circuit. He also stated that a local contractor would carry out the construction, and that all the 'crack' riders would participate in the sport when it opened at the circuit. Mr Dickinson was quoted as saying, 'As many as 60,000 spectators have attended one meeting in Manchester, and local riders will take part in the Knowle events. All will be given a sporting chance and there will be an opportunity for preliminary practices.' On 23 July, it was reported that the Knowle Stadium had been apportioned for up to two days per week for dirt-track racing. The races were to be held under ACU rules, and as much as £60 per week could be earned by those who got proficient in the art of skidding around the corners and getting a smart pick-up on the straight. The sport was described as a brilliant application of the possibilities of the motorcycle. To crank up the enthusiasm, such experts as Sprouts Elder would be taking part in the races, and there would also be Inter-City track events. The careful grading of competitions would cater for local enthusiasts, so that all would get the fairest of sporting chances. Clearly it would be correct to say that the opening of the Knowle track was awaited with eager anticipation.

1928

The amount of interest taken in the new dirt-track sport was evident at Knowle for the first meeting on 25 August, since a large crowd was present to witness the proceedings on the 344-yard raceway. The officials present were: E. Featherstone (ACU steward), M. Browning (BDTRA steward), W. Millman (judge), T. Dickinson (clerk of the course), B. Baxter (starter), C. King, L. Jacobs and V. Anstice (competitors' marshals) and G. Jenkins (timekeeper). Proceedings commenced with a short opening ceremony, during which Alderman F. Moore (acting as deputy Lord Mayor) explained that the Lord Mayor was unable to attend as he was away on holiday. Revealing a good sense of humour, Mr Moore went on to point out that he had had some hesitation about being present for fear that he might be asked to ride around the track. This was based on the fact that, nearly fifty years previously, he had ridden a penny farthing with great difficulty! He also hoped that the proceedings on the track would be carried out in a sportsmanlike manner, that there would be no accidents and that the venture would be a success. A vote of thanks to Alderman Moore was proposed by Mr Millman and seconded by Mr Wolfender from Manchester. Despite suffering from the effects of a broken wrist, ace speedster Stewie St George gave a demonstration of his broadsiding skills. The Kiwi dramatically came down on the first corner and, although he took several more falls, in between he gave a spectacular display, sending the dirt flying onto the terraces as he circumnavigated the new track. An announcement from the official box stated that, owing to rain, the dirt on the corners had got rather hard and it would have to be raked up a tad. That operation was not too successful at first but, undaunted, St George continued to provide the audience with thrill upon thrill. When the racing got underway, the Open Challenge was an entertaining affair, with the six heat winners meeting in the final. Overall victory went the way of the speedy Frank Smith, who just got home ahead of Les 'Smiler' Wotton after a wheel-to-wheel scrap. Mark 'Cyclone' Sheldon had come down from Manchester by aeroplane and he gave a breathtaking broadsiding demonstration. He initially endured machine problems before he had gone halfway around the circuit, but he soon found another steed and his exploits brought round after round of cheering from the enthusiastic onlookers. Later on, Sheldon had a mighty tussle for supremacy with Stewie St George in the International Challenge, but it was the New Zealander who just shaded it in the closing stages. There were six heats in the race for the Bristol Golden Helmet, which was to be competed for every fortnight. The first prize was £15, the golden helmet and an added bonus of £3 a week while holding the helmet! As with the Open Challenge, the six heat victors made it through to the final, which saw Len Parker establish a big lead to triumph ahead of Tommy Webb. In the Inter-City match, home representatives Parker and Wotton got away well, only for the latter to tumble at the first bend. Up front, St George battled past Parker for a stunning win, while Sheldon held off the remounted Wotton to give Manchester a 4-2 success. Billed as individual challenge matches, the three further heats served up more for the spectators to enjoy, including the sight of Sheldon establishing a track-record time of 100.4 seconds in the second race. Sidecar races were also featured in a packed programme, with Parker showing just why he had previously been victorious on three wheels in the 1925 Isle of Man TT event. Prior to that, in 1924, he had actually raced in the very first Senior TT race, then known as the Manx Amateur Road Race Championship. Parker, born in Bath on 30 September 1904, was to go on and win more titles than any other rider at the Knowle raceway.

On 1 September, the racing in meeting number two at Knowle provided plenty of spectacle, not least in heat two of the junior event when E.J. Mountstevens and Vic Anstice were involved in a terrific scrap. The duel ended abruptly when Anstice hit the deck on the first bend of the final lap, leaving his closely following opponent with no option but to ride over the grounded machine. Somehow, he accomplished the feat successfully and kept his seat to win the race. Prior to that, heat one had seen C.P. Clark hold the lead until the last lap, when he partially fell on the last corner. He recovered quickly, but not before D. Cameron had gone past to take victory by a matter of inches. The final saw Cameron lead the field, but after getting out of shape he tumbled on the last lap, leaving the impressive P.C. Smith to win by some distance from Mountstevens. The Challenge Vase gave Aussie Keith McKay the opportunity to demonstrate his broadsiding technique. He also revealed a keen sense of sportsmanship when he slowed up after Bath-born Stanley Gill had fallen on the opening lap, thus allowing his opponent to get back into contention. Heat one of the Senior Handicap saw some brilliant riding from Len Parker. He overhauled W.S. Waycott on the third lap, but the pair collided on the fourth bend, with Gordon Spalding on hand to take advantage and win from Smith, the earlier victor in the junior event. In heat three, McKay came from scratch and after riding furiously to get on terms, he unfortunately got into a wobble on the second bend and crashed into the wire fencing. He remounted, but was unable to finish due to machine problems. In the final, Cameron held sway for a couple of laps, before inexplicably making a mistake and running into the fence, with W. Spencer eventually taking the chequered flag from Spalding. Easily the best rider on the day was Arthur Sherlock of Manchester. Fearless and accomplished, he put up the best time of the meeting in his Golden Gauntlet heat, prior to making an attempt on the existing track record of 100.4 seconds. Cornering magnificently and keeping a wonderful balance, he was at the final bend in 96.0 seconds, only for disaster to strike when he grazed the wire fencing and fell. But for the mishap, it was a dead cert that he would have lowered the record, since he only had a few more yards to travel. In the Golden Gauntlet final, Parker was pressing Sherlock all the way until an untimely fall just before the finish. Mr William Douglas, the founder of Douglas Brothers Engineering, subsequently made the presentation of the trophy to Sherlock. The sidecar races gave the crowd more thrills, especially in heat two when Parker's passenger actually fell out of the outfit on the last lap. In the final, R. Lawson's Ariel overturned on the third lap and although he and his passenger continued on, there was no chance of catching the triumphant G.H. Tucker. Showing good promotional skills, Mr Thelluson, the manager of the greyhound track, staged a hurdle race during the interval and, with great interest shown by many who had not before witnessed the sport, it suggested there would be augmented audiences on dog nights.

The Knowle raceway drew another large crowd on 8 September and everyone present witnessed yet more thrilling racing. The meeting opened with the *Sunday Chronicle* Challenge Trophy, with the winner eligible to compete in a series of semi-finals to be held at the White City circuit in Manchester. Local man Bill Latchem emerged victorious, winning his heat before going on to take the final in great style from S.E. Webb. Prior to that, heat one had seen William 'Holy' Joy hold the lead for two laps, only to overslide spectacularly and put himself out of the race. In the challenge event, Cyclone Sheldon lost a lot of ground at the start but never gave up the chase, eventually losing only by a few yards to 'Old-em' Greenall. An interesting occurrence in heat two of the Senior Handicap saw R.G. Kelly disqualified after crossing the track and going onto the grass. Bath's Len Parker went on to take the final, defeating Tommy Webb by some margin, while Latchem came home in third position. Although the Inter-City challenge ended all square at 3 points apiece, Manchester were declared the winners by virtue of their rider, Arthur Sherlock, taking the race victory. Before the races for the Bristol Golden Helmet, Parker proudly rode around the circuit wearing the coveted trophy to great applause from the enthusiastic crowd. The day's best race just had to feature the man who had won the title in the opening meeting on 25 August and the popular racer didn't let his supporters down. Indeed, he overcame a sluggish start and, after allowing his opponents to build up a substantial lead, somehow reeled them in to amazingly post a fairly comfortable win in the end.

On 15 September, the chief attraction at Knowle lay in Arthur Sherlock's attempt at lowering the existing track record of 100.4 seconds, set by Cyclone Sheldon on 25 August. The Leicester man was successful too, providing a wonderful display of full-throttle racing to establish a new best time of 99.8 seconds for the 344-yard circuit. This followed on from his earlier victory in the Bristol Golden Gauntlet, as he retained the title he had previously won a fortnight earlier. Prior to that, the fans had been treated to some daring stuff from the Douglas-mounted Holy Joy, whose all-action efforts took him to victory in the final of the junior event. It must be said that he was a trifle fortunate, however, as Bill Latchem had led until 200 yards from the flag, only for his machine to lose power and leave him to trundle home in third place. In the Senior Handicap, a last-ditch spurt took Frank Smith to victory in his heat and, clearly inspired, he went on to win the final from Len Parker. It was close though, with the redoubtable Parker chasing all the way and very nearly catching his opponent in a sprint for the line. Cyclone Sheldon again excited those in attendance with his broadsiding skills, but regrettably had to retire from the meeting after crashing in the Senior Handicap final. That meant missing out on his scheduled showdown with Stanley Gill in the challenge event, although Smith was on hand to step in and gleefully add to his earlier triumph in a time of 111.4 seconds. Two sidecar races were programmed, but the one between H.J. Park (Brough Superior) and Jim Douglas (Douglas) was unfortunately cancelled after the former had experienced gearbox trouble. The other race went ahead though, and saw the multi-talented Parker defeat G.H. Tucker with some distance to spare. It was quite evident that members of the fair sex were taking a keen interest in dirt-track racing. In fact, quite a large proportion of the spectators were ladies and they weren't afraid of showing their excitement when the racing was in progress either!

A large crowd, estimated at over 8,000, turned up to witness the fifth meeting at Knowle on 22 September. The big event was the Bristol Golden Helmet, which had been won by Len Parker on its two previous stagings. However, on this occasion, the final saw Arthur Sherlock get away well and hold the lead from the challenging Gordon Spalding. It looked like finishing that way, only for Spalding to overslide on the last lap and allow Parker through for the runner-up spot. As the new holder, Sherlock then rode around the track wearing the Golden Helmet, which had been presented to him by William Douglas. For Sherlock it was a wonderful meeting, since he also took victory against Dick Hayman in the challenge event, as well as winning the Open Handicap. There was some consolation for Parker though, as he blitzed around the raceway to clock a new best time of 98.2 seconds in a successful track-record attempt. The Inter-City match ended in disappointment for the Bristolians when D. Cameron, lying second to Parker, collided with the fence and suffered facial injuries. The spectacular spill allowed Sherlock and Hayman through to force a draw, with Parker taking the winner's flag by the proverbial country mile.

Despite poor weather conditions, a decent crowd still turned out to view the Saturday afternoon fare at Knowle Stadium on 29 September.

Initially there was some doubt as to whether the meeting would go ahead but, after several loads of new ashes had been put down, it was decided to proceed with the racing. The first event was the *News of the World* Challenge Belt and it was evident how difficult track conditions were from the winning times, some of which were in excess of 2 minutes! The final saw Frank Smith make a rapid start and, after establishing his advantage, the exciting racer went on to win by some 20 yards. The circuit had clearly improved by the time Len Parker faced Cyclone Sheldon in a challenge race, as the crowd favourite led from the start and fairly streaked away to clock a new record time of 98.0 seconds. This time was set from a rolling start though, whereas the previous best had been established from a stationary position. Later on in the meeting, however, in an attack on the track record from a standing start, Arthur Sherlock amazingly equalled Parker's record time. Remarkably, in the final event of the day, Parker had another trick up his sleeve and again equalled his own record – in a sidecar outfit! Prior to that, Sherlock had retained the Bristol Golden Gauntlet ahead of Stanley Gill, after Parker had unfortunately suffered engine trouble in the early stages of the final. Well-known entertainer from the Princes' Theatre, George Grossmith, was the guest of honour and he was on hand to make the presentation to a delighted Arthur Sherlock, who had made it three wins out of three in the event.

The Knowle track record was once again under fire in the seventh meeting on 6 October, being lowered on no fewer than three occasions! Arthur Franklyn was the first to beat the clock, in heat four of the *Sunday Chronicle* Trophy, when he was timed at 95.4 seconds. Then, in the second semi-final, he went even quicker to record 94.2 seconds. Finally, the Manchester rider reduced the record time to 94.0 seconds, when taking victory in the Inter-City event. The *Sunday Chronicle* Trophy served up much in the way of entertainment for those in the stadium, with the first semi-final being particularly interesting. This saw George 'Clem' Beckett, Stanley Gill, Felix Dallimore and Holy Joy all come down in the initial running of the race. Joy was the unluckiest of the quartet, since he received a cut finger after somersaulting through the air and couldn't compete in the re-run. Dallimore was also unable to ride, while Beckett couldn't repair his battered machine in time. The super-fast Franklyn was untroubled in the final, taking the flag from Frank Smith, while D. Cameron came home in third place. In an exciting challenge race, Arthur Sherlock got a flying start to head Franklyn. Unfortunately, he lost control and fell, with Franklyn displaying a fine degree of sportsmanship in waiting for his opponent to remount before accelerating to victory. The Golden Helmet gave Franklyn a clean sweep on the day, with Len Parker having to settle for the runner-up position after a forlorn chase. Mr Johnstone, of Layton & Johnstone, the famous duettists from the Bristol Hippodrome, subsequently presented Franklyn with his prize.

Heavy rain rendered the Knowle raceway waterlogged on 10 October, leaving little option but to postpone the scheduled eighth meeting, which would have featured a galaxy of stars, including Clem Beckett, Arthur Sherlock, Billy Dallison and the Taft brothers from Birmingham. This was a great shame as the stadium management had made extensive alterations for the benefit of the public, with the lighting scheme enhanced by the use of powerful arc lamps.

With the weather much improved, local folk turned out in large numbers to enjoy the racing at Knowle Stadium on 13 October, despite the counter attractions of football and other sport in the area. Those present witnessed a number of falls and, while nobody was seriously injured, W.S. Waycott received a knock to the head through hitting the wire fence in the first race of the afternoon and took no further part in the proceedings. Disappointment was caused by the inability of Larry Boulton to participate fully after he had been delayed due to a railway accident at Charfield. The Manchester ace arrived late and without his steed, but did manage to borrow a machine so that he could pit his wits against Arthur Sherlock in a challenge race. Surprisingly, this resulted in a win for Boulton as Sherlock's mount had been left with bent forks from an earlier fall. Prior to that, the Open Handicap had seen Sherlock collect another victory at the Bristol raceway, with D. Cameron and Bill Latchem finishing second and third respectively. In the first challenge race of the day, Sherlock held the lead until the very last bend, when Len Parker found the drive to shoot through and post a popular success. The first running of the Bristol Golden Gauntlet final ended abruptly when Stanley Gill fell and Sherlock went over him, while Parker struck one of the stricken machines after finding himself with nowhere to go. None of the riders were badly injured, but Gill got cinder dust in his eyes and was unable to take his place in the restart. All the others took their places, with Parker scorching to glory from Felix Dallimore in a track-record time of 92.4 seconds. John Douglas, a partner in Douglas

Brothers Engineering, subsequently presented the Golden Gauntlet to Parker amid hearty applause from the appreciative audience.

Roughly 8,000 folk enjoyed a feast of action at Knowle Stadium on 17 October, when star visitor Arthur Jervis swept to victory in the *News of the World* Silver Challenge Belt, having postponed a trip to Denmark just to be able to participate. To all intents and purposes, it looked as though Arthur Franklyn had the race in the bag, but Jervis robustly forced his way inside on the last corner and just got the verdict on the line. Earlier, Franklyn had beaten Jervis in the final of the All-Star Scratch event, when he lowered the track record to a rapid 91.4 seconds. Len Parker was at his most sporting in heat one of the Challenge Belt, when he laid his machine down to avoid crashing into Arthur Sherlock and thus forfeited an excellent chance of winning. In the challenge event both Franklyn and Clem Beckett, who had also aborted the excursion to Denmark, got off the mark well, but the latter had a spill at the first bend and, after going on a few yards, stopped again. His steed was apparently only firing on one cylinder, but Franklyn experienced no such problems and carried on to claim an unchallenged success.

Owing to heavy rain, it was impossible to run the scheduled programme at Knowle on 24 October. Arthur Jervis, the Coventry ace, tested out the circuit, but understandably found the conditions hopeless for racing.

Billed as the final event of the year, the meeting on 31 October was staged in favourable weather conditions and a very good crowd witnessed some great racing. The first action on the race card was the Knowle Scratch event for local riders, which ended in victory for D. Cameron, who made a good start and sprinted away to win the final with ease. The first challenge race initially saw Len Parker hold the lead, only for Arthur Sherlock to fall and cause a restart. At the second attempt, Sherlock showed no mercy and stormed home. Billy Dallison leapt away to lead the first two laps in the other challenge event, but some clever riding took Arthur Franklyn ahead and he cantered on to cross the line in a new track-record time of 89.4 seconds. In the Silver Challenge Belt, Frank Smith experienced mechanical problems at the start, leaving Franklyn and Larry Boulton to battle for supremacy. Although Franklyn just stayed ahead for the duration, Boulton was always right on his tail, but the Durham star proved just too good for him. The last event in a busy programme was the Bristol Golden Helmet and this saw the quicker-starting Dallison eventually overhauled by Franklyn after a ding-dong scrap, with the holder going on to retain the title he had won on 6 October. Well-known TT rider Fred Dickson subsequently presented the coveted trophy to Franklyn.

The dirt-track season had been scheduled to end on 31 October at Knowle but, owing to the number of requests received by the management, it was decided to hold an extra event on 7 November. The main item on the card, apart from the race for the Bristol Golden Gauntlet, was a friendly encounter between Bristol and Leicester. This was a great match for the fans and featured the skilled riding of Skid Skinner and Cyril 'Squib' Burton, who led their team to a 9-3 success. The Knowle Scratch Race resulted in victory for the fast-starting Bill Latchem from Harold 'Spiller' Cook, with Holy Joy remounting to fill third place after he and Tommy Webb had crashed together. In the Bristol Golden Gauntlet, Len Parker burst past Arthur Sherlock on the opening lap prior to powering away to retain the title he had won on 13 October.

SUMMARY OF 1928 MEETINGS

Date	Event	Winner/Result
25 August	Bristol Golden Helmet	Len Parker
	Open Challenge	Frank Smith
	Bristol v. Manchester	Bristol 2 Manchester 4
1 September	Bristol Golden Gauntlet	Arthur Sherlock
	Senior Handicap	W. Spencer
	Bristol v. Manchester	Bristol 2 Manchester 4
8 September	Bristol Golden Helmet	Len Parker
	Sunday Chronicle Challenge Trophy	Bill Latchem
	Senior Handicap	Len Parker
	Bristol v. Manchester	Bristol 3 Manchester 3
15 September	Bristol Golden Gauntlet	Arthur Sherlock
	Senior Handicap	Frank Smith
22 September	Bristol Golden Helmet	Arthur Sherlock
	Open Handicap	Arthur Sherlock
	Bristol v. Manchester	Bristol 3 Manchester 3
29 September	Bristol Golden Gauntlet	Arthur Sherlock
	News of the World Challenge Belt	Frank Smith
	Bristol v. Manchester	Bristol 2 Manchester 4
6 October	Bristol Golden Helmet	Arthur Franklyn
	Sunday Chronicle Trophy	Arthur Franklyn

	Bristol v. Manchester	Bristol 3 Manchester 3
10 October	Meeting Postponed	
13 October	Bristol Golden Gauntlet	Len Parker
	Open Handicap	Arthur Sherlock
17 October	News of the World Challenge Belt	Arthur Jervis
	Bristol Handicap	Gordon Spalding
	All-Star Scratch Race	Arthur Franklyn
24 October	Meeting Postponed	
31 October	Bristol Golden Helmet	Arthur Franklyn
	News of the World Challenge Belt	Arthur Franklyn
	Knowle Scratch Race	D. Cameron
	All-Star Scratch Race	Larry Boulton
7 November	Bristol Golden Gauntlet	Len Parker
	Knowle Scratch Race	Bill Latchem
	Bristol v. Leicester	Bristol 3 Leicester 9

1929

Amid perfect weather conditions, the dirt-track season commenced at Knowle Stadium on 6 April and a galaxy of stars helped to draw a huge crowd. Among the quality field were Austrian Champion Rudolph Runtsch and the American Sprouts Elder, who thrilled the enthusiastic crowd with his clever riding, particularly on the corners. In the Challenge Match Race, Elder was pushed all the way by Len Parker, but held on to win by the smallest of margins in a track-record time of 88.8 seconds. Elder repeated his success over Parker in the Bristol Golden Helmet, being subsequently presented with the trophy by Major Vernon Brook of the ACU. The Knowle Scratch Race saw a remarkable effort from Runtsch in heat five when, after falling, he quickly remounted and came through to claim a fine victory. The first semi-final provided a ding-dong tussle between Stewie St George and Len Parker, with the New Zealander just getting the verdict on the line. Jim Douglas looked like winning the other semi-final, but took a nasty tumble into the safety fence. He immediately recovered, however, and gave chase to snatch a good second place. Douglas led in the final, only for the ultra-competitive Parker to overhaul him and speed on to triumph. However, what had promised to be a great spectacle was ruined somewhat as St George struggled around with engine trouble.

Despite unpleasant weather, there was a good crowd for the next meeting on 13 April, when there was plenty to enthuse over. Four London riders were present, namely Reg Pointer, Dicky Bird, Leo Ralph and Ray Ralph, while Cardiff were represented by Champ Upham and Ivor Hill. Another notable participant was Rudolph Runtsch, who again rode magnificently, although he met with more than his fair share of ill luck. The Bristol Open Handicap saw a spectacular accident when both Tommy Webb and W.S. Tregarthen crashed through the safety fence in heat three. Later, in the second semi-final, Runtsch rode well to grab the runner-up spot following a fall in the early stages. In the final, Len Parker fell while leading, leaving Holy Joy to go on and win from Runtsch. The Inter-City races proved enjoyable, with Bristol beating London 8-4, having earlier ended all-square with Cardiff at 3 points apiece.

There were a number of stars on show for the third meeting of the year on 20 April, including Pat Creaney, Brian Donkin, Crawley Rous, Ed Bradley and Al Wilkinson. The programme was busy and varied, beginning with the Knowle Open Handicap. The opening heat was a disaster for Creaney, since he was unable to get his engine started. However, local rider Jim Douglas showed plenty of promise in trying to overhaul his handicap, losing second place by only a wheel. Victory in the final eventually went the way of Wilkinson, with Stanley Gill scooping a good second place. The Golden Helmet went the way of Gordon Spalding, who won the trophy from Turnip Owen in great style to become only the second local rider to win the coveted title after Len Parker. Bradley made three attempts to break the track record but, in giving it his all, he crashed down on each occasion. His efforts were greatly appreciated by an enthusiastic audience though, with much applause reverberating around the stadium.

Knowle Stadium was again packed on 27 April and those present witnessed thrills and spills galore in a pulsating meeting. The programme began with a Challenge Match series and, in heat one, Eric Spencer came from behind and tore up the racing strip to beat Len Parker in a new track-record time of 87.4 seconds. The second race also went the way of Spencer, after the chasing Parker had fallen and remounted some distance behind. In the Wells Road Handicap, Bill Hamblin was unfortunate to crash after crossing the line to win heat five, suffering a collarbone injury in the process. In the second semi-final, Parker brilliantly cut through the pack to take the lead, only to overcook a corner and lose position. The Bathonian wasn't finished though and came back to grab second place by half a wheel on the line. Turnip Owen rode well to take the final from Harold 'Spiller' Cook, while Parker remounted to finish third, having taken another tumble on the last lap. The Bristol Golden Gauntlet resulted in triumph for local boy Jim Douglas, his success ahead of W. Spencer and Will Dennis being enthusiastically cheered by the large audience.

On 4 May, Jupiter Pluvius struck with a vengeance and, with the track in a saturated state, there was no way the scheduled programme of events could take place. Despite the conditions, a considerable number of folk still arrived at the track. When the rain finally abated, the supporters were admitted free to witness Billy Dallison and others at practice.

The first evening meeting of the year took place at Knowle Stadium on 7 May and, with a large crowd in attendance, the weather was in complete contrast to that experienced three days previously. A nasty incident in the final of the Knowle Open Handicap saw Len Parker and Stanley Gill collide. Thankfully, there weren't any serious injuries, although the latter did receive cuts and bruises. Taking advantage of the situation was Felix Dallimore, who took victory from Turnip Owen. Parker got back to winning ways in the Bristol Golden Helmet, comfortably defeating Holy Joy and Champ Upham to take the title for the first time since 8 September the previous year.

Len Parker again proved the man to beat on 11 May, with a large crowd in place to see him in action, as well as the Wembley duo of Crawley Rous and Charlie Briggs. The racing began with the Bristol Open Handicap and there were just two finishers in the final as Ted Bravery took victory from Bill Clibbett. Prior to that, the event had seen the first track appearance of local boy Edwin (Teddie) Douglas and he was an instant hit in winning heat five. Looking at the Golden Gauntlet, another local lad, Gordon Spalding, rode a Triumph in his heat, but borrowed Stanley Gill's Douglas for the latter stages. It was his first experience of a Douglas but, in an excellent display, he managed to finish second in the semi-final and third in the final. Victory went the way of that man Parker, while Felix Dallimore filled the runner-up position.

Uncertain weather led to a lower-than-usual turnout for the meeting on 14 May, but those present saw some fine racing. The riders included the popular Arthur Sherlock, plus fellow Midlands stars Neville Wheeler and Alec Bowerman. Meanwhile, Cardiff were represented by Ronnie 'Whirlwind' Baker, George Gregor, Champ Upham and Johnny George. The Bath Open Handicap provided some exciting stuff for the spectators to drool over, with the final eventually going to Frank Smith, but only by the smallest of margins from Len Parker. In the Bath Scratch Race the finalists were the evening's four best performers, namely Parker, Sherlock, Upham and Wheeler. Naturally, the fastest time of the meeting was clocked in this race, which initially saw Parker lead from Sherlock, only for the latter to encounter engine trouble on the second lap. That left Parker to win comfortably in 97.0 seconds, with Wheeler filling second place.

A large holiday crowd was present for the next meeting on 18 May, which was run amid perfect weather conditions. The only drawback was the dry state of the track, caused by restrictions on water usage, which resulted in slow times and much billowing dust. The chief attraction was the appearance of a couple of Wembley aces in Harry '£100' Whitfield and Bert Fairweather. In the Kingswood Open Handicap Bill Clibbett and Whitfield were due to contest the first semi-final, but neither could get his machine to fire, leaving Len Parker to win from Felix Dallimore. Surprisingly though, the final went the way of Dallimore, with S.E. Webb beating Parker for second place. The redoubtable Parker gained revenge in the Kingswood Open Scratch, however, taking victory in the final ahead of Dallimore in the fastest time of the meeting.

A galaxy of stars attracted a crowd of over 3,000 to Bristol Speedway on 21 May, when a well-watered track and beautiful weather combined to make for an entertaining meeting. Among the visitors were the Australian duo of Jack Chapman and Frank Duckett, the latter becoming the first man to ride a Harley Peashooter at Knowle. Meanwhile, Bob Harrison, Neville Wheeler and old favourite Arthur Sherlock completed the list of illustrious visitors. Wheeler went on to win the Whitchurch Open Scratch Race after S.E. Webb had taken victory in the Whitchurch Open Handicap. The one the fans had waited to see, however, was the Challenge Match Race between Harrison, Chapman, Sherlock and local hero Len Parker. Despite being on board a borrowed

Douglas, Parker still dashed home ahead of Sherlock, his success sending the fans home happy once more.

The meeting on 25 May saw the introduction of a new contest, namely the Wrington Rollers Scratch Race, which unsurprisingly was run from a rolling start, with three evenly matched riders in each heat. So well matched were the riders that the event provided several really exciting races, with very close finishes instead of the processions that were usually seen when the stars were matched against less experienced speedsters. The result in the final had a very familiar ring about it though, with Len Parker claiming another win ahead of Frank Smith in a fast time of 95.0 seconds. Prior to that, the Sunshine Open Handicap had seen Australian Les 'Ned' Kelly post victory in his heat but, to the disappointment of the crowd, he was unable to ride again due to machine damage sustained when he had lent his steed to another rider. Also making an appearance in the Sunshine Open Handicap, which somewhat inevitably resulted in another final victory for Parker, was the originally named 'Cigarette' Player. He was an Australian who first came over in 1928 and actually helped construct the track at Knowle before becoming a rider himself. His real name was Ben Player and he was to subsequently meet and marry Betty Copson, whose family had moved to Bristol from Swansea. She was a package designer at Fry's factory and, following their marriage, they lived at Pembroke Villas in Bristol.

Although very inexperienced, Teddie Douglas did so well in the meeting on 28 May as to arouse great enthusiasm among a large crowd. Indeed, he revealed superb form as he won his heat, semi-final and the final of the Woodstock Open Handicap, defeating Len Parker and Ted Bravery in the big showdown. He then won his heat in the Golden Gauntlet in a time of 98.6 seconds, a time that was only bettered by Parker in the Inter-City event against Exeter and Cardiff. As Golden Gauntlet holder, Parker did not have to ride until the final but, after sweeping ahead of the field, his chain came off, leaving visiting rider Nick Carter to take the trophy ahead of Bill Clibbett. In the team event, Bristol held their own to tie with Exeter on 16 points apiece, while Cardiff scored 10. Star riders in town included Richard 'Buggie' Fleeman, Les 'Kernel' Barker, Champ Upham, Charlie Swift, Johnny George, Frank 'Buster' Buckland and Ray 'Sunshine' Cannell.

The meeting on 1 June featured only the locally based riders and a fair-sized crowd witnessed plenty of keen racing. This was emphasised in the final of the Somerset Open Handicap, when Ted Bravery and Jim Douglas fought neck-and-neck for much of the way, with Len Parker close on their heels. Unfortunately, Parker shed a chain in a late bid for the lead, leaving Bravery to win by the smallest of margins from Douglas. Parker did at least have the consolation of taking victory later on though, when he beat Felix Dallimore in the final of the Somerset Scratch Race. Parker also set the fastest time of the day when clocking 95.0 seconds in the Inter-City match, his efforts helping Bath to triumph 13-11 over Bristol.

On 4 June, the heats of the Evening Open Handicap provided plenty of spectacle for an enthusiastic audience. The best race was a tight scrap in heat three which eventually saw Teddie Douglas defeat Len Parker. The first semi-final resulted in victory for Ted Bravery from Holy Joy, while Jim Douglas crashed out in spectacular fashion. Parker then put his earlier disappointment out of mind to win the second semi-final, with Turnip Owen following him across the line. The final provided the unusual sight of Parker hitting the deck, while Teddie Douglas collided with the fence not that far short of the finish. Thankfully neither was hurt and, despite a severely buckled wheel, Douglas managed to push home for second position. There was much more top-notch racing in the Bristol Golden Gauntlet and among the competitors was Nick Carter, who had won the previous staging of the event at Knowle Stadium on 28 May. Carter, however, did not even make it to the semi-finals, instead going out in the heats. Teddie Douglas replaced his damaged machine with a borrowed one, but he also went out of the running in the heats. The brilliant Parker went on to triumph in the final, thereby regaining the title he had last won on 11 May.

The riders at the meeting on 8 June were again all local men, the experiment of seven days previous having proved a great success. Before the action got underway, there was a grand parade of all the competitors and it was an imposing sight, with some twenty-five riders going around the raceway. Yet another member of the Douglas family, the fourth, made his first appearance on the track in this meeting, namely William, who was more commonly referred to as Billy. The youngster went very well after a bad start had seen him take a spectacular spill and land some 10 yards from his machine, having turned a complete somersault through the air. W. Spencer got the better of a tight tussle to narrowly win the Derby Open Handicap from Gordon Spalding, with track master Len Parker surprisingly at the rear. Parker gained some consolation in the

Oakes Scratch event, however, taking victory ahead of Ted Bravery and Jack Douglas.

Australian Freddie Hore was a welcome visitor to Knowle on 11 June and he certainly made a mark in his heat of the TT Open Handicap, when he very nearly snatched second place despite a fall earlier in the race. Al Wilkinson, having won the first semi-final, went on to take the final ahead of Frank Smith. Prior to that, in the Track Championship, Jim Douglas beat Ted Bravery in great style. Meanwhile, the Bristol Golden Gauntlet ended in a fine win for Bill Clibbett, with Frank Smith securing second place on board a brand-new Douglas machine. Another feature of the evening was the Flying Nine Scratch Race, run from rolling starts, with three riders in each of three heats. Len Parker just held on to take the final of this contest, with the pressing Smith again having to settle for the runner-up spot.

A novel feature of the meeting on 15 June was a race in which the competitors were selected by two lady spectators, who picked the names from a hat! The contestants turned out to be Holy Joy and Alan Collier from Exeter, with the former being the eventual victor. The lucky lady who had drawn his name subsequently announced Joy's success on the microphone and decorated his bike with a doll and ribbons. The two visitors from Exeter, Roy Reeves and Collier, found the Bristol boys more than their match. On his new mount, Frank Smith put in some very fine riding, including the fastest time of the afternoon. He won the June Open Handicap, but had a fall in the semi-final of the Newbury Scratch Race, which was won by the favourite Len Parker. Teddie Douglas had been expected to make a track return after a spill on 4 June, but in the end wasn't quite fit enough to do so.

The meeting on 18 June commenced with an international event, namely a match race between Arthur Sherlock and Australian ace Syd Parsons. Run from a flying start, it proved to be one of the finest seen on the Knowle circuit since its opening almost ten months previously. Both men raced wheel-to-wheel all through the second and third laps, before Parsons passed the post just two tyre widths in front of the Englishman. In fact the pair were racing so hard that they crashed after crossing the line, although thankfully no damage was done to the men or their machines. Len Parker started as favourite for the Clifton Open Handicap but, having won his semi-final, he was unable to catch Jack Douglas in the final. In his heat of the Bristol Golden Helmet, Genial Hindle crashed right through the fence, although thankfully he emerged without injury. Ted Bravery was involved in a wonderful race with Len Parker in the final, with the latter holding the lead until the final bend, when Bravery cut inside to win the coveted trophy by no more than 12 inches.

The highlight of a packed programme on 25 June was undoubtedly the final of the Grand Prix Open Handicap, in which Bill Clibbett rode extremely well to win despite Len Parker being right on his tail for the duration. This was after Gordon Spalding and Jack Douglas had collided in spectacular fashion. Meanwhile, in the Flying Sixteen event, Frank Smith surged to victory and clocked the fastest time of the meeting. His task was made a little easier though, since Parker had earlier crashed out in his heat. In the Bristol Golden Gauntlet, John (Jack) Douglas won a no-holds-barred final, which looked like being anybody's race, until the local youngster edged ahead to win from Ted Bravery.

The meeting on 2 July featured an appearance by Australian ace Syd Jackson, who rode well to win his heat in the July Open Handicap. In the final, however, he wrenched a leg and the race was re-run with Jim Douglas taking his place. It was fortunate for Douglas though, as he went on to win the restart ahead of Frank Smith and Champ Upham. Meanwhile, in the Star Scratch Race, Len Parker again revealed a thirst for winning as he dashed home from Ted Bravery. Amazingly, that was the Bath man's eighteenth success since the track had opened and there were a lot more to come besides!

On 9 July, Englishman Gus Kuhn, who had ridden on the Isle of Man and was a prominent member of the Stamford Bridge team, appeared at Knowle. He was in great form too, winning both the Speedway Open Handicap and the Bristol Golden Gauntlet. Len Parker put up a terrific effort in the latter event, but in the end was well beaten by Kuhn. There were many spills on the night, though thankfully there were no serious injuries to report. Ted Bravery was one to take a nasty fall owing to the forks of his machine snapping, this being the consequence of a tumble in an earlier race. Three heats of the Track Championship were staged, with Len Parker having the misfortune to lose his chain while leading heat two. By way of some consolation, Parker at least managed to take the Flying Sixteen contest ahead of Jack Douglas.

A large crowd was present for the meeting at Knowle on 16 July, which featured visiting riders from Cardiff, including Nobby Key, Champ Upham, Nick Carter and George Gregor. The Inter-Track event against the Welsh side saw Bristol collect a 6-4 success, due chiefly to Len Parker, who won the race in magnificent style. In heat five of the Westbury Scratch Race, much amusement was caused when the three riders left in the race all crashed in a heap. This was followed by a mad scramble to be the first to get up and running again, with Turnip Owen being the one to emerge as the winner. In the second semi-final, Owen made a very sporting gesture after being awarded second place. He went up to the judges' box and informed the officials that he should be disqualified for cutting across the grass. Jack Douglas subsequently won the final, after Len Parker had lost a chain for the second week running.

The meeting on 23 July attracted a vast number of spectators, due in no small part to the presence of Jack Parker, one of the leading riders in England. Indeed, at Stamford Bridge the previous week Parker had shattered the track record and in the process stormed away from Gus Kuhn, who had been so dominant at Knowle on 9 July. Parker's first race of the evening was in his heat of the Sandown Open Handicap, when he fully demonstrated his speed, clocking an extraordinary 92.6 seconds. He was even quicker in the first semi-final, winning by a huge distance in 91.8 seconds. In the final, Turnip Owen actually led for two laps but Parker, in spite of nearly overdoing a broadside, caught and passed the local man on the last lap. Len Parker made a gallant effort to oust his namesake in the semi-final of the Bristol Golden Gauntlet but, as he was about to pass, he unfortunately fell. Despite this, he still managed to remount and finish second. The final featured another great scrap between the Parkers but, once again, Jack was the victor. Watching the action were a group of sea scouts from Jamaica, who had recently disembarked at Avonmouth. At the end of an entertaining meeting, one of the party was selected to proudly present the Golden Gauntlet to Jack Parker.

The first event of the programme on 30 July was an attempt on the track record by Syd Jackson of Leicester Stadium fame. He clocked a very quick time too, 91.4 seconds, beating Jack Parker's time set the previous week as the fastest of the season but 4 seconds outside the all-time track record set by Eric Spencer from a rolling start. Showing his class, Jackson went on to win both the Flying Nine event and the Kingsway Scratch, after local favourite Len Parker had earlier taken the Leicester Open Handicap by some margin from Turnip Owen.

Following his impressive performance the previous week, Syd Jackson was back in town on 6 August and he certainly made his presence felt, lowering the all-time track record to 86.4 seconds while on his way to victory over Len Parker in heat three of their challenge series. That gave the Leicester star a 2-1 success overall, although Parker could be considered somewhat unlucky since he had stopped while well ahead in the opening race after noticing that his opponent had fallen while attempting a broadside. Jackson made no mistake in the re-run, going on to win easily. In front of a bumper crowd, Parker raced away to triumph in heat two, thereby squaring the series at one win apiece. In the deciding race, however, Jackson wasn't extended and won with nearly half a lap to spare, shattering the track record in the process.

The large crowd which gathered at Knowle Stadium on 13 August was agreeably surprised when it was announced that Gus Kuhn was to appear in the meeting. The Stamford Bridge ace took the place of Halifax's Geoff Taylor, who was unable to ride. On a very dry raceway, Kuhn, in his heat of the Pendine Open Handicap, clocked a very fine 92.0 seconds. Unfortunately though, he was forced to retire in the semi-final when his steed shed a chain. Bill Clibbett subsequently went on to take the final from Ted Bravery. There was some consolation for Kuhn, however, as he managed to repair his machine and went on to win the final of the Weston Open Scratch event. Also featured in the schedule of events was lady rider Fay Taylour but, despite quick machinery, she failed to hold Turnip Owen over a three-heat challenge series.

The meeting on 20 August included the final of the Knowle Track Championship, with the competitors being Frank Smith and Felix Dallimore, both of whom had emerged successfully from the preliminary rounds spread throughout the season. The two were evenly matched, although Dallimore had a two-second start, giving him 20 yards on his opponent. Smith went all-out to make up the ground but it was only on the last corner that he drew level and cut back underneath brilliantly to win by half a wheel. The winner's trophy was duly presented to Smith by the Sheriff of Bristol, who was witnessing dirt-track racing for the first time in his life. To the delight of the spectators, Gordon Spalding was back on track following a long lay-off after a bad crash at Cardiff. The Wrington racer won his first race with ease and went on to take the Manchester Open Handicap in great style. Another highlight saw Bill Clibbett ride a magnificent race to beat Arthur Franklyn in heat one of the Flying Nine Race when clocking a wonderful time of 90.0 seconds. Revenge was sweet for Clibbett, who had previously lost out to Franklyn in the final of the Bristol Open Scratch event. Meanwhile, the remarkable Len Parker chalked up yet another Knowle success, his victory over Jack Douglas in the Flying Nine final being his twenty-second title at the Bristol venue in little under a year.

Once again, a large Knowle crowd witnessed plenty of keen racing on 27 August. In addition to the usual local riders, some well-known visitors were present, notably the Stamford Bridge duo of Gus Kuhn and Les Blakeborough. Meanwhile, Cardiff boys Nobby Key and Champ Upham were also in town. Kuhn was an early faller in the final of the Knowle Open Handicap, leaving a great scrap between three local boys for the coveted title. Ted Bravery went on to take victory after Turnip Owen and Bill Clibbett had crashed, although both escaped injury and pushed their machines home for second and third positions respectively. Clibbett showed no ill effects, as he later took a smart victory from Blakeborough and Kuhn in the final of the Bristol Golden Gauntlet. Heat one of the Badman Cup resulted in victory for Stanley Gill, with subsequent wins following for Turnip Owen and Cigarette Player. This was an interesting competition, sponsored by Mr W.J. Badman of Weston-super-Mare, which was to be spread out over several meetings.

Female fans screamed aloud at Knowle Stadium on 3 September when Turnip Owen lost control of his machine and ploughed into the officials' area, actually hitting one of the judges. The incident occurred in one of the heats of the Flying Twelve Scratch Race, when Owen and Len Parker, who had been riding neck-and-neck for the lead, hit the last bend together. Owen suddenly mounted the grass and headed straight for the judge, Mr R. Baxter of the Black Horse Hotel, Redfield. There was a nasty collision, and at first it seemed as if Mr Baxter had been seriously injured, but fortunately he eventually clambered to his feet. When spoken to by a *Bristol Times and Mirror* representative, Mr Baxter said that, apart from shock, he was thankfully unhurt. Visitors for the meeting included Nobby Key, Jack Barber, Nick Carter and George Gregor, but none could match the pace of the home lads, who cleaned up in all the evening's events. Prior to his spectacular crash, Turnip Owen had won the Cardiff Open Handicap, while Len Parker had taken the Flying Twelve Scratch event. Parker also went on to land the Cardiff Open Scratch Race in a great evening's racing.

The meeting on 10 September opened with another three heats of the Badman Cup, Len Parker winning the first with ease in 97.8 seconds.

Parker went on to win the final of the London Open Handicap after just getting the better of a ding-dong struggle with Ted Bravery in the last few yards. The great event of the evening was the Inter-Track challenge match between Bristol and Stamford Bridge. The visitors' line-up featured Gus Kuhn, Les Blakeborough, Nick Nicol and Wal Phillips, so a tough contest was expected. The local boys, Len Parker, Bill Clibbett, Ted Bravery and Jack Douglas, rode well though, coming out on top by 18 points to 9. After the close of racing, the wireless music continued, with many folk joining in the dancing on the centre green!

The chief item of an interesting programme on 17 September was the Inter-Track match between Bristol and Birmingham (Perry Barr). The visiting team included Wally Lloyd, Bill Ashcroft, Geoff Siddaway and Arthur Johnson, while Len Parker, Ted Bravery, Bill Clibbett and Jack Douglas represented the home side. As they had done the previous week against Stamford Bridge, it was the local boys who ran out comfortable winners by 17 points to 10. Prior to that, the meeting had opened with the semi-finals of the Badman Cup. Cigarette Player won heat one in fine style from Ted Bravery and Jack Douglas, with subsequent victories following for Felix Dallimore and Len Parker. The Birmingham Open Handicap saw Parker add to his long list of triumphs, while Frank Smith was an easy winner of the Bristol Golden Gauntlet after both Parker and holder Bill Clibbett had surprisingly come to grief on the opening lap.

Bristol riders again carried all before them on 24 September, narrowly defeating Crystal Palace 12-11 in a challenge match despite stiff opposition from the London boys. Meanwhile, in the Crystal Palace Handicap, Jack Douglas secured a good win from Len Parker and Bill Clibbett in the final. The finest race of the evening, however, occurred in the final of the Crystal Palace Scratch event, which featured a terrific tussle between Parker and Triss Sharp, with the local favourite just coming out on top. This was sweet revenge for Parker, who had lost to Sharp in one of the heats of the team match. Prior to that, Parker had started the meeting in style, taking victory in the Badman Cup ahead of Cigarette Player and Felix Dallimore. The heats and semi-final of this contest had been staged over a number of weeks and a great struggle had been expected in the final. As it turned out though, Parker gained the advantage from the start and went on to triumph with relative ease.

The scheduled meeting at Knowle Stadium on 1 October had to be postponed due to the effects of heavy rain, which had left the track in a saturated state. The management issued vouchers to all spectators on leaving the stadium, allowing entrance to the following week's event.

After the previous week's rain-off, fine evening weather and an exciting programme attracted a large crowd to the Bristol raceway on 8 October. The Wembley riders were in town but it was the 'King of Knowle' Len Parker who produced a fantastic ride to beat Roger Frogley in the final of the Wembley Open Scratch Race. His winning time was a scorching 89.8 seconds. This rounded the evening off in perfect style for Parker, who had previously taken victory in both the Wembley Handicap and the Challenge Sash.

The meeting on 15 October got underway with the Crystal Palace Open Handicap, which saw Jack Douglas, Wally Lloyd, Ted Bravery and Len Parker safely negotiate the semi-finals. The four star riders duly made a very fine race of the final, with Douglas coming out on top ahead of Bravery while, somewhat surprisingly, Parker could only manage third position. The big event of the evening was the team event between Bristol and Crystal Palace, with the homesters winning the nine-heat encounter 33-20. Prior to that, the victor in the Bristol Golden Gauntlet was the one and only Len Parker, ahead of Jack Douglas. For the prolific Parker, it was actually the fifth time he had won the Golden Gauntlet since the track had opened in August 1928. Parker's getaway from the start in the final was a tribute to the accelerating powers of his Douglas and he literally screamed around the circuit to win handsomely by very nearly half-a-lap. Meanwhile, Frank Smith, the previous holder, had to settle for third place behind Jack Douglas.

An impressive list of visiting riders for the meeting on 22 October included Triss Sharp, Neville Wheeler, Art Warren and Alec Bowerman. Proceedings began with the *Evening Times and Echo* Sash, which saw Sharp clock a fast 89.6 seconds in heat five, despite damaging his gearbox in the process. The Crystal Palace skipper hastily fitted another but in the semi-final this unfortunately also 'went west'. The final brought together Len Parker, Jack Douglas, Cigarette Player and Neville Wheeler. All four made a big dive for the first corner, with Douglas emerging ahead. At the start of the second lap, Player was thrown from his machine, while Parker also fell. Douglas remained untroubled, however, and went on to win ahead of Wheeler, with the remounted Parker trailing in third. Next up were the heats of the Leicester Handicap and this featured some fast and furious racing. Ted Bravery rode well in the final to defeat Parker by just a few yards. Sharp had been close to Parker and Bravery at the start but he fell awkwardly and hurt his foot. During the evening, several attempts were made to lower the track record, with a new best time established by Les 'Smiler' Wotton, who clocked 84.8 seconds from a flying start.

SUMMARY OF 1929 MEETINGS

Date	Event	Winner/Result
6 April	Bristol Golden Helmet	Sprouts Elder
	Knowle Scratch Race	Len Parker
13 April	Bristol Golden Gauntlet	Leo Ralph
	Bristol Open Handicap	Holy Joy
	Bristol v. Cardiff	Bristol 3 Cardiff 3
	Bristol v. London	Bristol 8 London 4
20 April	Bristol Golden Helmet	Gordon Spalding
	Knowle Open Handicap	A. Wilkinson
	Bristol v. London	Bristol 5 London 1
	Bristol v. London	Bristol 3 London 3
27 April	Bristol Golden Gauntlet	Jim Douglas
	Wells Road Handicap	Turnip Owen
4 May	Meeting postponed	
7 May	Bristol Golden Helmet	Len Parker
	Knowle Open Handicap	Felix Dallimore
	Bristol v. Cardiff	Bristol 6 Cardiff 6
11 May	Bristol Golden Gauntlet	Len Parker
	Bristol Open Handicap	Ted Bravery
	Bristol v. Wembley	Bristol 5 Wembley 1
14 May	Bath Handicap	Frank Smith
	Bath Scratch Race	Len Parker
18 May	Kingswood Open Handicap	Felix Dallimore
	Kingswood Open Scratch Race	Len Parker
21 May	Whitchurch Open Handicap	S.E. Webb
	Whitchurch Open Scratch Race	Neville Wheeler
25 May	Sunshine Open Handicap	Len Parker
	Wrington Rollers Scratch Race	Len Parker
28 May	Bristol Golden Gauntlet	Nick Carter
	Woodstock Open Handicap	Teddie Douglas
	Bristol v. Exeter v. Cardiff	Bristol 16 Exeter 16 Cardiff 10
1 June	Somerset Open Handicap	Ted Bravery
	Somerset Scratch Race	Len Parker
	Bristol v. Bath	Bristol 11 Bath 13

4 June	Bristol Golden Gauntlet	Len Parker
	Evening Open Handicap	Holy Joy
	Bristol v. Leicester	Bristol 3 Leicester 4
	Exeter v. Cardiff	Exeter 5 Cardiff 4
	Leicester v. Exeter	Leicester 7 Exeter 2
8 June	Derby Open Handicap	W. Spencer
	Oakes Scratch Race	Len Parker
11 June	Bristol Golden Gauntlet	Bill Clibbett
	TT Open Handicap	A. Wilkinson
	Flying Nine Race	Len Parker
15 June	June Open Handicap	Frank Smith
	Newbury Scratch Race	Len Parker
18 June	Bristol Golden Helmet	Ted Bravery
	Clifton Open Handicap	Jack Douglas
	Bristol v. Cardiff	Bristol 6 Cardiff 4
	Leicester v. Exeter	Leicester 7 Exeter 3
	Bristol v. Leicester	Bristol 5 Leicester 5
25 June	Bristol Golden Gauntlet	Jack Douglas
	Grand Prix Open Handicap	Bill Clibbett
	Flying Sixteen Race	Frank Smith
2 July	July Open Handicap	Jim Douglas
	Star Scratch Race	Len Parker
	Flying Sixteen Race	Ted Bravery
9 July	Bristol Golden Gauntlet	Gus Kuhn
	Speedway Open Handicap	Gus Kuhn
	Flying Sixteen Race	Len Parker
16 July	Midsummer Handicap	Frank Smith
	Westbury Scratch Race	Jack Douglas
	Bristol v. Cardiff	Bristol 6 Cardiff 4
23 July	Bristol Golden Gauntlet	Jack Parker
	Sandown Open Handicap	Jack Parker
	Flying Sixteen Race	Jack Parker
30 July	Leicester Open Handicap	Len Parker
	Kingsway Scratch Race	Syd Jackson
	Flying Nine Race	Syd Jackson
6 August	Bristol Golden Gauntlet	Syd Jackson
	Holiday Open Handicap	Len Parker
13 August	Pendine Open Handicap	Bill Clibbett
	Weston Open Scratch Race	Gus Kuhn
20 August	Knowle Track Championship Final	Frank Smith
	Manchester Open Handicap	Gordon Spalding
	Bristol Open Scratch Race	Arthur Franklyn

	Flying Nine Race	Len Parker
27 August	Bristol Golden Gauntlet	Bill Clibbett
	Knowle Open Handicap	Ted Bravery
	Flying Nine Scratch Race	Gus Kuhn
3 September	Cardiff Open Handicap	Turnip Owen
	Cardiff Open Scratch Race	Len Parker
	Flying Twelve Scratch Race	Len Parker
10 September	London Open Handicap	Len Parker
	London Open Scratch Race	Len Parker
	Bristol v. Stamford Bridge	Bristol 18 Stamford Bridge 9
17 September	Bristol Golden Gauntlet	Frank Smith
	Birmingham Open Handicap	Len Parker
	Bristol v. Perry Barr	Bristol 17 Perry Barr 10
24 September	Badman Cup Final	Len Parker
	Crystal Palace Handicap	Jack Douglas
	Crystal Palace Scratch Race	Len Parker
	Bristol v. Crystal Palace	Bristol 12 Crystal Palace 11
1 October	Meeting postponed	
8 October	Wembley Handicap	Len Parker
	Wembley Open Scratch Race	Len Parker
15 October	Bristol Golden Gauntlet	Len Parker
	Crystal Palace Open Handicap	Jack Douglas
	Bristol v. Crystal Palace	Bristol 33 Crystal Palace 20
22 October	Evening Times and Echo Sash	Jack Douglas
	Leicester Handicap	Ted Bravery

1930

Following major work on the circuit during the winter, the Sheriff of Bristol, Mr H.J.G. Rudman, officially opened the third dirt-track season at Knowle on 29 April. A large turnout of supporters enjoyed an abundance of thrills from both the local riders and guest speed-sters, who included George Greenwood, Cyclone Sheldon and Charlie Barrett. One of the most intriguing events on the programme was a gripping tussle between Ted Bravery and Bill Clibbett in the final of the Open Handicap. Bravery tore around the track in a reckless manner, with Clibbett roaring along behind. On every bend, Clibbett threatened to take the lead but each time Bravery, with a gigantic skid that sent the cinders flying, held his position in front. Going into the last lap, Clibbett made a final bid and succeeded in getting alongside Bravery on the first bend. Down the straight they raced neck-and-neck and, on the last bend, Clibbett drove through on the inside to take the win. Having missed out in the Open Handicap, track maestro Len Parker soon pocketed his first Knowle success of the season, beating Leeds rider George Greenwood across the line to win the Bristol Scratch event in a swift time of 91.2 seconds. The heats for the Big 8 Race were rather spoilt by spills and mechanical trouble, but what they lacked in close finishes the riders certainly made up for with thrilling broadsides. Charlie Barrett seemed to have heat one well in hand, but was thrown from his machine on the last lap. At first, it appeared he was badly hurt, but fortunately that wasn't the case and he rode several more times, displaying the same daring he had previously shown. Jack Douglas took advantage of Barrett's misfortune, coming through from some distance behind to take victory. Wembley's Arthur 'Buster' Frogley was in sparkling mood in heat two of this event, blasting to victory from Cyclone Sheldon. In the final, Sheldon again had to settle for second place, with Jack Douglas scooping top spot.

Persistent rainfall failed to dampen the enthusiasm of the spectators for the second meeting of the year on 6 May, although it did leave the track in a somewhat waterlogged state. Indeed, with no let up in the wet stuff, the riders were sliding in liquid cinders towards the end of the meeting. Despite the tricky conditions, some fine racing was witnessed, with the Stamford Bridge boys, Gus Kuhn, Les Blakeborough, Nick Nicol and Colin Ford, giving great value for money. The star event was the Big 8 event, in which the local lads were matched against the visitors. In heat one, Kuhn and Ford lined up alongside Len Parker and Jack Douglas. A quick getaway gave Kuhn an early advantage and the Stamford Bridge skipper was to maintain his lead throughout the race. Douglas wasn't far behind though, as he pressed all the way, never more than a few feet adrift of the Birmingham-born racer. Behind, Parker was an easy third, as Ford's motor was clearly feeling the effects of the wet weather. Heat two brought out Nicol and Blakeborough against the Bristol boys Bill Clibbett and Ted Bravery. This resulted in a Bristol one-two, with Clibbett getting home first, while Nicol's engine gave up the ghost and Blakeborough was out-ridden by the local lads. The result of the final turned out to be a reverse of heat two, with Bravery getting the verdict over Clibbett. In third place was Kuhn, who, having had problems with the transmission on his own machine, had to borrow another steed, which regrettably lacked the necessary power. Meanwhile the other finalist, Douglas, fell on the third lap and failed to remount. The Stamford Handicap and the Stamford Scratch events provided some fine racing, especially in the final of the former. This initially saw Kuhn lying second to W. Spencer, with Clibbett close on his heels. By the final bend Kuhn had edged to the fore, when Clibbett entered the turn at great speed, leaning his Douglas at an unbelievable angle and showering cinders into the crowd. His spectacular efforts were to no avail though, as he failed to make up any ground. However, the sudden shock of seeing Clibbett at full-throttle must have upset Kuhn's concentration, as it was Spencer who pulled away to take the win.

The scheduled meeting on 13 May had to be postponed due to the effects of wet weather and, in spite of the unpleasant conditions, a large number of fans still assembled outside Knowle Stadium. Both the Bristol boys and the visitors from Portsmouth had been eager to race, but it was the seemingly endless rainfall that eventually prevailed.

On 20 May comparatively low speeds but plenty of thrills rewarded a large crowd when the Portsmouth boys arrived to dice with the local favourites. Regrettably, the track was a little on the bumpy side and minor spills were common, with the visiting duo of Phil 'Tiger' Hart and Australian Steve Langton looking somewhat uncomfortable on the circuit. In the Portsmouth Handicap, the final provided a thrilling duel between Len Parker and Bill Clibbett, with the latter making a bold move to overhaul the multi-Knowle victor on the final bend. His efforts were ultimately in vain, since Parker hung on to narrowly win in 96.2 seconds. Clibbett did taste victory in the final of the Bristol Golden Gauntlet, however, after a great ride had seen him squeeze past early leader Felix Dallimore. Later in the race, W. Spencer also ousted Dallimore, but there was simply no catching the speedy Clibbett. Heat one of the Big 8 event saw Clibbett and Ted Bravery lead the 'Pompey' lads from the start, and they were soon left out on their own when the two visitors tumbled. Heat two saw the redoubtable Parker cut across the grass on the first bend to take the lead, although he sportingly shut off to go behind again. Despite the ground he had lost, he still managed to beat Langton for third place. Up front, Jack Douglas took the heat ahead of Portsmouth rider Reg Clark in a time of 102.0 seconds. The final had a promising start, with Douglas leading from Clibbett, closely followed by Bravery and Clark. The second lap brought disaster for Clibbett, for, just after working his way into the lead, he lost control and crashed, with Bravery running into the wreckage. Clark, following closely, had nowhere to go and also ended up among the mangle of men and machines on the track. Clibbett, Bravery and Clark all picked themselves up and got going again, but by then Douglas was well on his way to victory.

Before an attendance of some 5,000, Australian Vic Huxley was certainly the star of the show at Knowle on 27 May. Even though the track was badly waterlogged on the inner line, Huxley showed that he was thoroughly the master of his bucking, roaring machine, when he laid it over in the most perfectly controlled slides. His first appearance occurred in heat two of the Bristol Handicap, which he won with ease in 94.0 seconds. The Aussie went on to win the first semi-final but, in the final, Jim Douglas and Jack 'Lightning' Luke surprisingly relegated him back into third place. However, in heat three of the Big 16 event, Huxley came from behind to beat Cigarette Player, prior to taking victory in the final, ahead of both Felix Dallimore and Luke. The Cardiff boys, Champ Upham, Fred 'Hurricane' Hampson, Lightning Luke and Ivor Hill, were not always in the first three positions, but all rode well. Hampson ended the evening with a nasty spill, which required medical attention, but, despite head injuries, he was later able to return to Cardiff. Bill Clibbett, who had won a warm place in the hearts of the Knowle public, had a surprise package on his tail in the first semi-final of the Bristol Scratch event. On the second bend, he recovered brilliantly from a wobble and just managed to hold his lead from W. Spencer. However, the Bristol-born racer probably hadn't realised just how close Spencer had got and was completely surprised when his rival roared past on the last bend to win by a length. Disappointingly for the crowd, Huxley had toured round with a dead motor in his semi-final, thereby missing out on a final place. In the showpiece race though, Clibbett gained revenge on Spencer, triumphing in a slick time of 90.6 seconds.

Four Birmingham boys from Hall Green Speedway featured among the competitors at Knowle Stadium on 3 June, with Billy Dallison and 'Bunny' Wilcox, plus brothers Harry and Cyril Taft, all showing them-selves capable of spraying the cinders with the best of them. In particular,

Harry Taft appeared to have some real pep on board his snappy red Douglas. There was a fairly good attendance too, despite the counter attraction of Bristol French week. J.K. Lucas had some bad luck in the Birmingham Handicap semi-final, when, with the race seemingly in the bag, he came a cropper and hit the safety fence. During the whole of the next heat, the St John Ambulance men were kept busy attending to a cut over his eye and removing the cinders from it. It was the only real spill of the evening and Lucas didn't ride again. The final saw the local speedsters to the fore, with Bill Clibbett getting the better of Len Parker for a fine success, while visitor Harry Taft came home third. There was a thrilling duel in the first semi-final of the Birmingham Scratch event, when Harry Taft and Felix Dallimore battled for the lead. It looked as though Dallimore had done enough to prevail when, suddenly, the Birmingham lad took a large lump of twist-grip and shot inside the local rider to take the win. Taft's move was rather too close to be altogether pleasant for Dallimore, who had to be content with second place. In the second semi-final, Cyril Taft started quickly and gave Parker plenty to think about, leading all the way to win in 96.0 seconds. The final, however, was the highlight of the evening, with Dallimore, Parker and the Taft boys lining up at the start. Harry Taft initially took the lead, with Dallimore in hot pursuit behind. Cyril Taft lay third, with Parker, who had struggled out of the start, bringing up the rear. Harry Taft was to develop motor trouble, which cost him the lead on lap two, as Dallimore roared past. Suddenly though, Harry Taft's bike started to fire again and he pressed Dallimore for the rest of the lap, eventually retaking the lead. Parker, meanwhile, had put on a spurt to displace Cyril Taft, prior to edging ahead of Dallimore entering the final lap. Parker then began to haul in Harry Taft and, in an amazing finish, he snatched first place, getting home in 95.2 seconds. The final of the Big 16 event brought another victory for Clibbett, while M. Elliott rode a fine race to finish second after passing Dallison on the last lap.

On 10 June, the meeting at Knowle Stadium opened in unfamiliar fashion, with the track unusually bumpy at the start. Emphasising this, even Bill Clibbett took a fall, as the first five heats of the Bristol Handicap were completed in very slow times. The programme featured a variety of events and included several visiting riders, such as Ivor Hill, Lightning Luke, Tom Lougher, Norman Evans, Harold 'Ginger' Lees and Art Warren. In particular, Lees did his best to liven things up, but the raceway was a little too much for him as he bumped around from scratch in hectic style without gaining a place. Regrettably it was not until the heats of the Bristol *v.* Visitors event that racing assumed its customary brightness. M. Elliott rode splendidly in the second semi-final of the Bristol Handicap when finishing as runner-up to Bill Latchem. The final saw a terrific battle between Felix Dallimore, Elliott and Latchem, although it was a shame that Len Parker dropped out of the running through engine problems. A mistake cost Latchem dear, with Dallimore and Elliott nipping through to fill the leading two positions respectively. In the first semi-final of the Bristol Golden Gauntlet, Elliott overcame a poor start to snatch second place behind Ted Bravery, with Parker subsequently wrapping up the second semi ahead of Norman Evans. The brilliant Parker continued in that vein in the final, again beating Evans to win the event for a sixth time. Meanwhile, Clibbett, the previous holder, had an off-day and could only manage third place. Parker also went on to take the final of the Bristol *v.* Visitors challenge, beating Lees in 93.4 seconds. A varied programme of events also featured two attempts at the rolling-start track record, but both failed. Firstly, Clibbett completed three laps prior to crashing, then Hill tried but twice fell before calling it a day.

Hot and sunny weather made track preparation difficult at Knowle on 17 June, and the visitors from Preston, namely Hamlet 'Ham' Burrill, Joe Abbott, Jack Tye and George Reynard, were clearly ill at ease. The home lads too didn't seem to be quite as happy as usual with the racing surface. In the Preston Handicap, the final saw Jack Douglas put in a valiant effort to catch Bill Hamblin and Felix Dallimore. All his ducking and diving proved to be in vain though, as Hamblin held on to take the win from Dallimore. Young Hamblin hadn't previously been among the winners but, on the evidence of this showing, he certainly looked like another local boy with a bright future. He would, of course, later go on to become team manager of Bristol Bulldogs and was to faithfully serve the club for many years. The Preston Scratch event saw Len Parker win the final ahead of a battling Abbott, with Vic King occupying third spot. Parker and Burrill had a dust-up in heat one of the Bristol *v.* Preston event, but the flying home man eventually pulled away to win in 91.6 seconds. The last race on the programme was also the best, as Parker posted his fifth win of the night, leading Abbott home in the fractionally quicker time of 91.4 seconds. Behind, Ted Bravery plugged away for the duration and succeeded in passing Burrill on the third lap but, despite his frantic efforts, he was unable to catch the second-placed Abbott.

The meeting on 24 June featured a team match, although regrettably it didn't prove much of a spectacle, since Bristol posted a monotonously decisive victory over their West Country rivals from Exeter, winning by 42 points to 10. The match comprised nine heats, run from rolling starts, with a conventional scoring system of 3 points for a race win, 2 for second and 1 for third place. In every race, the Knowle boys secured first place, and in only two heats did they fail to gain second spot as well. It was obvious that the Exeter riders, coming from their much larger track, were over-geared for Bristol's smaller 344-yard circuit. Australian Noel Johnson, whose JAP had a fast reputation on the Exeter track, found it particularly hard adapting to the Knowle raceway. The finest race of the evening brought Knowle regulars Bill Clibbett and Ted Bravery face to face with the Exeter pair of Johnson and Charlie Swift in heat eight. It was very much a Bristol affair, however, for the home duo fought tooth and nail all the way, leaving the visitors out in the cold. Bravery managed to find that bit of extra horsepower to pip his teammate by a tyre width, while Johnson finished some way behind in third place. Bravery and Clibbett also enjoyed a similar tussle in an earlier heat against the Exeter pair of Jack Addison and Fred Hawken, when the first two positions were again filled in the same order. Reg Beer was Exeter's star hope and, in the last team race, he rode splendidly to lead from Felix Dallimore, until a mistake saw him clatter into the safety fence with an almighty clout. That left the way clear for Dallimore to collect the win ahead of visitor Frank Jarman, who had previously secured the only other second place for his team, when only just losing out to Len Parker in heat four. The Exeter Handicap produced some entertaining racing, particularly in the final, which saw W. Spencer beat Bill Latchem in 97.0 seconds. Earlier, Harry Bamford had bitten the dust in front of Cigarette Player, but it could have been much more unpleasant had the latter not sportingly slid to the ground to avoid the stricken rider. In the Exeter Scratch event, Jimmy Haines recorded his first win on the track, when beating Beer in the last of the heats. Track maestro Len Parker went on to take the final of this event, comprehensively beating W. Spencer, with Jarman following behind.

With the sole exception of Billy Lamont, the Wimbledon stars failed to twinkle in their visit to Knowle on 1 July. Lamont, the idol of Australia and acclaimed as one of the world's most spectacular riders, flared up like a meteor in one race, before bad luck set in. The thrill of the evening occurred in heat two of the Flying 8 event, when Lamont met and defeated Bill Clibbett. After numerous false starts and mechanical failures, Lamont got going and, with the throttle wide open, roared around in his characteristic style, crouched low over the handlebars and sliding in wide broadsides close to the safety fence. He held a consistent speed and won in a swift time of 86.8 seconds. In heat three, Jack Douglas eventually came home ahead of Ray Tauser after both had fallen together, while heat four saw Len Parker put one over Dicky Case in no uncertain fashion. In the semi-final, Ted Bravery beat Lamont after the Aussie had fallen – the home rider being flagged as the winner after three laps. A close encounter had been expected in the final, but Parker made it look easy as he defeated Bravery in 88.6 seconds. The amazing Parker went on to complete a clean sweep, beating Clibbett to retain the Golden Gauntlet, prior to taking the Bristol Handicap ahead of Felix Dallimore.

On 8 July, the meeting at Knowle featured some excellent racing, with Arthur Sherlock and Neville Wheeler being the best of the visitors, while Gordon Spalding was also one of the successes of the evening. It wasn't the same for all the competitors, however, since Fred Wilkinson, usually another great rider, struggled to get to grips with the circuit. The first semi-final of the Bristol Handicap produced a super scrap between Turnip Owen and Bill Hamblin, with the former showing great determination to hold off his pursuer after an excellent start. The battle was to end abruptly, when Hamblin fell after overcooking one of the bends and left Ernie Edwards to take up the ultimately unsuccessful chase of Owen. The second semi-final produced close racing too, with Bill Latchem, Spalding, Bill Clibbett and Sherlock battling neck-and-neck, before Clibbett fell and brought down Sherlock. With just two competitors remaining, Spalding cornered at great speed to round Latchem on the last bend to post a fine victory. The final subsequently went to Owen, who managed to get a good getaway and rode with a high degree of skill to come home ahead of Spalding. The Golden Helmet brought out the best in the local boys as Felix Dallimore, Clibbett and Len Parker all won their preliminary races. Dallimore then accounted for the first semi-final after gaining a 50-yard lead, which Clibbett found too much to cope with. In the other semi-final, Parker was a long way ahead when his engine failed and allowed Edwards to take the victory. The final saw Dallimore take the lead on lap one, before brilliantly blocking the attempts of Edwards and Wheeler throughout the rest of the race to come home in pole position. In the Big 12 event, Dallimore reached his second final of the meeting by defeating Alec Bowerman, with Parker and Clibbett also reaching the big showdown. However, Dallimore failed to live up to his earlier standard, leaving Wheeler to battle it out with Parker. Somewhat predictably, the race was to result in another triumph for Parker, who took the lead on the second lap and sailed away to win in 95.0 seconds.

Although the greater part of the meeting on 15 July was run in pouring rain, the Knowle raceway still produced much in the way of entertainment. The visiting boys from Wembley were fired up from the start and all rode well, particularly Colin Watson and the redoubtable Harry '£100' Whitfield. Among the most thrilling races were those in which Len Parker and Watson were engaged. Both men favoured the inside line, but also managed to combine daring with clever tactics. As such, the second semi-final of the Wembley Scratch was a classic, with Watson producing a fabulous last-bend swoop to pass Bill Clibbett for victory. Clibbett, who actually came down as Watson sped past, strained a cartilage, but pluckily took his place in the final. The big race subsequently featured a tussle between Parker and Watson, but the Wembley man fell on the second lap, leaving the popular home favourite to cruise home ahead of Felix Dallimore in 93.6 seconds. In heat one of the Big 16 event, the fastest time of the evening was returned in what was arguably the finest race ever seen at Knowle. Watson got away second to Parker and set after the local man, cutting through on the inside to marginally take the lead after two laps. The two riders remained locked together until the last bend, when Parker found an extra bit of drive to pull ahead and win brilliantly in 92.0 seconds. Parker went on to triumph in the final ahead of Whitfield, who thrilled the crowd in breathless fashion, standing up on his footrest as he entered the turns. In what was a tremendous night's racing, Parker totally dominated proceedings by winning all eight races that he appeared in. Another feature of an excellent meeting was the tactical riding of comparative newcomer Vic King.

Triss Sharp, a Knowle track expert of old, led the visitors from Crystal Palace in a very entertaining meeting on 22 July. Sharp and future Bristol rider Harry 'Shep' Shepherd were easily the best of the visiting boys, although the home lads held sway through the excellent riding of Len Parker, Bill Clibbett and Jack Douglas. Indeed, Parker again proved himself to be the master of the circuit by taking the Visitors' Handicap. Sharp, last away in the first semi-final, strove vainly to gain the lead, but ultimately failed as he trailed in behind Cliff Bamford and Ernie Edwards. The final saw the other Bamford, Harry, fighting hard to keep the lead after a good start. However, he was unable to withstand the pressure from Parker, who stormed through to win, with Edwards subsequently just pipping Bamford for second place. The Big 16 event attracted a good field and saw Parker establish an early lead in heat one despite the efforts of Turnip Owen and Sharp. In heat two, Joe Francis and Bill Latchem failed to retain their seats, which gave Clibbett all the time in the world to take victory. Jack Douglas took a first-lap lead in heat three and could have walked home, such was the huge gap he opened up. Heat four saw Shepherd give of his best, which was sufficient to get him past the post in first place. So to the final, which looked certain to be a straight battle between Parker and Clibbett. Unfortunately, for the latter, he dropped his machine, leaving Parker to romp away and win from Jack Douglas. The Golden Gauntlet provided a keen contest, with Felix Dallimore and Shepherd winning their respective semi-finals. Parker made no mistake in the final, screaming from the start and pulling away to win from Shepherd in 93.4 seconds. This was Parker's eighth victory in the event and capped yet another fine evening for the local man.

Despite rain, there was some eventful racing at Knowle on 29 July, when the visiting riders included Gus Kuhn of Stamford Bridge, plus the Leicester boys Alec Bowerman, Neville Wheeler, Bert Spencer and Hal Herbert. Mounted on board a Rudge, Kuhn noticeably wasn't quite so happy as when riding a Douglas on his previous visit to the track. Tommy Webb cleaned up in the final of the Leicester Handicap, winning in dashing style from E. Taylor and Cliff Bamford. Meanwhile, Bill Clibbett, riding from scratch, was unable to catch the leaders and finished in an unusual position for him… stone last! The final of the Bristol Scratch looked like developing into a super duel between Len Parker and Clibbett. The two speedsters traded places a couple of times, before Clibbett came down heavily on the straight. Almost simultaneously the closely following Felix Dallimore also fell, leaving Gordon Spalding to weave his way through the debris to take second place. A Match Race series between W. Spencer and Ernie Edwards produced some good riding, as the former took the first two heats. However, as Edwards had fallen in their second encounter, Spencer generously decided that there should be a third race. In the extra heat, Edwards brilliantly snatched the lead on the last lap to win, after Spencer had held sway all the way from the start. The fastest time of the evening was 91.2 seconds and this was twice clocked. The first to achieve the time was Clibbett, when he just got home ahead of Ted Bravery in heat two of the Bristol *v.* Visitors event. Then, in the very next race, Jack Douglas recorded the exact same time in defeating Wheeler. Immediately after the race, Douglas came off in a most unpleasant mix-up with Tommy Webb, suffering a damaged knee. Bravely, he took his place in the final, but he was unable to live with the hot pace of Kuhn and Clibbett. Initially, Kuhn led, but only just. Then, the chasing Clibbett fell, and after remounting, he managed to regain second place. By then, however, Kuhn was out of sight and over the line for an easier than expected victory.

On 5 August, in front of a large and appreciative attendance, Stamford Bridge's Gus Kuhn again revealed a liking for the Knowle raceway to clinch a hat-trick of successes. Meanwhile, Jack Ormston, Charlie Barrett, Jack Jackson and Norman Evans of Wembley all rode as well as any visitors had all season in Bristol. Indeed, Ormston was particularly unlucky to have his chain come off when holding a useful position, not just once, but on two occasions. The final of the Bristol Handicap was a Gus Kuhn affair. From scratch, he roared through the field, leaving Evans and Harry Bamford to battle for the minor places. The all-action Ted Bravery had been expected to challenge Kuhn, but he unfortunately bit the dust on the opening lap. However, prior to falling, he again showed himself to be one of the most spectacular riders ever to grace the Knowle circuit. Bravery did have another go at Kuhn in one of the heats for the Golden Helmet but, despite running him close, he had to settle for second place. Len Parker and Bill Clibbett were the two central figures in the first semi-final of the Bristol Golden Helmet, as they raced shoulder-to-shoulder. Clibbett held a slight lead as they hit the last lap and the crowd lifted in anticipation of the usual last-bend swoop from Parker. However, it wasn't to be as the twist grip came off in his hand and he uncharacteristically hit the deck. Kuhn won the other semi-final to set up a scrap against local men Clibbett and Felix Dallimore, with the Wembley duo of Evans and Jackson completing a cracking line-up. It turned out to be a disaster for the local fans though, as Clibbett over-slid on the first bend and Dallimore appeared to encounter motor problems. Dallimore plugged away, but could only secure third place after Jackson had fallen on the last lap. Up front, Kuhn won with ease, ahead of Evans, in a quick 93.4 seconds. The Big 16 final looked like being another thriller, with Kuhn, Parker and Clibbett at the start line. However, Clibbett again overcooked a corner, while Parker just couldn't seem to get going in his customary fashion. Kuhn went on to win in style, with Evans again filling the runner-up spot.

Ted Bravery was the star of the show at Knowle on 12 August, when he took victory in a Match Race series against Gordon Spalding. However, although his riding was brilliantly daring, at times he tended to be a little overzealous. Heat one saw Bravery steer his Rudge to an easy victory in 91.4 seconds, which turned out to be the fastest recorded time of the evening. Holding the inside line in superb fashion throughout, Spalding squared the series in heat two, setting up a dramatic decider. This was to provide fabulous entertainment for the crowd, as Bravery flung himself into the corners with Spalding right on his tail. On the last bend, Spalding ripped around on his favoured inside line and it looked for a moment as if he would do it, but Bravery brilliantly held on to get the verdict by half a wheel. In the Bristol Scratch event, one of the heats saw Bill Clibbett slide off, with the closely following Harry Taft quickly laying his machine down to avoid the stricken rider. Unfortunately, Bravery was unable to avoid the melee and, after hitting the pile of men and machines, he took off, flying at least six feet into the air. It looked as though he was going to clear the safety fence, but he landed with a thud on the track, just in front of the barrier. Unbelievably, no one was hurt and they all walked back to the pits unaided. The Bamford brothers supplied something of a comedy touch after they had both qualified for the Bristol Scratch final. Since they only had one machine and one crash helmet between them, it was a dilemma as to what would happen. As they scratched their heads, Vic Worlock came to the rescue with the loan of his bike but, as it turned out, Harry Bamford was unable to get his borrowed steed to go. Birmingham's Harry Taft subsequently went on to win the final ahead of Jack Douglas, while Cliff Bamford occupied third spot. Clibbett and Taft were later involved in a great duel in the final of the Big 16 event, with the local man coming home in front following a typically dashing ride.

The combination of good weather and a well-prepared circuit made for some splendid racing at Knowle on 19 August. A Match Race series between Len Parker and Bill Clibbett was the main feature and a record crowd was present to witness the long-awaited duel. However, Clibbett had been to the dentist during the afternoon and wasn't feeling 100 per cent fit. In heat one, he fell off on the opening lap and the race had to be restarted. Clibbett slightly led the re-run, but went wide on the pits bend, allowing Parker to slip inside and, from there, he made no mistake. Heat two saw Clibbett again fall, having been on Parker's rear wheel for three laps, with the 'King of Knowle' going on to triumph in a super-fast 86.4 seconds. The second top-notch performance of the evening came from Ted Bravery, who won four races, including the August Scratch final. He only just lost out in the final of the Big 16 event to Parker, having ridden his Rudge in a masterful style, sliding really fast into the turns before wrenching it away from the fence by sheer brute force. Despite his battling efforts, he couldn't prevent the flying Parker from winning yet another Knowle final. Earlier on, W. Spencer had taken victory ahead of Felix Dallimore in the August Handicap. Spencer in fact, had a great evening, winning five out of the six races in which he participated. Another welcome addition to the programme was D. Cameron, who had taken up racing again after an elongated rest. He won a handicap heat in 95.0 seconds and was second to Spencer in a scratch heat. Wal Hicklin and Del Forster were the visiting riders for the evening and both rode well. Hicklin, who had appeared at the previous Knowle meeting was a little unlucky, although he did gain two race wins in the heats and took third place in the final of the August Scratch event.

Wal Hicklin made his third successive visit to Knowle on 26 August and he had obviously mastered the tightness of the track, which had been the undoing of many a visitor. He secured a number of firsts in the heats and ran a second to Len Parker in the final of the Big 16 event. Aside from Hicklin, there were several other visiting riders, including Charlie Barrett, Ron Thompson and Champ Upham. But, Hicklin apart, none of them got to grips at all well with the Knowle raceway. A welcome addition to those participating was J.C. Bamford, the third member of the family, who put in a fine effort to finish fourth in one of the Golden Gauntlet heats. A Match Race challenge between the popular Felix Dallimore and E. Taylor provided much spectacle for those in attendance. The series had to go to a decider after Dallimore had overdone a corner and come down just before the end of lap two. Dallimore duly wrapped up a 2-1 victory and was much the faster of the two on the straights, although Taylor was always able to make up lots of ground on the turns. Meanwhile, Parker again retained the Golden Gauntlet, but only after Gordon Spalding had chased him hard the whole way round. Spalding was very much on form, but tended to drift across the bends throughout the evening and that cost him several races. This was Parker's fourth successive triumph in the Golden Gauntlet and the ninth time overall he had won the event. It was a mixed bag for a couple of the other Bristol regulars though, as old favourite Bill Clibbett continued to go through a bit of a rough patch, winning just one heat all night. However, the crowd-pleasing Ted Bravery rode in his usual hectic manner and cleaned up in the Visitors' Handicap, winning the second semi-final and the final from scratch.

The first round of the Challenge Cup Track Championship, sponsored by the *Evening Times*, was included among a busy programme at Knowle on 3 September. Ted Bravery won heat one, although Turnip Owen tried very hard and pushed him all the way. Heat two saw Jack Douglas come from behind to defeat Harry Bamford, who had led the way over the first two laps. In heat three, Ernie Edwards took victory from Stanley Gill, with E. Taylor subsequently winning heat four from Cliff Bamford. Heat five was a walkover for W. Spencer after D. Cameron had been unable to get his machine going. The last heat of the scheduled six saw Tommy Webb initially hold sway, only for a fall to let Vic Worlock through for an unchallenged win. Miss 'Sunny' Somerset, alias Vera Hole from Watchet, along with Art Warren and Bill Crouch were the visitors to Knowle for the meeting. Miss Somerset was involved in a Match Race with Art Warren, but mechanical problems turned the event into a fiasco for the local girl and she was unable to mount a competitive challenge, losing 2-0. W. Spencer and Edwards, who previously had a challenge race series on 29 July, were at it again, albeit in just one heat rather than three. Following several restarts after both riders had taken tumbles, Spencer was again to triumph, although he was clocked at a somewhat slow 112.6 seconds. The most memorable moment of the evening occurred when Jack Douglas lost control of his steed and made a beeline for the officials' hut on the centre green. Those inside the box made a mighty quick escape although, regrettably, their time off the mark wasn't recorded! Luckily, Douglas managed to avoid all the officials, but he was something of a hero on the night since, in the Somerset Handicap, he won the first semi-final and went on to take the final ahead of the great Len Parker. It just wasn't Parker's night for, despite winning the first semi-final of the Bristol Scratch event, it was Bill Latchem who crossed the line ahead in the final, with W. Spencer in second spot.

On 9 September, the meeting at Knowle provided spectators with a real mixed bag. The second series of heats for the *Evening Times* Challenge Cup Track Championship produced some good races, whereas the Best Broadsiders' event failed lamentably. A number of heats with an award for the best slider were run, while there was also a first prize for the man who sprayed the most cinders over the safety fence. Ted Bravery took this idea a little too far, when a spectacular fall resulted in a flight over the fence before he came to rest on the dog track. Members of the supporters' club judged these events and E. Taylor was certainly the most consistent broadsider on show. However, it generally appeared as though the riders had learned the art of white-lining too thoroughly to take kindly again to the more spectacular but slightly slower broadsiding method. In heat seven of the Track Championship, M. Elliott jetted from the start to lead, but a fall was to cost him dear, with Jim Douglas taking advantage to win in 95.6 seconds. Heat eight saw Bill Hamblin surprisingly beat Felix Dallimore in 94.2 seconds. Bill Latchem took heat nine after J. Bamford had fallen, but then came the real race of the night. Bill Clibbett led Jimmy Haines, only to crash down and give his opponent a five-second lead as he remounted. Amazingly, Clibbett had reclaimed the lead by the end of the first lap, only to hit the deck once more. As he picked himself up, Haines again went by, but Clibbett got back on his steed and took up the chase, eventually retaking the lead and going on for a fine victory. Amazingly, he was clocked at 98.2 seconds, which was nothing short of remarkable under the circumstances. Heat eleven saw Gordon Spalding return the excellent time of 91.6 seconds in defeating Vic King. To conclude the series for the evening, Len Parker allowed Cigarette Player to lead him for two laps, before bursting through to win in 95.0 seconds. Parker followed that up by winning his semi-final and the final of the Bristol Scratch event, once again proving himself to be the champion of the Bristol circuit. The visiting riders included John Deeley, Arthur 'Tiny' Tims, Bill Ashcroft and Cyril Taft from the Midlands, but none of them fared too well throughout the evening.

Jack Douglas put up a tremendous show at Knowle on 16 September, racing home ahead of Len Parker in the fast time of 91.4 seconds to win the final of the Bristol Scratch event. Earlier, the second round of the *Evening Times* Challenge Cup Track Championship produced some good races. In heat one Gordon Spalding beat Jim Douglas handsomely, while E. Taylor cleaned up the second race after Jack Douglas had twice fallen.

Bill Clibbett also fell a couple of times in his heat with Ted Bravery, as the latter stormed home in 93.4 seconds. In heat five, W. Spencer enjoyed a runaway win from Bill Hamblin, who finished a good way behind due to having to hold his flywheel on with his foot! Then Len Parker gave Ernie Edwards a four-second start in heat six and his win was made doubly sure when his opponent came down on the last lap. The Autumn Handicap final provided much in the way of entertainment, with Stanley Gill leading the way until he fell. That allowed surprise package Vic King to take over up front and he held on grimly until right near the end, when Parker inevitably slid gracefully through to win by just a few yards. A Match Race between Spalding and E. Taylor showed just how much the latter had improved, as he rode to two straight wins by handsome margins, although it must be said that his motor was much the hotter of the two. The visitors for the meeting were Wal Hicklin, Ron Thompson, Lew Lancaster and Wilmot Evans, all of whom tried hard but enjoyed little in the way of success.

No one was at all surprised when Len Parker crossed the line to add the *Evening Times* Challenge Cup Track Championship to his long list of achievements at Knowle Stadium on 23 September. The final had seen Gordon Spalding tenaciously hold the lead until the second lap, with Parker then slipping through on the inside of the pits bend before powering on to triumph with aplomb. The other finalist, W. Spencer, was misfiring badly and finished a good distance behind in third place. Previously, in the final qualifying round, Spencer had beaten Vic Worlock, while Parker had put paid to the hopes of E. Taylor. The third and last qualifier unfortunately led to an altercation between the crowd and the stewards after it was announced that the highly popular Ted Bravery wouldn't be permitted to ride against Spalding. This was because Bravery rode a Rudge machine and the powers that be had decreed that the meeting should be an all-Douglas affair! As Bravery either couldn't or wouldn't ride a Douglas, he decided not to compete. It was to turn into another wonderful evening for Parker though, as he also went on to win the Big 16 event ahead of Jack Douglas, before defeating Turnip Owen to take the September Handicap. Jack Douglas achieved the almost impossible, beating Parker in the first semi-final of the Bristol Scratch event, but the Bathonian had his revenge, winning the final by the proverbial mile in 91.0 seconds. Stressing his dominance, the win took Parker's tally of heat victories on the night to nine out of the ten races in which he participated. Further emphasising his brilliance at the Bristol raceway, his four final successes on the night took his grand total of title wins at the circuit to sixty-one! Four visiting riders were present, namely Joe Dallison, Tiny Tims, John Deeley and Arthur Johnson, but none of them really got a look in against the local lads. Among a large crowd, many women could be seen sporting the attractive beret in the colours of the Bristol Speedway Supporters' Club. Regrettably, this proved to be the last meeting at Knowle for six years. All the initial enthusiasm seemed to have waned, due, it seemed, to the combination of an unvaried race programme, poor track preparation and the lack of suitable machinery. More clues regarding these aspects could be gleaned from an article entitled 'The swing of the pendulum' by R.I.M. Samuel, which appeared in the Olympia special edition of the *Conrod* in 1930. In it, Mr Samuel stated that 'despite its increasing popularity, there are many enthusiasts who feel that, notwithstanding an all-round increase in the quality of the racing, its spectacular appeal is not so great. Why? The reason is not hard to find. Broadsiding – the skilful sliding round the bends with the machine at a wide angle to the line of travel – has largely disappeared, and with it the visible demonstration of riding skill which used to get the crowd on its toes. Undoubtedly the skill is still with us, but it is no longer so obvious, and speedway racing is the poorer for its disappearance.' He went on: 'To appreciate what has happened, it is necessary to trace briefly the history of the sport in this country. When, in 1928, the first promoters endeavored to interest the public, their riders were a pretty hopeless lot of novices using, for the most part, touring machines of a variety of makes and accessories. Little wonder then that the great *Daily Mail*, which has now given the sport its blessing in the very practical form of putting up the National Trophy, described the earlier meetings as being nothing better than circuses.' Mr Samuel continued: 'Then the Australian contingent arrived, mounted, most of them, on Douglas machines. Immediately the racing took on a new aspect, and the public was given its introduction to broadsiding, with all its thrills. The success of speedway racing in this country was established when the first expert Australians showed us how a combination of speed and skill, heavily spiced with spectacular broadsiding, could raise the hair on our heads! It is significant that Douglases were essential to success in those days, and it is no idle boast to say that the Kingswood factory put the new sport on the map. To modernise an old saying, every motorcycle has its day. The Douglas certainly had its year so far as speedway racing is concerned, for 1928-29 saw the famous twin almost universally used on the cinders. But competition was bound to come, and public favour is notoriously fickle. The big single began to appear. It is only scant justice to say that it proved fast and easy to handle. Some of the more successful riders abandoned their speedy twins and the season, which has just closed, saw the temporary eclipse of the Douglas at speedway.' He concluded: 'I can afford to be candid, for everyone who has a lengthy connection with the motorcycle industry knows and appreciates at their proper value these swings of the pendulum. I am convinced, and I am voicing an opinion, which is shared by competent judges including many of the more successful riders, that the Douglas will quickly regain its popular position on the track. The promoters recognise the loss of spectacular effect due to the temporary eclipse of the Douglas on the track, and this is obvious from the suggestions that the use of Douglases should be made imperative. This, however would be impracticable and it is very much better that the Douglas should win its way back to universal use by sheer merit, as it assuredly will. Meanwhile, it is significant that many of the big stars who have gone to Buenos Aires for the winter months have taken Douglases with them. These include such famous riders as Sprouts Elder, Billy Lamont, Eric and Oliver Langton, and Arthur Westwood.'

The outstanding figure from the early days of Bristol Speedway was without doubt Len Parker. He took victory in most of the leading events, having graduated as a skilled road rider and won numerous awards in all sorts of open trials, as well as the sidecar TT. He also competed in several junior and senior TT races on the Isle of Man, although he was unable to repeat his 1925 sidecar success due to engine malfunctions. How fitting it was that he should have won all four titles on the race card of what turned out to be the last dirt-track event at Knowle until 1936.

SUMMARY OF 1930 MEETINGS

Date	Event	Winner/Result
29 April	Open Handicap	Bill Clibbett
	Bristol Scratch Race	Len Parker
	Big 8 Race	Jack Douglas
6 May	Stamford Handicap	W. Spencer
	Stamford Scratch Race	Ted Bravery
	Big 8 Race	Ted Bravery
13 May	Meeting postponed	

20 May	Bristol Golden Gauntlet	Bill Clibbett
	Portsmouth Handicap	Len Parker
	Big 8 Race	Jack Douglas
27 May	Bristol Handicap	Jim Douglas
	Bristol Scratch Race	Bill Clibbett
	Big 16 Race	Vic Huxley
3 June	Birmingham Handicap	Bill Clibbett
	Birmingham Scratch Race	Len Parker
	Big 16 Race	Bill Clibbett
10 June	Bristol Golden Gauntlet	Len Parker
	Bristol Handicap	Felix Dallimore
	Bristol v. Visitors' Race	Len Parker
17 June	Preston Handicap	Bill Hamblin
	Preston Scratch Race	Len Parker
	Bristol v. Preston Race	Len Parker
24 June	Exeter Handicap	W. Spencer
	Exeter Scratch Race	Len Parker
	Bristol v. Exeter	Bristol 42 Exeter 10
1 July	Bristol Golden Gauntlet	Len Parker
	Bristol Handicap	Len Parker
	Flying 8 Match Race	Len Parker
8 July	Bristol Golden Helmet	Felix Dallimore
	Bristol Handicap	Turnip Owen
	Big 12 Race	Len Parker
15 July	Midsummer Handicap	Len Parker
	Wembley Scratch Race	Len Parker
	Big 16 Race	Len Parker
22 July	Bristol Golden Gauntlet	Len Parker
	Visitors' Handicap	Len Parker
	Big 16 Race	Len Parker
29 July	Leicester Handicap	Tommy Webb
	Bristol Scratch Race	Len Parker
	Bristol v. Visitors Race	Gus Kuhn
5 August	Bristol Golden Helmet	Gus Kuhn
	Bristol Handicap	Gus Kuhn
	Big 16 Race	Gus Kuhn
12 August	Bristol Handicap	Harry Bamford
	Bristol Scratch Race	Harry Taft
	Big 16 Race	Bill Clibbett
19 August	August Handicap	W. Spencer
	August Scratch Race	Ted Bravery
	Big 16 Race	Len Parker
26 August	Bristol Golden Gauntlet	Len Parker

	Visitors' Handicap	Ted Bravery
	Big 16 Race	Len Parker
3 September	Somerset Handicap	Jack Douglas
	Bristol Scratch Race	Bill Latchem
9 September	Bristol Scratch Race	Len Parker
	Broadsiding Handicap	Len Parker
16 September	Autumn Handicap	Len Parker
	Bristol Scratch Race	Jack Douglas
23 September	*Evening Times* Track Championship	Len Parker
	September Handicap	Len Parker
	Bristol Scratch Race	Len Parker
	Big 16 Race	Len Parker

1936

After an absence of five-and-a-half years, it was announced that speedway was to return to Bristol, promoted by 'Knowle Greyhound Stadium' and managed locally by Ronnie Greene. Primarily, Bristol Speedway would be a nursery for Wimbledon assets, who made up the bulk of the 1936 side that entered the National Provincial League – British speedway's then equivalent of the Second Division. Indeed, mainstays of the team Eric Collins, Bill Rogers, Fred Leavis, Bert Spencer and Mike Erskine were all borrowed from Wimbledon. Spencer, incidentally, was mistakenly thought to be of Australian origin, but had actually been born in Richmond, Surrey in 1908. He emigrated to Brisbane with his family as a three year old and subsequently rode as an Australian international. Meanwhile, Roy Dook and Harry Shepherd were loaned from New Cross, a fact that Mr Greene was extremely grateful for, acknowledging the help received from Fred Mockford, promoter at the circuit affectionately known as the 'Frying Pan'. Due to the Wimbledon connection, the motif on the Bristol race jacket was a star similar to the one used by the Dons. However, instead of the London club's red-and-yellow colours, Bristol used black and orange.

The dawning of the new era didn't begin at Knowle, however, for Bristol's first meeting back in action was a Provincial League fixture at Nottingham on 28 April. And what a start it was, as the newcomers claimed a marvellous 34-33 victory, with skipper Roy Dook establishing a new track record of 75.36 seconds in the opening heat, on his way to a four-ride maximum. His best support came from Harry Shepherd, who weighed in with 10 points, while Australian Bill Rogers scored 8. For Nottingham, Bill Stanley recorded 10 points, while Chun Moore notched 9. Stanley in fact, was involved in the strangest race of the meeting, when he proved the only finisher in heat eleven, clocking 82.33 seconds – the slowest time of the match.

The eagerly awaited first meeting back at Knowle Stadium took place on 8 May, when Southampton were the visitors for a league fixture. Bristol ran out winners by 38 points to 32, with Eric Collins storming to a full tally of 12 points and clocking the fastest time of the match, 74.0 seconds, to create a new track record for the revamped 290-yard circuit. The rest of the home side scored solidly throughout, with Roy Dook gathering 8 points, Harry Shepherd 7, Fred Leavis 5 and Bill Rogers 4. Meanwhile, for Southampton, Alec Statham was top man with 11 points. A link with the first period of racing at the stadium came in the shape of former rider Bill Hamblin, who was the starting-line marshal. Hamblin had in fact participated in the sidecar event in the very first meeting at Knowle on 25 August 1928. Another tie-up with the initial period of track action saw former rider Vic Anstice installed as the regular ACU timekeeper and judge. Other regular meeting officials during 1936 were: Frank Lewis (announcer), Dr N.P. Eskell (honorary medical officer), F.E.B. Fellows (chief pit marshal), W. Mortimer (flag steward), G. Tucker and S. Harrison (lap scorers), while Ronnie Greene also acted as clerk of the course.

A week later on 15 May, Cardiff were the visitors to Knowle in another league match, which Bristol won 38-33. Top scorer in the home camp was Mike Erskine with 11 points, while George Greenwood thumped in a 12-point maximum for the visitors and posted the fastest time of the match in heat three when timed at 76.4 seconds. The return match with Cardiff took place five days later, when Bristol suffered defeat for the first time since their return to track action, losing 39-33. Flying Aussie Eric Collins was top scorer for Bristol with 11 points and, although Harry Shepherd chipped in with 8, the rest of the side failed to score sufficiently to save the match. The defeat didn't really matter though, as Cardiff later resigned, with all their results being expunged from the league table.

Back home at Knowle on 22 May, Bristol entertained Liverpool in their fifth Provincial League match, running out winners by 41 points to 30. Harry Shepherd topped the scoring, plundering 11 points, with Fred Leavis next in line on 8. Jack Hargreaves was Liverpool's best, recording 10 points in a side that also included Oliver Hart and the Lancashire-born Tommy Price. Next on the agenda was a trip to Southampton for league business on 28 May, where Bristol went down to a heavy 43-29 defeat. Only Harry Shepherd showed any real resistance in scoring 9 points. The Bristol boys soon put the memory of that loss behind them though, easily beating Nottingham 43-29 the following night at Knowle. Eric Collins returned to the top of the Bristol scorechart, gleaning 11 points from the match. For the beleaguered Nottingham side, South African Cecil De La Porte was the only rider to show any real form, scoring 6 points.

Plymouth were the visitors to Knowle on 5 June, but the homesters again ran out winners by 40 points to 32. Eric Collins was back to maximum form with another 12-point haul, while Dick Wise topped the Plymouth scoring with 10 points. Collins also clocked a new track-record time of 70.5 seconds in heat two. A week later on 12 June, Bristol's impressive home record was left in tatters, as Southampton returned in a Provincial Trophy match and won by 38 points to 32. Although super Aussie Eric Collins recorded another unbeaten 12 points, he received little in the way of support from his teammates. It should be pointed out that Bristol were below strength, with Mike Erskine absent through illness while Roy Dook and Harry Shepherd had to ride in a National Trophy tie at Hackney for their 'first claim' team New Cross. Nevertheless, Southampton gained much credit as they rode with great determination throughout and, having built up a lead of 9 points during the first half of the meeting, they kept a grip to win fairly comfortably in the end. Owing to bad weather, times were slower than usual, with Bristol's acting captain Eric Collins recording the best time of 75.2 seconds. Fred Strecker and Billy Dallison led the way for the solid-scoring Saints with 8 points apiece, while both Frank Goulden and Syd Griffiths tallied 7.

Returning to league action on 15 June, Bristol travelled up to Liverpool where they lost by a single point, 36-35. It was a great effort though, with Eric Collins bagging another 12-point maximum and Harry Shepherd scoring 10. All America visited Knowle four days later in a challenge match, boasting a side that included Putt Mossman (captain), Sam Arena, Byrd McKinney, Manuel Trujillo, Pete Colman, Bo Lisman, Roy Grant and a certain Pee Wee Cullum, who went on to ride for Belle Vue. In an action-packed meeting, Bristol ran out 57-49 winners, with three riders in double figures, namely Ernie Evans (11), Shepherd (10) and Roy Dook (10), while Arena (16) and Mossman (11) were America's top men.

On 23 June, Bristol ventured back to Nottingham for a Provincial Trophy meeting and raced to a brilliant 43-27 victory. The side was led superbly by Wal Morton, who weighed in with a 12-point full-house, while Eric Collins and Roy Dook recorded 10 apiece. Next up at Knowle were Liverpool in another Provincial Trophy fixture on 26 June, but it was a disastrous night for the homesters, who went down by 40 points to 32. The track wasn't in the best of conditions, with a very slick patch coming out of the first bend, and this was to cause the Bristol boys far more problems than their visitors. Eric Collins fell in heat two and was pinned under his machine, resulting in him missing his next ride. Although Collins later came out to win heat nine from the back, the 3 points he gained from the race were his only contribution on the night. In another heat, Harry Shepherd fell and brought down Liverpool's Ernie Price, with Bert Spencer running onto the grass to avoid the carnage. The race eventually resulted in a share of the points, after Shepherd had remounted to take third spot behind winner Jack Hargreaves of Liverpool and the second-placed Spencer. Man of the Match Tommy Price won each of his four starts, as well as his heat and the final of the scratch race event in the second half. Oliver Hart also chipped in with 12 points for Liverpool, while Shepherd (8) and Ernie Evans (7) were Bristol's top performers.

The popular American tourists returned to Knowle for another challenge match on 3 July, but again Bristol were victorious, winning 62-43, with Roy Dook chalking up 14 points, while Eric Collins weighed in with 13 and Harry Shepherd scored 10. Dook also recorded the fastest time of the meeting, winning heat one in 72.8 seconds. As with the previous American visit on 19 June, Putt Mossman and Sam Arena were the tourists' best riders on the night.

H.R. Hatsell, speedway correspondent for the *Evening World*, explained in an article that Bristol had by this time already established a thriving supporters' club with several thousand members, each of whom proudly wore the club badge at meetings. Meanwhile, flags were available for cars and motorcycles, and there was also a club tie! Later in the same article, 'HRH', as he was known, mentioned the training diets of riders. Apparently the Hackney team had 'trained' on beer at the start of the season, but had later wisely changed to tomato juice!

After a month of Provincial Trophy and challenge match action, Bristol returned to important league business when visiting Plymouth on 7 July. It was a triumphant return too, as they claimed a narrow 37-35 victory. Bill Rogers and Roy Dook led the Bristol scoring, each recording 11 points, while Dick Wise top scored for Plymouth with a tally of 9. Australian Billy Lamont rode for the Panthers but only scored 3 points and it would be fair to comment that his career was unfortunately on the wane after he had been one of the great pioneer riders in the 1920s. Bristol skipper Roy Dook also had the distinction of recording the fastest time of the night in heat twelve, when clocked at 79.2 seconds.

The Plymouth boys visited Knowle three days later for what was supposed to be a Provincial Trophy meeting; however, it was altered to a challenge match after heat seven due to adverse weather conditions. Bristol went on to win easily 46-22 but, as an indication of the poor conditions, every recorded time throughout the match was over 85.0 seconds – some 15 seconds outside the track record! Fred Leavis recorded 11 points for Bristol, with Harry Shepherd and Roy Dook each scoring 9. For Plymouth, Fred Tuck contributed 8 points, while reserve Billy Lamont wasn't given any rides at all!

Bristol once again ventured to Nottingham on 14 July, but were hammered out of sight, 53-19, in a Provincial League encounter, with Eric Collins and Roy Dook being the joint top scorers on 5 points apiece. This was followed by individual action at Knowle on 17 July, when a round of the Provincial League Riders' Championship was staged. A good field was assembled and Southampton's Frank Goulden emerged as the winner with 14 points. Full result: Goulden 14; Tommy Price 12; Billy Dallison 12; Eric Collins 10; Dick Wise 9; George Greenwood 9; Roy Dook 8; Harry Shepherd 7; Fred Leavis 7; Jack Hobson 6; Tiger Hart 5; Les Gregory 5; Ted Bravery 4; Stan Hart 4; Bert Jones 3; Eric Blain 1. Bravery was, of course, another link with the past, having ridden at Knowle in the initial period of action between 1928 and 1930.

Liverpool beckoned on 20 July, as the Bristol boys travelled north for a Provincial Trophy match that they gleefully won 42-30. In scoring

10 points, Bert Spencer was their best performer on the night, his tally including a win over Tommy Price in heat eleven to dash the Liverpool star's hoped-for maximum. Instead, Price had to be satisfied with 11 points and the fastest time of the night in the opening race, when clocked at 86.6 seconds. The main meeting was followed by a match race, which saw Price defeat Les Wotton.

Back at Knowle on 24 July, West Ham Hawks visited in another Provincial Trophy match. Bristol won easily though, taking the meeting by a 43-29 scoreline, with both Eric Collins and Harry Shepherd storming to 11-point totals. For what amounted to West Ham's second side, Eric Chitty claimed 11 points, while other team members included Rol Stobart, Charlie Spinks and George Saunders.

Four days later, Bristol visited Plymouth for more Provincial Trophy action, losing heavily by 46 points to 25. On what must have been a difficult track surface, winning times ranged from 84.8 seconds in heat eleven, by Les Bowden, to 96.0 seconds in heat three, by Harry Shepherd. Conditions must have improved as the meeting went along, although things clearly didn't get better for Bristol, who felt the brunt of the Plymouth onslaught. Only Bill Rogers and Harry Shepherd were able to return with any credit, each finishing with 8 points. Meanwhile, for the rampant Plymouth side, Australian Les Bowden flew to a 12-point full house, while Les Gregory (10), Jack Bibby (8) and Dick Wise (8) also made solid contributions.

On 31 July, Liverpool journeyed down to Knowle on Provincial League business. It was a field night for the homesters though, as they trounced their Merseyside rivals 52-19. On a night of misery for the visitors, Bristol riders crossed the finishing line first in every single heat. Fred Leavis rocketed to a 12-point maximum, while Harry Shepherd (11), Eric Collins (8), Bill Rogers (8) and Mike Erskine (8) all scored heavily. For the beleaguered Liverpool side, Tommy Price was totally outclassed and only Alan Butler (4), Ernie Price (4) and Jack Hargreaves (4) offered token resistance.

Legendary manager Johnnie Hoskins brought his West Ham side to Knowle for a challenge match on Bank Holiday Monday 3 August, when a Bristol & New Cross composite side comfortably won 43-29. Then again, they did have George Newton, Jack Milne and Norman Evans riding for them! Harry Shepherd and Mike Erskine, the only two Bristol representatives in the match, understandably found the opposition a bit too hot – Shepherd gaining just 3 points, while Erskine could only muster 1. It was the first opportunity of seeing riders from the National League in opposition at Knowle and the start of the meeting had to be delayed so as to let in the crowd of some 10,000. The track record was broken three times on the night, with England international George Newton recording 70.4 seconds in heats one and eight, while Norman Evans matched that time in heat nine. It was a marvellous night for the faithful Knowle fans, as they also got to see the likes of Tiger Stevenson, Mike Murphy, Tommy Croombs and Arthur Atkinson in action.

Next on the agenda was the visit of Nottingham for a Provincial League encounter on 7 August, and this was actually the night that the 'Bulldogs' were born. The programme for the meeting contained an interesting letter from supporters' club member no. 1289, with the writer suggesting that, as Southampton had a saint, and Plymouth had a panther, why didn't Bristol have a bulldog? Presumably it was Ronnie Greene who replied and he had no objection, so from then on the team was known as 'Bristol Bulldogs'. Anyway, the match resulted in a 43-29 success, with both Eric Collins and Wal Morton netting 10-point tallies. For Nottingham, George Greenwood grabbed 10 points, while Tiger Hart recorded 9. Also, on an historic night, the flying Collins further lowered the track record in heat one, scorching around in 69.2 seconds.

Three days later, the Bulldogs travelled up to Merseyside and lost 39-33 to a Tommy Price-inspired Liverpool side in a Provincial League match. Wal Morton recorded a quite superb maximum for the visitors but, aside from Eric Collins (8), he received scant support, with Bill Rogers (5) next in line on the scorechart. Back at Knowle for a third time came the Americans on 14 August, and this time the visitors pulled off a 57-49 victory. The full list of scorers for the tourists was: Manuel Trujillo 17; Sam Arena 15; Pete Colman 11; Putt Mossman 9; Dick Ince 3; Pee Wee Cullum 2. Trujillo was in sensational form, further lowering the track record to 69.0 seconds on his way to that 17-point haul. Meanwhile, Eric Collins recorded 13 points for the Bulldogs, with Wal Morton (11) and Harry Shepherd (10) providing the backbone of the team. In the second half, Collins created a new one-lap (clutch start) track record of 18.4 seconds.

The Bulldogs bounced back from their American setback, defeating Nottingham 45-24 in a Provincial Trophy match at Knowle one week later on 21 August. The visitors were weakened by the fact that

Ted Bravery was ineligible to ride, having already ridden for another team in the competition. Eric Collins passed George Greenwood to win heat one in the fastest time of the evening, 70.6 seconds. However, the best race of the night occurred in heat nine, when Bill Stanley and Wal Morton were involved in a three-and-a-half-lap battle. This culminated in an outside blast from Morton, only for Stanley to drift out and cause the home man to fall. The steward disqualified Stanley for foul riding and, although the Bristol fans were happy, this was certainly not a popular decision with the visiting supporters. Top man for the Bulldogs was Collins with 11 points, while Bill Rogers and Harry Shepherd chipped in with tallies of 9 apiece. For Nottingham, Cliff Parkinson rode brilliantly to record 10 points, with Greenwood scoring 9. After the main match, Eric Chitty broke the two-lap track record when clocked at 34.6 seconds.

Six days later on 27 August, the Bulldogs visited Banister Court, Southampton for the return fixture *v.* West Ham Hawks in the Provincial Trophy, and returned with a 39-33 victory under their belts. It was a win that put Bristol equal with Plymouth and Liverpool at the top of the table. Bill Rogers led the way with 10 points, while Wal Morton scored 9. Meanwhile, Eric Chitty rode well for the Hawks, winning each of his first three rides, but machine problems in his fourth outing restricted his score to 9 points. Charlie Spinks also notched 9 points for West Ham, while George Saunders recorded 8. Prior to the match, Chitty made a special attempt on the rolling-start track record and managed to establish a new best time of 67.6 seconds.

The following night, Bristol entertained Plymouth at Knowle in the rearranged Provincial Trophy fixture, running out winners by 50 points to 22. Bill Rogers had little difficulty in recording a maximum, receiving able support from Harry Shepherd, who weighed in with 11 points, while Australian Dick Wise was the visitors' best, netting just 6 points.

Southampton arrived at Knowle for league action on 4 September, when the Bulldogs suffered their fourth home reverse of the season, going down 37-35. Although Eric Collins thundered to a 12-point full-house, he received little back-up, as the solid-scoring Saints took the spoils of victory with Syd Griffiths (9), Frank Goulden (8), Fred Strecker (8) and Billy Dallison (8) recording the bulk of their points.

Next for the Bulldogs was a visit to Pennycross Stadium for a Provincial League fixture *v.* Plymouth on 8 September. Bristol were made to fight all the way for a single-point victory, 36-35, and the feature of the meeting was a dramatic return to form by Australian Billy Lamont. Indeed, the 'Cyclone' fairly scorched to a 12-point maximum and knocked two-fifths of a second off the track record, lowering it to 78.6 seconds in heat twelve. The homesters suffered several instances of bad luck during the match and could perhaps point this out as a reason for slipping to defeat. In heat three, Jack Bibby was disqualified for breaking the tapes and, in his third ride, heat eight, his machine gave up the ghost while he was leading. Another problem saw Les Bowden's bike stop as the tapes rose in heat six. However, Bristol also had some misfortune of their own in heat ten, when Bill Rogers went too wide and struck the fence while lying a comfortable second to Bowden. That unfortunately allowed Bibby through to join his partner on a Panthers 5-1. Top of the Bristol scorechart was Wal Morton on 10 points, while Bill Rogers accumulated 8. The Bulldogs' victory kept them in contention at the top of the league table and this was a wonderful achievement in their first season of competitive team racing.

For a fourth time in 1936, the Americans returned to Knowle on 11 September, but it was Bristol who avenged their previous defeat at the hands of the tourists with a comprehensive 63-43 success. Eric Collins scorched to 16 points for the Bulldogs and was well supported by both Wal Morton and Fred Leavis, who each recorded 12. For America, Eric Chitty carded 15 points, with skipper Putt Mossman and Manuel Trujillo gathering 11 apiece.

Bristol completed their Provincial Trophy fixtures with another trip to Southampton on 17 September, and a successful visit it was too, as they came away with a 40-29 victory. Leading the way was Eric Collins with a four-ride maximum, while another Wimbledon asset Jack Sharp, making his Bristol debut, grabbed 9 points. The Saints' top man on the night was Frank Goulden, whose 10-point haul included wins in heats one, six and twelve. A quite remarkable start to the match saw Wal Morton fall and Jack Goldberg drop out with engine trouble to present Southampton with a 5-0 victory. In heat two, Bert Jones fell and Art Fenn suffered motor problems, so Bristol gained a 5-0 of their own. Despite losing, the Saints were later presented with the National Provincial Trophy, having built an unassailable lead at the top of the table, much to the delight of the 9,000 enthusiastic supporters packed into Banister Court.

The following day, Plymouth arrived at Knowle on Provincial League business and the Bulldogs had no difficulty in collecting a 49-23 victory to move above Southampton at the head of the table. Top Australians Eric Collins and Bill Rogers both recorded fine 12-point maximums, and Fred Leavis weighed in with 10. Aussie Jack Hobson topped the Panthers' scorechart with 7 points, while club skipper and fellow countryman Dick Wise could only muster 5. The second part of a double-header featured a nine-heat international challenge match between England and Australia, which the host nation won by 33 points to 21. For England, George Newton scored a maximum 9 points from his three starts, while the other points were scored as follows: Roy Dook 6; Wal Morton 6; Harry Shepherd 5; Fred Leavis 5; Dick Hollis 2. For some unexplained reason, Australia were captained by Englishman Norman Evans, who headed their scoring with 7 points! The rest of the Australian side was made up thus: Bill Rogers (7), Bert Spencer (5), Jack Hobson (2), Eric Collins (0) and Dick Wise (0). Newton also had a go at the two-lap track record (with rolling start), and he didn't disappoint the fans, setting a new best figure of 34.4 seconds.

The twenty-second meeting of the season at Knowle, coincidentally on 22 September, was a very special event indeed, as the world-famous Belle Vue side visited for a grand challenge match. Not surprisingly, the Bulldogs went down 40-32 to the 'Cock of the North', for whom Australian Max Grosskreutz roared to a four-ride maximum, while both skipper Eric Langton and stylish white-liner Bill Kitchen gathered 10-point returns. Also included in the visitors' side were Bob Harrison (3), Walter Hull (3) and Acorn Dobson (2). Bristol's best on the night were Harry Shepherd and Jack Sharp, both of whom registered 8 points. After the team racing had been completed, Grosskreutz set another new track record for two-laps (with rolling start), when clocking 33.4 seconds. The thought of seeing the Aces obviously fuelled the fans' imagination, for the meeting was witnessed by a record Knowle gate of some 19,000 enthusiastic supporters.

On 24 September, it was back to serious Provincial League business, with a further trip to Southampton, and this was the 'big one' that would determine the Champions for 1936. The Saints merely had to win the match to claim the title by virtue of having a greater race-points difference. Bristol's hopes were high though, following their victory at Banister Court the previous week. Regrettably, things went horribly wrong and they crashed to a 41.5-29.5 defeat. The Bulldogs were hampered from the start due to the absence of Eric Collins, who had to appear for parent club Wimbledon in a match at Wembley. However, it was a great night for the homesters as, throughout the whole evening, the Banister Court Stadium resounded to prolonged cheering and the scenes at the end were of the wildest enthusiasm. The Saints' hero of the hour was skipper Frank Goulden, who took victory in each of his four races. After the match, Goulden gleefully accepted the Provincial League Championship trophy from Jack Parker.

Southampton had opened the meeting with a 5-1 advantage, courtesy of Frank Goulden and Dick Smythe over Wal Morton and Fred Leavis. A re-run heat two was shared after a three-man spill, with Roy Dook eventually winning from Syd Griffiths and Art Fenn. Heat three was a thriller, with Fred Strecker just holding off a bold challenge from Harry Shepherd, while Bill Rogers filled third place. Morton and Leavis were sat on maximum points in the next race until Welshman Griffiths superbly split them on the last bend, restricting the Bulldogs to a 4-2. Dook took heat five from Bert Jones, while there was an incredible dead-heat for third place, as Strecker and Spencer flashed across the line in unison. That left the Saints holding a single-point lead at 15.5-14.5, as the tension mounted. Heat six saw Shepherd leading from Rogers, with the home pairing of Smythe and Goulden bringing up the rear. Amazingly Goulden won the race as, firstly, Shepherd's machine spluttered to a halt, then Smythe fell on the back straight of the final lap, before Rogers tumbled on the very last bend! Incredibly, Goulden toured home first, while Rogers remounted for second place, as only the two finished. Southampton then increased their lead to 23.5-17.5, as Strecker and Jones romped to maximum points in the next heat. Two shared races followed, before Smythe won heat ten from Leavis, and with Strecker in third position, Southampton inched closer to the title, leading 33.5-25.5. They duly wrapped it up in the penultimate heat, courtesy of a 4-2 from Jones and Griffiths, with Rogers providing the sandwich filling. Finally, Goulden took heat twelve from Shepherd, while Fenn came home third. For Southampton, aside from Goulden's fine 12-point maximum, their remaining points came from: Strecker 7.5; Jones 7; Griffiths 6; Smythe 5; Fenn 4. Meanwhile, the Bulldogs' scorers in a battling performance were as follows: Rogers 8; Dook 8; Morton 5; Shepherd 4; Leavis 3; Spencer 1.5.

The night after the great league decider, America paid a fifth and final visit of the season to Knowle for another challenge match, emerging with a slender 37-35 victory. Stan Greatrex stepped in to captain the Bulldogs and topped their scoring with 10 points, while Harry Shepherd gleaned 8. The Americans were well led by Eric Chitty with a maximum from four starts, while the legendary Jack Milne weighed in with 11.

On 2 October, a composite side made up from Bristol and Wimbledon riders defeated an All Nations team 37-34 at Knowle. For the home side, the points were plundered thus: Eric Collins 9; Vic Huxley 8; Jack Sharp 8; Wal Phillips 6; Harry Shepherd 5; Bill Rogers 1; Roy Dook 0. Meanwhile, All Nations comprised the following: Bill Kitchen 12 (maximum); Jack Milne 7; Eric Chitty 7; Bluey Wilkinson 5; Tommy Croombs 3; Cecil De La Porte 0. After the main business of the evening, Wilkinson established a new track record of 16.6 seconds for one lap (with a flying start).

Next up was a visit from West Ham on 9 October in another end-of-season challenge match, which saw the visitors take a 41-31 victory. Harry Shepherd (8) and Bill Rogers (7) were Bristol's top men, while West Ham were best served by Tiger Stevenson (11), Bluey Wilkinson (10) and Arthur Atkinson (9). The following evening, the Bulldogs ventured to Harringay for a nine-heat challenge match v. Southampton, which resulted in a 27-27 draw. Eric Collins led the Bristol scoring on 9 points, while Fred Leavis collected 7.

The twenty-sixth and final event of the season at Knowle again featured Southampton in a challenge match on 16 October, and Bristol duly rounded off their campaign with a tidy 34-20 victory from the nine-heat encounter. Once more, Eric Collins was the leading Bulldog in amassing 8 points, while Alec Statham was the best visitor with 7. Speedway manager Ronnie Greene's notes from the programme expressed his gratitude to the supporters who had turned out at Knowle throughout the season, revealing that the average attendance had been over 9,000, a figure that was believed to be the highest in the Provincial League. That meant an aggregate gate of 250,000 during the course of the season. He stated: 'It can safely be said that the first season's racing in the Provincial League has been extremely popular and successful. Unfortunately, some tracks have not been so successful as ourselves. That alone is a source of envy to them, but what would they not give to possess such an amazingly loyal and enthusiastic band of supporters as those at Bristol?'

So, a highly successful campaign ended with the Bulldogs taking the runners-up spot in the National Provincial League, in fact only losing out on the Championship by race-points difference. League winners

Southampton also won the National Provincial Trophy, with Bristol again finishing second. With the exception of the expunged fixtures *v.* Cardiff, the Bulldogs participated in a total of thirty-eight fixtures (sixteen National Provincial League, ten National Provincial Trophy and twelve challenge). From these, Eric Collins was the top man in the side, scoring 275 points from thirty-one meetings for a match average of 8.87. Harry Shepherd was the next best with 235 points, also from thirty-one matches, while Bill Rogers notched 202 points from thirty-three appearances.

Bristol skipper Roy Dook revealed that, after the season, he reverted to his other business in the bailiff and hire-purchase line. Apparently he was a partner in a firm, but his colleague took care of the 'rough stuff', although on one occasion Dook apparently came up against a troublesome customer and was chased down the street with his enemy brandishing a razor in his hand. How the Bristol captain must have longed for his speedway steed at the time! Meanwhile, Harry Shepherd, who made many hundreds of friends in Bristol during the campaign, revealed that he preferred something a little less exciting outside the racing season. He was actually a partner in a firm of London builders and decorators. Other off-track occupations included: Fred Leavis (car sales), Mike Erskine (engineer), while Ernie Evans and Stan Greatrex had a motorcycle business in London, with their showroom decorated in the black-and-orange colours of Bristol Speedway.

1936 STATISTICS

(Bristol's score shown first unless otherwise stated)

NATIONAL PROVINCIAL LEAGUE

Opponents	Home	Away
Cardiff	W38-33	L33-39
	Not staged	Not staged
Liverpool	W41-30	L35-36
	W52-19	L33-39
Nottingham	W43-29	W34-33
	W43-29	L19-53
Plymouth	W40-32	W37-35
	W49-23	W36-35

SPEEDWAY IN BRISTOL 1928-1949

Southampton	W38-32	L29-43
	L35-37	L29.5-41.5

MATCH AVERAGES

Rider	Matches	Points	Average
Eric Collins	15	126	8.40
Harry Shepherd	15	102	6.80
Wal Morton	11	70	6.36
Bill Rogers	15	93	6.20
Roy Dook	12	68	5.67
Fred Leavis	14	68	4.86
Mike Erskine	8	30	3.75
Ernie Evans	3	10	3.33
Bert Spencer	11	24.5	2.23
Henry Collins	1	1	1.00
Syd Farndon	1	1	1.00

NOTE: Match averages do not include expunged matches v. Cardiff, or reserve appearances when a rider took no rides.

NATIONAL PROVINCIAL LEAGUE TABLE

Team	Matches	Won	Drawn	Lost	For	Against	Pts
Southampton	16	10	0	6	619	519	20
Bristol	16	10	0	6	593.5	546.5	20
Nottingham	16	9	0	7	599	538	18
Liverpool	16	9	0	7	555	577	18
Plymouth	16	2	0	14	476.5	662.5	4

NOTE: Cardiff resigned in mid-season, with their record expunged from the final league table.

NATIONAL PROVINCIAL TROPHY

Opponents	Home	Away
Liverpool	L32-40	W42-30
Nottingham	W45-24	W43-27
Plymouth	W50-22	L25-46

1936

Southampton	L32-38	W40-29
West Ham Hawks	W43-29	W39-33

MATCH AVERAGES

Rider	Matches	Points	Average
Eric Collins	7	65	9.29
Harry Shepherd	6	55	9.17
Jack Sharp	1	9	9.00
Bill Rogers	9	66	7.33
Wal Morton	5	33	6.60
Roy Dook	7	44	6.29
Jack Goldberg	1	5	5.00
Bert Spencer	9	43	4.78
Ernie Evans	3	14	4.67
Mike Erskine	5	19	3.80
Fred Leavis	9	32	3.56
Henry Collins	1	3	3.00
Tommy Allott	1	1	1.00
Jack Dalton	1	1	1.00
Will Lowther	1	1	1.00
Syd Edmunds	1	0	0.00

NOTE: Match averages do not include reserve appearances when a rider took no rides.

NATIONAL PROVINCIAL TROPHY TABLE

Team	Matches	Won	Drawn	Lost	For	Against	Pts
Southampton	10	8	0	2	400	308	16
Bristol	10	7	0	3	391	318	14
Liverpool	10	5	0	5	376	335	10
Plymouth	10	4	1	5	318	319	9
Nottingham	10	4	0	6	290	343	8
West Ham Hawks	10	1	1	8	280	432	3

CHALLENGE

Opponents	Home	Away
All Nations	W37-34	–
America	(1) W57-49	–
America	(2) W62-43	–
America	(3) L49-57	–
America	(4) W63-43	–
America	(5) L35-37	–
Belle Vue	L32-40	–
Plymouth	W46-22	–
Southampton	W34-20	D27–27
West Ham	(1) W43-29	–
West Ham	(2) L31-41	–

NOTE: The challenge match v. Plymouth started as a scheduled Provincial Trophy meeting. However, after heat seven, it was changed to a challenge due to adverse weather conditions; The first match v. West Ham featured a composite side made up of Bristol and New Cross riders; The match v. All Nations featured a composite side made up of Bristol and Wimbledon riders; The away match v. Southampton was staged at Harringay.

MATCH AVERAGES

Rider	Matches	Points	Average
Ernie Evans	2	20	10.00
Stan Greatrex	1	10	10.00
Eric Collins	9	84	9.33
Harry Shepherd	10	78	7.80
Roy Dook	8	54	6.75
Bert Spencer	5	29	5.80
Wal Morton	7	39	5.57
Fred Leavis	10	55	5.50
Jack Sharp	5	27	5.40
Nobby Key	1	5	5.00
Bill Rogers	9	43	4.78
Jack Dalton	2	8	4.00
Henry Collins	1	3	3.00
Mike Erskine	5	8	1.60

NOTE: Match averages do not include reserve appearances when a rider took no rides.

1937

After the obvious success of operating speedway at Bristol in 1936, Ronnie Greene negotiated for and took over the control of First Division Wimbledon, which he would run along with his Second Division operation at Knowle.

Knowle opened for the season on Good Friday 26 March, when a challenge match pitched a Bristol and Wimbledon composite side against New Cross. The meeting resulted in a 46-35 victory for Ronnie Greene's men, with Gus Kuhn and Eric Collins grabbing 10 points apiece. For New Cross, Norman Evans also weighed in with 10 points, while Stan Greatrex scored 7. Surprisingly, George Newton only managed to score 6 points, but he did have the distinction of lowering the track record to 68.0 seconds in the second-half Easter Scratch event. There was chaos prior to the start of the meeting, with a traffic queue of over a quarter of a mile in length. The speedway-starved folk of Bristol were obviously keen to get going again, despite the bitterness of a snowy night, as some 15,000 hardy souls were actually in attendance!

In the programme for the opener, Ronnie Greene went into great detail when explaining that in 1936 Bristol had borrowed riders from Wimbledon and New Cross as they had no assets of their own. He went on to point out that this was an unsound basis on which to operate, and that at the end of the season there had been some doubt as to whether speedway racing would even continue at Knowle. Greene continued: 'I immediately approached the greyhound company and, after protracted negotiations, I secured a lease to operate speedway racing here. The result was that I was then faced with the practical impossibility of obtaining a team, as the Speedway Control Board had brought out a rule to the effect that no Second Division track could borrow riders from First Division tracks or from any other tracks. In other words, any Second Division track operating this season must have their own riders, who were not eligible to ride for any other team. This meant that I was faced with a track on my hands, but no team. I tried to buy riders, in fact, I offered exorbitant sums, but not one track would dispose of one man.'

Greene went on to explain that he had approached Fred Mockford at New Cross and suggested that they joined forces in promoting at Knowle in 1937. Mockford agreed and, as a result, Bristol were able to track their own riders, with the promoting company being known as 'The Bristol Motor Sports Ltd'. Greene stated: 'We have secured the very best that we can possibly obtain. We have gone further, we have brought two riders from Canada, and two from Australia. We have in every way possible endeavoured to obtain riders from other tracks but, once again, I repeat to you, the position is that no track can possibly afford to sell a rider.'

On 2 April, before a crowd of 8,000, Knowle hosted a Best Pairs event, with the Bulldogs' pairing of Harry Shepherd and Fred Leavis totalling 18 points to come out on top. Meanwhile, another Bristol twosome, Roy Dook and Harold Bain, took the runners-up spot with a combined total of 15 points. Full result: Shepherd (11) and Leavis (7) 18; Dook (11) and Bain (4) 15; Johnnie Millett (7) and Bill Maddern (6) 13; Sam Marsland (8) and Tommy Allott (2) 10; Bert Jones (6) and Alec Statham (3) 9; Syd Farndon (4) and Fred Wiseman (1) 5.

West Ham Reserves were the visitors to Bristol for a challenge match on 9 April and it proved a big payday for the Bulldogs, who ran riot to triumph 60-23. Some 7,000 spectators witnessed Fred Leavis amass a 12-point maximum, with solid support supplied by Roy Dook and Rol Stobart, each of whom scored 10. With a tally of 6 points, George Saunders top scored for a West Ham side who also included a couple of interesting names in Phil Bishop (5) and Lloyd Goffe (3).

Four days later, the Bulldogs journeyed to Southampton for their first Provincial League fixture of the season. Rain fell throughout the match, but the racing was every bit as good as it had been on Bristol's previous visits to Banister Court in 1936. Home boys Frank Goulden and Syd Griffiths seemed set for maximum points in the opening heat, until Harry Shepherd cleverly slipped past Goulden for second spot. Despite missing the start, Roy Dook then took the flag in heat two. A close finish in the third race saw Jack Hobson and Ivor Creek inflict a 5-1 over Fred Leavis, before Goulden won a processional heat four. Bert Jones and Jack Riddle zoomed to maximum points in the next, following a fall from Shepherd. A tight battle in heat six resulted in a win for Hobson, ahead of Dook and Bill Maddern. Saints' linchpin Goulden then took another comfortable win in the next, prior to Bill Rogers winning a ding-dong battle with Jones in heat eight. Shepherd then won the ninth race for the Bulldogs, out-pacing Hobson, with Rogers in third position. Goulden took his score on to 10 points in the next, but Dook and Maddern held on to share the race. Jones and Riddle were sat on a 5-1 in heat eleven, only for Jones to tumble on the last lap, with Rol Stobart and Leavis gratefully accepting the gift points in what became a shared result. Shepherd took victory in the race that followed, before Riddle stormed home in the penultimate heat. Reserve Cyril Anderson gleefully wrapped up a Saints success in heat fourteen as he sped away from Bristol new boy Johnnie Millett. So it was a losing start for Bristol, 46-38, with Shepherd (9), Rogers (8) and Dook (8) being the pick of the side. Goulden was well supported in the home camp, while Riddle and Hobson recorded 9 points apiece.

The return match against Southampton was staged at Knowle on 16 April, and was equally as exciting, with the Bulldogs racing to a 45-36 victory in front of 9,000 fans. Saints' skipper Frank Goulden gave an outstanding display, scorching to an unbeaten 12 points, while also twice clocking the fastest time of the night, 70.8 seconds, in heats two and ten. Southampton's fast-gating main man received scant support from his teammates, however, and three exclusions for exceeding the time allowance certainly didn't help their cause. For Bristol, Harry Shepherd top-scored with 11 points, while Rol Stobart recorded 10. Making his home debut for the club was Toronto-born Johnnie Millett, but he had an inauspicious start, scoring but a single point before crashing out spectacularly in heat twelve.

The Bulldogs were scheduled to appear at Nottingham in the National Trophy on 20 April, but the meeting was unfortunately postponed due to adverse weather. Staying with the competition, Bristol entertained Nottingham in what became the first leg of the tie at Knowle on 23 April and they claimed a convincing victory too, running out winners by 48 points to 36. Indeed, the Bulldogs were really on-song, finishing first in twelve out of the fourteen heats as another huge Knowle crowd of some 10,000 thrilled to the spectacle before them. Nottingham opened the meeting in sensational style though, with Tommy Allott and Sam Marsland romping to maximum points over Bristol's Australian recruit

Bill Maddern; this after Harry Shepherd had pulled up with machine problems. Bill Rogers and Fred Leavis quickly avenged the early setback in heat two, dashing to a 5-1 to level the scores. Frank Hodgson led the next heat for three laps, until Roy Dook brilliantly took victory after cutting inside on the pits bend and rocketing into the lead on the straight. Shepherd, on a borrowed steed, took superb wins in heats four and seven and at the halfway stage Bristol led 25-17. The Bulldogs' newest recruit, Reg Gore, collected a maiden victory in heat eight, albeit in the very slow time of 79.2 seconds. That was after George Dykes had been excluded for anticipating the start, leaving Don Hemingway to do battle with Fred Leavis and Gore. Brilliant tactics from Leavis allowed Gore to take and hold the lead, while Hemingway was blocked in at the rear. Rol Stobart clocked the swiftest time of the night, 70.0 seconds, in winning heat nine, and with Dook scooping third place after Marsland had crashed, Bristol's advantage stood at 34-20. Shepherd, Rogers and Dook were triumphant in heats ten, eleven and twelve respectively, before Hodgson became only the visitors' second race winner in heat thirteen, denying Rogers his maximum in the process. Stobart rounded things off in heat fourteen, after Maddern had dropped out with machine problems on the first lap. Top scorers on the night for Bristol were Rogers (11), Dook (10) and Shepherd (9), while Allott and Hodgson were Nottingham's best representatives, scoring 8 points apiece.

Three days later, it was off to the 440-yard Stanley Stadium raceway in Liverpool for a Provincial League encounter. It was a pleasant experience for the Bulldogs too, as they stormed to a stunning 55-29 victory. Setting the pace right from the start, they gained an opening heat 4-2, courtesy of Harry Shepherd and Bill Maddern over Ernie Price, and a heat two maximum from Bill Rogers and Fred Leavis, before cruising to success. So emphatic was the victory that a Bristol rider crossed the line ahead in each and every heat of the match. No fewer than three of the side recorded full maximums, with Rogers, Shepherd and Roy Dook going through the card. For the hapless Liverpool side, Stan Hart and Eric Blain recorded 6 points apiece, while skipper Tommy Price could muster just 2.

Leicester arrived at Knowle for league business on 30 April, only to find the Bulldogs in rampant form, as they carried on from where they had left off at Liverpool, thundering to a 68-15 victory. The newcomers to the Provincial League offered little resistance to the onslaught, with the first eleven heats all resulting in maximum wins. The best Leicester could do was second-place finishes in heats twelve and thirteen, as a Bristol rider again took the flag in every race. Bill Maddern finished on top of the pile with an unbeaten 12 points, while Bill Rogers (11), Roy Dook (11), Fred Leavis (9), Rol Stobart (9) and Harry Shepherd (8) all contributed heavily. Meanwhile, with just 4 points, Harry Bowler was Leicester's best performer on the night. There was more for those on the terracing to enthuse over in the second half, when Dook equalled Bluey Wilkinson's record time for one lap (with flying start) of 16.6 seconds. As a matter of interest, the aforementioned Stobart was actually based in Carlisle and faced a round trip of some 600 miles for each home meeting, which was a monumental journey to have undertaken at the time.

The West Country boys faced another trip to Nottingham on 4 May, for the return leg of their National Trophy tie. The Lacemen, as they had become generically known, made a tremendous effort to overturn Bristol's 12-point advantage from the first leg, with the Bulldogs grateful for a slender 3-point aggregate success in the end. The homesters took a 46-37 victory on the night, but the undoubted star of the show was Bristol skipper Harry Shepherd, who plundered another maximum to safely see his side through to the next round. Tommy Allott (11), George Dykes (10) and Fred Strecker (9) led the way for Nottingham, with Allott recording the fastest time of the night for the 380-yard circuit, when clocked at 76.16 seconds in heat eight.

The Bulldogs continued their barnstorming run on 6 May, winning 57-23 at Leicester in a Provincial League match. Harry Shepherd posted a superb 12-point maximum, while backing him solidly were Roy Dook (11) and Bill Rogers (10), both of whom remained unbeaten by an opponent. Meanwhile, Fred Leavis (10) and Rol Stobart (9) also weighed in with hefty contributions to the rout. Top man for Leicester on a desperate night was Wilf Plant, who gained his side's solitary race win on the way to an 8-point tally. It came as no surprise later in the season, though, when the totally under-strength Midlands outfit resigned from the league, with their results being expunged from the records. Back at Knowle the following night for more league activity, a gate of 9,200 saw Liverpool become the latest victims of the 'Bristol Massacre', as the Bulldogs walloped in a 58-25 success. The visitors were restricted to just one race winner all night, when Stan Hart took the flag in heat ten. Youngster Reg Lambourne made his league debut for Bristol in the match, riding steadily to collect

2 points, while George Saunders, a recent recruit from West Ham, won his first race for the club when taking the opening heat. It was a scrappy race though, with Saunders, Eric Blain and Oliver Hart all coming to grief at the first time of asking. The re-run saw Harry Shepherd tumble, before Saunders went on to take his initial victory ahead of Blain, while the remounted Shepherd eventually made it home in third place. Top men for the Bulldogs on the night were Rol Stobart (11), Fred Leavis (11), Roy Dook (10) and Shepherd (9), while Stan Hart and Tommy Price both notched 7 points for the beleaguered visitors.

Bristol were due to contest a league fixture at Birmingham on 11 May but, with the Midlands taking a battering from the weather, the meeting was postponed. They were soon back in action on 14 May though, when Norwich arrived at Knowle for a Coronation Cup fixture and the Bulldogs continued their remarkable home form with a crushing 53-29 win. The Norfolk outfit were hampered, however, when a heat-two spill ruled Chun Moore out of the meeting. Heat nine featured a dead-heat for first place, with Fred Leavis and Bill Rogers flashing across the line in unison. The visitors gained their first win of the match in heat ten, when Wilf Jay took the flag, with Jock Sweet repeating the success in heat eleven. That though, was the only joy of the evening for the latest side to feel the full brunt of the Bulldogs. Skipper Harry Shepherd was again Bristol's highest scorer, with 11 points, while Jay headed the Norwich scoring on 8. Rather interestingly, a certain Charlie Dugard appeared in the visiting side, but scored just 1 point from his four starts. Dugard had purchased a share in Eastbourne Speedway in 1934 and the Arlington-based club has, of course, been synonymous with his family ever since.

On 15 May, Bristol travelled to East Anglia for the second leg against Norwich, and they were again triumphant, recording a 47-35 victory. The Bulldogs were inspired by the tremendous riding of Roy Dook, who scorched to a maximum and twice broke The Firs Stadium track record. In heats six and ten, he clocked 79.8 seconds for the 425-yard circuit, knocking one-fifth of a second off the previous best. Later on, in the second-half scratch event, George Saunders further lowered the track record to 79.6 seconds.

On Bank Holiday Monday, 17 May, Knowle Stadium hosted a grand challenge match between Fred Mockford's Team and Ronnie Greene's Team, with the latter side coming out on top by 45 points to 39. Both outfits included some star names, with Stan Greatrex (9) and Jack Milne (9) doing the business for Greene's side, while Rol Stobart (10) was Mockford's main man. News in the programme indicated that the supporters' club had reached the 9,000 mark and that over 800 members had travelled to Birmingham on 11 May for a rain-off! Meanwhile, Ronnie Greene's page appeared to be addressing comments made by the Bulldogs' opponents, suggesting that the Bristol riders were on superior machines to any other teams. Needless to say, Mr Greene simply explained it was just a case of regular maintenance and keeping things in tip-top condition.

Friday 21 May saw another special twelve-heat challenge match at Knowle, with the Bulldogs up against mighty Wimbledon, as Ronnie Greene pitted his National League team against his Provincial League side. Despite unsettled weather, the meeting attracted another bumper gate of almost 10,000 and those present witnessed the Provincial League leaders put up a terrific scrap before going down by 39 points to 33. Former Bristol rider Eric Collins proved he hadn't forgotten the quickest way around the Knowle raceway as he stormed to maximum points for the London side. Indeed, the final heat saw Collins complete his full-house after a tight struggle with Harry Shepherd. Both captains raced neck-and-neck for three laps, until the Wimbledon man drew away to finish ahead of his old clubmate. Wilbur Lamoreaux also felt at home, flying to 11 points, while Bristol's best were Bill Rogers (10) and Shepherd (9).

Having previously been rained off at Birmingham earlier in the month, the Bulldogs' rescheduled away league fixture at the Hall Green venue was set for 26 May. Unfortunately, the weather was again unkind and, for a second time, the meeting was called off without a wheel being turned. Putting the disappointment behind them, Bristol entertained Nottingham in a league match on 28 May and they were in no mood for charity, running out convincing 49-31 winners. Regrettably, the visitors were without Sam Marsland for most of the match after he had been involved in a car crash on his journey down. In fact, Marsland only arrived in time to take his place in the final heat, which he duly won. One can only wonder what the score might have been had Marsland been there from the start, although it is hard to imagine Bristol losing their unbeaten league record at Knowle. The Bulldogs won ten of the fourteen heats, claiming maximum points in four of them. Scoring

11 points apiece, Bill Rogers, Harry Shepherd and Roy Dook topped the score grid, while Frank Hodgson compiled an impressive tally of 11 for Nottingham. The match was marred by a bad crash in heat eight, when Billy Lamont fell in front of Reg Lambourne, with both riders ending in an untidy heap. Lambourne was carried off on a stretcher with concussion and a shoulder injury, while Lamont was able to return to the pits after medical attention.

On 1 June Bristol raced in the return league fixture at Nottingham but, despite a full maximum from Roy Dook, they slipped to a slender 42-40 defeat. Unfortunately, Dook received little support from his teammates, with Bill Rogers next in line on 7 points. Three days after the trip to Trent Lane, the Bulldogs entertained Southampton in a National Trophy tie. A Knowle crowd of 15,000 suffered a rather severe shock though, as the visitors won by the narrowest of margins, 42-41. It was a disastrous meeting for the homesters, with Harry Shepherd having an off-night and Bill Rogers twice falling while holding the lead. Rol Stobart also had problems, having somehow 'lost' his machine on the train journey to Bristol, while the bike he had to borrow did nothing but play up. With the scores tied at 6 points apiece, Billy Dallison and Bert Jones scored a 5-1 in heat three after Rogers had tumbled out. Heat four then saw Shepherd and Jack Riddle crash on the pits bend, allowing Cyril Anderson to win from Jack Dalton and extend Southampton's advantage to 14-9. Dook had to miss the next race, having been hit in the face by flying cinders in heat two. As it was, Frank Goulden took the race from Stobart and Bill Maddern, thereby maintaining the Saints' lead. Bristol came back in heat six though, as Rogers teamed up with Fred Leavis to inflict maximum points over Riddle and Syd Griffiths. With heat seven shared, Southampton held a narrow 21-20 lead at the halfway stage. Dook was back to take heat eight from Griffiths in what was the fastest time of the night (70.0 seconds) and with Maddern in third place, Bristol moved 24-23 in front. Rogers again fell in heat nine, gifting Southampton a 4-2, before Griffiths and Riddle plundered another 4-2 in the race that followed. Dallison and Jones then recorded a third 4-2 on the bounce for the visitors, leaving Bristol trailing 35-30. The Bulldogs hit back with a maximum from Rogers and Maddern to bring them within a point. Dallison won the penultimate heat from Stobart and Dalton to leave things balanced on a knife-edge going into the final heat. However, Jones held his nerve to defeat Leavis and Saunders in heat fourteen, bringing the curtain down on a pulsating meeting. Bristol's top men on the night were Dook and Leavis with 7 points each, while Jones and Dallison gleaned 9 apiece for the victorious Saints.

The return leg of the National Trophy tie v. Southampton was staged at Banister Court on 8 June, when the home side cantered to a 51–32 victory. The meeting was staged amid a tremendous atmosphere, with the Saints firing on all cylinders. In spite of this, all the bad luck on the night actually went the way of Southampton, so Bristol couldn't make any excuses and were a well-beaten side. At one stage of the proceedings, Ronnie Greene protested about track conditions and was roundly booed by the home supporters. However, the referee deemed the track fit and the meeting proceeded with race times akin to normal. The Bulldogs' best performer on the night was Roy Dook (7), while Syd Griffiths and Billy Dallison both romped to 12-point maximums for Southampton.

Bristol returned to winning ways on 11 June, when 9,000 fans saw them take Norwich to the cleaners in a league match at Knowle. Back at their very best, they romped to a 64–18 victory and took the first nine heats with maximum points. Norwich though, were severely handicapped, having turned up without sufficient riders and machines, and they were also minus manager Max Grosskreutz. Home boss Ronnie Greene had to loan the unfortunate visitors several riders in an effort to ensure the meeting went ahead. For a second time in the season, there was a dead-heat at Knowle, when Roy Dook and Rol Stobart couldn't be separated as they crossed the line in heat eleven. Stobart headed the Bulldogs' scoring with 11.5 points, with Harry Shepherd (11) and Bill Rogers (10) supplying great support. Meanwhile, out of Norwich's meagre total, Alan Smith was top man with just 5 points. Stobart continued to enjoy himself in the second half, equalling the time set by Max Grosskreutz the previous year of 33.4 seconds for the two-lap (rolling start) track record.

The following evening, Bristol journeyed to The Firs Stadium for the return league match against Norwich and coasted to a 54–27 victory. Roy Dook headed the scoring with 11 points, while Bill Rogers grabbed 10, along with Harry Shepherd, who also recorded the fastest time of the match in heat one, when clocked at 80.6 seconds. For the beleaguered Norwich side, Bert Spencer occupied pole position on the scorecard with 8 points.

Next on the Bulldogs' agenda was a trip to National League Wimbledon for a challenge match and, not surprisingly, they went down by 48 points to 36 on the 343-yard Plough Lane circuit. Bill Rogers rode very well for Bristol, topping the scoring with 10 points, while the home side were best served by a maximum from Wilbur Lamoreaux and a tally of 10 from Alfred Rumrich. Prior to the meeting, George Newton of New Cross set no fewer than three new track records: 67.8 seconds for four laps with clutch start, 65.6 seconds for four laps with flying start and 16.2 seconds for one lap with flying start.

League pacesetters Southampton made another trip to Knowle on 18 June for the Bulldogs' first National Provincial Trophy fixture of the campaign. Twelve thousand supporters witnessed the two sides again produce a thrilling contest, with Bristol just shading the result by 54 points to 50. Captain Harry Shepherd was involved in several crashes on the night; firstly with Billy Dallison in heat six and later in heat seventeen when challenging Syd Griffiths for the lead on the final bend, he took a heavy tumble and had to be assisted from the track. Griffiths subsequently took the flag, only to be excluded for foul riding by the meeting steward. Heat ten saw a remarkable turn of events, with Frank Goulden suffering an engine failure as he took the lead, while Shepherd and Ivor Creek both fell. That let George Saunders through to win in 72.0 seconds, with Shepherd remounting to take second place ahead of Creek, who pushed home for the odd point. The principal scorers were: (Bristol) Rol Stobart 12 (6 rides); Roy Dook 10; Shepherd 9; (Southampton) Bert Jones 14; Griffiths 12; Goulden 8.

The Bulldogs' busy schedule then took them back to Banister Court for a difficult league match against the super Saints on 22 June. It was a good night for the powerful Southampton side though, who strengthened their position at the top of the league with a decisive 52-31 victory. The homesters were without the recently injured Syd Griffiths, but it made little difference as they chalked up a succession of heat wins. Indeed, such was their dominance that Bristol provided just two race winners in Roy Dook, heat ten, and Bill Rogers, heat thirteen. Dook's race win over Frank Goulden and Ivor Creek was achieved in one of the fastest times of the match, 69.6 seconds, but he did little else on the night, only registering 5 points in total. Instead, Bristol's best was Rogers with 9 points, while Billy Dallison and Bert Jones both romped to full maximums for the victorious Saints.

The following day, the Bulldogs made another trip to Birmingham on league business, and it was third time lucky, having been rained off on two previous occasions in May. The 302-yard Hall Green circuit produced an entertaining scrap, with Bristol returning to winning ways by 44 points to 39. They were brilliantly led by maximum points from Bill Rogers and 11 from Rol Stobart, while Steve Langton and Tiger Hart netted 10 apiece for Birmingham.

On 25 June, the last home action of the month saw the Bulldogs face Liverpool in a Provincial Trophy match, and the men in orange and black recorded yet another comfortable victory, 67-41, in front of 11,000 enthusiastic cinder fans. Bill Rogers produced a stunning display, scorching to a six-ride maximum, while Harry Shepherd was only just short, accruing 17 points from his six starts. For Liverpool, Stan Hart was the leading performer, recording 13 points from his six outings. The meeting was preceded by a special best-of-three challenge between World Champion Lionel Van Praag of Wembley and George Newton of New Cross. Van Praag took the first heat after Newton had fallen, but the New Cross man squared the challenge, just heading his opponent home in heat two. In the decider, Van Praag lost his footrest after two laps but still rode tremendously despite the handicap to win easily in 69.4 seconds.

Bristol made their second visit of the year to Liverpool for a Provincial Trophy encounter on 28 June and they fairly ran riot, winning by a massive 62-43 margin, with Bill Rogers (15-point maximum) and Rol Stobart (11) being the leading lights. Next up was another Provincial Trophy match v. Nottingham at Knowle on 2 July, when the Bulldogs gave another fine team display to win 60-47. Rol Stobart had a miserable night though, falling in each of his first three rides, while Harry Shepherd twice tumbled out, in heats eight and ten. Bristol's man of the moment Bill Rogers fell in heat twelve and, although the steward disqualified Tommy Allott after the race, it spelt the end of a tremendous run of nineteen successive race wins for the durable Australian. Rogers, however, quickly gathered his composure to win heat sixteen in the fastest time of the night, 70.2 seconds. The meeting's top scorers were: (Bristol) Fred Leavis 14; Shepherd 12; Rogers 12; (Nottingham) Fred Strecker 11; Ted Bravery 10; Sam Marsland 9. As an added bonus, a special match-race challenge between Wimbledon's Eric Collins and Bristol-born Les Wotton of Harringay resulted in a 2-0 victory to the Bulldogs' star man of 1936.

Bristol were on their travels again on 3 July and duly arrived at The Firs Stadium for an important league fixture *v.* Norwich. An attendance of more than 6,000 witnessed the Bulldogs go down by 44 points to 39 in a pulsating match. The Stars never looked like losing on the night and fully merited their success. Bert Spencer led the way for the victors with 10 points, receiving solid support from Jock Sweet (8) and Alec Peel (7). In fact, Peel was a real surprise package and also recorded the fastest time of the night, 79.0 seconds, when winning heat seven. In what was something of an indifferent Bulldogs' display, Jack Dalton emerged as their top scorer with 9 points, while usual star turns Roy Dook (8), Harry Shepherd (7) and Bill Rogers (5) were all a little off colour.

On 9 July, just two weeks after their previous visit, Liverpool returned to Knowle for a league match, but again the Bulldogs had the upper hand, hammering the Merseyside outfit 59-24. A Bristol rider took the chequered flag in each of the fourteen heats, with six of the races ending in 5-1 successes. Liverpool's cause wasn't helped by their failure to turn up with any reserves and this resulted in four races taking place with three riders only. The crowd of 9,000 witnessed several crashes, including a heat-three spill for Bill Rogers and a spectacular fall from Liverpool's Eric Blain two races later, when he ended up on the centre green. Fred Leavis grabbed a fine maximum for the Bulldogs, being ably backed by Rol Stobart (11) and Harry Shepherd (10), while the beleaguered visitors' leading rider was Tommy Price with 7 points. After the match, Jack Milne of New Cross gained a 2-0 victory over Wimbledon's Wilbur Lamoreaux in a match-race challenge. The race-day programme advertised a range of souvenirs available at the kiosk, including car mascots (chromium) 8*s*; car badges (chromium) 5*s*; car pennants 1*s*; cycle pennants 6*d*; badges 6*d*; rosettes 6*d*; ties 1*s* 6*d* and 2*s* 6*d*; team jigsaw puzzles 1*s* and photographs 2*d*.

Bristol were on the road again on 13 July, with a trip to Custom House Stadium for a four-heat mini-match, which took place after West Ham had defeated Belle Vue 52-42 in the ACU Cup. The Bulldogs met the West Ham junior side (known as the Hawks), going down by a single point, 12-11, on the 440-yard circuit. The Hawks were represented by Ken Brett (6), Danny Lee (3), Lloyd Goffe (2) and Kid Curtis (1), while Bristol lined up as follows: George Saunders (5); Roy Dook (4); Fred Leavis (2); Rol Stobart (0); George Pepper (0). The mini-match was marred by a crash involving Stobart in his only ride, which unfortunately resulted in him breaking an arm and dislocating a shoulder.

It was back to important league business on 14 July, when Bristol travelled up to Hall Green to take on Birmingham. Another great night for the Bulldogs saw them chalk up a 45-38 victory, this being their fifth away success of the league campaign. In actual fact, it was their second win at Hall Green inside three weeks, the West Country boys having previously won at the venue on 23 June. This time, Bristol took charge of the meeting from the opening heat, with Bill Rogers, Roy Dook and Fred Leavis leading the way on 9 points apiece, while Steve Langton weighed in with 11 for Birmingham. The win catapulted the Bulldogs to the top of the Provincial League standings as they leapfrogged early pacesetters Southampton.

There was a real treat at Knowle on 16 July when more than 11,500 folk assembled to watch the brilliant West Ham side in a grand challenge match. Although the Bulldogs went down by 72 points to 36, they put up a plucky fight against the senior league team. As it was, the Hammers roared to no less than eight maximum advantages during the course of the eighteen-heat match. Their star riders proved a big hit amongst the Bristol fans, with Bluey Wilkinson scorching to 17 points from six starts. His only dropped point occurred in heat five and, even then, he came home behind colleague Bronco Dixon. As a matter of interest, the remainder of the West Ham side scored thus: Eric Chitty 15; Tommy Croombs 14; Arthur Atkinson 12; Bronco Dixon 9; Tiger Stevenson 3; Charlie Spinks 2; Lloyd Goffe (Res) DNR. In posting 12 points, Aussie Bill Rogers was the only Bristol rider to offer any real resistance, his performance including a superb victory over Atkinson in heat twelve, when he clocked 68.2 seconds, just two-fifths of a second outside George Newton's track record.

The Bulldogs' bulging fixture list next took them to the White City Speedway at Nottingham for a Coronation Cup semi-final tie on 20 July. Although Bristol were at full strength, they were never in with a shout and crashed to a disappointing 55-29 reverse. The home side provided the race winner in no less than twelve of the fourteen heats, gaining maximum points on five occasions. Fred Strecker and Ted Bravery both collected full 12-point returns for the homesters, while skipper George Greenwood rattled up a tally of 11, his only loss being at the hands of teammate Billy Lamont in heat ten. Aside from his maximum, Bravery also clocked the fastest time of the match in heat three, when scorching around the 380-yard circuit in 74.44 seconds. Bristol's leading lights on a poor evening were Bill Rogers and Bill Maddern with just 6 points each. In a special attempt on Manuel Trujillo's track record of 72.5 seconds, Greenwood just missed out when returning an impressive 72.85 seconds.

The return Coronation Cup fixture with Nottingham took place at Knowle three nights later, with the Bulldogs gaining a 47-37 victory. Regrettably, the 10-point win wasn't sufficient to win the tie, with Bristol tumbling out on the wrong end of a 92-76 scoreline on aggregate. Riding sensibly throughout, Nottingham consistently packed the minor places to curtail the Bulldogs' progress in the competition. Bill Rogers and Roy Dook led the Bristol scorechart with 11 points apiece, while Fred Strecker (10) topped the pile for Nottingham. Newcomer Reg Vigor made his home debut for the Bulldogs and impressed greatly with two race wins included in his 7-point total. After the meeting, a series of match races took place, when those present witnessed the leading Bristol lads being challenged by some of the American aces. Manuel Trujillo was the only tourist to win one of the five heats when avenging an earlier defeat by Rogers, in the fastest time of the evening, 69.8 seconds. The other heats saw Harry Shepherd defeat Earl Farrand, while Fred Leavis beat Pete Colman and Roy Dook outpaced Shorty Campbell. It was revealed in the match programme that, when riding in South Africa some years previously, the Bulldogs' captain Harry Shepherd had taught the natives how to ride and, because the Zulus thought so much of him, they still possessed an old crash helmet of his as a mascot. Apparently the chairman of the Zulu Control Board put the helmet on when he had to sentence one of the lads for riding on an unlicensed track! In another feature, it was revealed that membership of the Bristol Supporters' Club had increased and, incredibly, fell just short of the 12,000 mark.

On 24 July, Bristol journeyed to Norwich for the second time in a matter of three weeks for a Provincial Trophy match. The Stars were already handicapped by an injury to Wilf Jay, when skipper Dick Wise fell heavily in the opening race. Although Wise rode in one further heat, he was suffering from concussion and had to withdraw from the remainder of the meeting. Bill Rogers was again in sensational form for the Bulldogs, scorching to an unbeaten 18-point tally, while providing sound assistance were Fred Leavis (11), Roy Dook (10) and George Saunders

(10) as the Bulldogs cantered to a 62-45 success. Norwich, meanwhile, were led by Bert Spencer (16) and Alec Peel (10), who scored more than half their side's total between them. Bravely, Jay did compete despite his injury, but could only muster 4 points.

Knowle hosted the second Test match of a series between England and Australia on 30 July, when 12,723 fans turned up to witness the men from Down Under overwhelm the host nation by a staggering 79 points to 29. England could only manage a solitary race win via George Greenwood in heat ten, while their opponents rampaged to eleven 5-1s during the course of the eighteen heats. Full result: England 29 (Greenwood 7; Harry Shepherd 7; Frank Goulden 5; Fred Leavis 4; Tommy Allott 3; Billy Dallison 2; Stan Hart 1; Roy Dook 0) Australia 79 (Lionel Van Praag 17; Bluey Wilkinson 17; Eric Collins 14; Bill Rogers 12; Ron Johnson 10; Ernie Evans 8; Mick Murphy 1; Charlie Spinks 0). There was bad news for the Bristol supporters, since Dook crashed in heat two, unfortunately suffering a dislocated shoulder and a broken wrist. There was a strange occurrence in heat three when Wilkinson led Rogers home, only for it to be discovered that five laps had actually been completed. The corrected result, after four laps, made Rogers the winner and ultimately denied Wilkinson a full 18-point maximum!

The wonderful Bristol fans didn't have long to wait for their next speedway fix, with some 8,600 of them assembling to see the popular American tourists in town for a 3 p.m. start on Bank Holiday Monday, 2 August. Already missing Rol Stobart, and with Roy Dook out injured following his Test match crash, the Bulldogs drafted in Ron Johnson and also gave Eric Collins a guest team berth, although it was to no avail as the Americans snatched a narrow 37.5-34.5 victory in the special twelve-heat match. Collins led the home scoring with 9 points, while Harry Shepherd, Reg Vigor and Bill Rogers all contributed 6 apiece. The Americans' scorechart was headed by a four-ride maximum from Wilbur Lamoreaux, while Jack Milne netted 9 points and Pete Colman recorded 8. Meanwhile, former track-record holder Manuel Trujillo had a poor night, only scoring 3 points from his four starts.

On 4 August, Bristol put up a tremendous effort at Southampton in a Provincial Trophy fixture. Things looked ominous as the Saints took maximum points in the first two races, but the Bulldogs rallied, finally going down by 59 points to 48. Once again, Bill Rogers topped the Bristol scoring on 13 points, with Harry Shepherd (11) supplying excellent support. Meanwhile, the Saints were best served by free-scoring Frank Goulden (17) and Syd Griffiths (14). Surprisingly, Goulden's only defeat came at the hands of Reg Vigor in heat fifteen, since the relative new boy in the Bulldogs' line-up did little else in the match, totalling just 5 points.

Further Provincial Trophy action was served up at Knowle two nights later, when the Bulldogs entertained Birmingham. An under-strength Bristol side were shocked by the visitors though and suffered defeat by 58 points to 50. The match was fought out in a thrilling manner and it wasn't until after heat seventeen that the visitors had victory in the bag. The highlight of the evening was the tremendous riding of Birmingham's Malcolm Craven, a rider who had started the season at reserve for Norwich. He simply stormed to 15 points from six starts, his fabulous performance including victories over Bill Rogers, Harry Shepherd (twice) and Fred Leavis, as well as clocking the fastest time of the night in heat thirteen, 69.8 seconds. However, Craven wasn't his side's top scorer; that honour went to Tiger Hart with 16 points, while Steve Langton backed the duo, tallying 10 points. For the homesters, Rogers led the way on 14 points, with Shepherd and Fred Leavis each notching 10. The meeting also included a best-of-three match-race series between Tiger Hart and Geoff Pymar, with the latter winning 2-1. A cause for concern was the attendance figure at this meeting, which slumped to just 7,800.

Norwich were the next opponents at Knowle for a Provincial Trophy clash on 13 August and, after two home defeats on the bounce, Bristol got back to winning ways in no uncertain terms. On a wet and greasy surface, they pulverised the Stars by 72 points to 34, with eight races resulting in 5-1 successes. The only visitor to offer any resistance was former Bristol rider Wal Morton, who gleaned 13 points in spectacular fashion. Despite the rain, Reg Vigor and Fred Leavis roared around to card victories in 70.0 seconds flat in heats ten and twelve respectively. The conditions did account for several nasty spills though, the worst of which saw Norwich reserve Bill Birtwell carried off on a stretcher with concussion and a shoulder injury. The Bulldogs' huge success was achieved by virtue of having five men in double figures: Bill Rogers 14; Vigor 13; Bill Maddern 12; George Saunders 11; Harry Shepherd 10. After the main meeting, a special match-race challenge resulted in a 2-0 victory for Jack Milne over Lionel Van Praag. It was probably due to the adverse weather conditions, but the attendance dropped again for this meeting, with a season's low of 7,000 recorded. Ronnie Greene's programme notes praised the efforts of Bill Maddern in heat twelve of the previous week's match *v.* Birmingham, when he came through from fourth position to win the race. Mr Greene suggested that some kind supporters might like to hand the flying Australian a large packet of toffee in praise of his fine efforts.

The battle at the top of the Provincial League hotted up on 20 August when, before a much-improved gate of 10,300, the Bulldogs entertained their main challengers Southampton. It was imperative that Bristol put one over on their bogey team and they didn't disappoint in what was actually the fiftieth meeting at the stadium since the sport had been reintroduced the previous year. Running out 55-28 winners, the Bristol boys had a field night, crossing the finishing line first in all but two of the fourteen heats, the crucial victory putting them 2 points ahead of the Saints in the race for the Championship. Youngster Reg Vigor did particularly well, continuing his rapid progress with an unbeaten 12-point haul. He was well supported by Bill Rogers (9), Fred Leavis (9), Harry Shepherd (8) and George Saunders (8) in a very solid team performance. In heat three, Leavis scorched around the 290-yard circuit in 68.6 seconds; a mere 0.6 of a second outside the track record. Turning briefly to Southampton, their best showing came from Syd Griffiths, who notched 9 points. The programme advertised a trip to Wembley for the World Final on 2 September, with a return train fare of 5*s* being charged, while admission to the big meeting was available at 2*s* 6*d*, 5*s* and 10*s* 6*d* depending where you sat or stood. Supporters' club members were offered very good rates of discount on the prices, with the 10*s* 6*d* ticket available at just 7*s* 6*d* for example.

Bristol made their fourth trip of the season to Trent Lane, Nottingham for a Provincial Trophy fixture on 24 August. It wasn't a good night for the Bulldogs, however, as they succumbed by 68 points to 40. Bill Rogers headed the Bristol scoring for the umpteenth time with 14 points, but his only real support came from Harry Shepherd (10). Meanwhile, the home side featured five riders in double figures as they simply overwhelmed their opponents, namely: George Greenwood 15; Fred Strecker 15; Ted Bravery 12; Tommy Bateman 10; Billy Lamont 10. Nottingham captain Greenwood also posted the fastest time of the match in heat eight, when clocked at 75.40 seconds.

All America returned to Knowle once more on 27 August, with the tourists stealing away with their second victory inside four weeks. In a keenly contested match, it wasn't until heat eleven that the 'Stars and Stripes' took a grip, when Wilbur Lamoreaux and Manuel Trujillo walloped home a 5-1 over Reg Vigor and Bill Rogers. The Bulldogs were again bolstered by the inclusion of Wimbledon's Eric Collins and Ron Johnson of New Cross for the match, and Collins certainly enjoyed the return to his old stamping ground, tearing round the circuit in 67.8 seconds in heat four to equal the track record. He also went on to top the side's scoring with 8 points, while Johnson and Bill Rogers each recorded 7. For the American outfit, Jack Milne (10), Lamoreaux (10) and Byrd McKinney (9) were the leading men in their 40-32 victory. Prior to the start of the meeting, the 13,500 gate stood in silence to pay tribute to twenty-three-year-old Belle Vue Merseysiders rider Stan Hart, who had tragically lost his life in a track accident at Birmingham on 25 August. Liverpool had transferred their home fixtures to Belle Vue in mid-season, hence the change of team name.

Before a Knowle audience of 10,300, the Bulldogs consolidated their position at the head of the Provincial League standings on 3 September, when they raced to a 48-35 success over Nottingham. The meeting signalled the return of Roy Dook to track action, following his spill in the Test match on 30 July. Bill Rogers coasted to a maximum, winning his four rides with ease, while Reg Vigor continued to shine with an 11-point tally. Meanwhile, Tommy Allott and Ted Bravery were the visitors' best, netting 9 points apiece. Ronnie Greene's programme notes were written with great enthusiasm, as he informed the public that the BBC would be at Knowle the following week, broadcasting live race commentary from the league encounter *v.* Birmingham.

Prior to that, the Bulldogs faced two crucial away league matches at Nottingham and Belle Vue. Firstly, on 7 September, they ventured to White City for the fifth time in the season and disappointingly lost by 45 points to 35. The home side took half the match to build up a 4-point lead, but gradually increased it thereafter to run out comfortable victors in the end. Home skipper George Greenwood flew back from honeymoon in Ostend to plunder a 12-point maximum, receiving solid support from Fred Strecker (9) and Ted Bravery (8). Leading the way for the Bulldogs were Bill Rogers (11) and Harry Shepherd (8); the rest of the side had a bad time of it. In the second half, Nottingham defeated

Belle Vue 21-15 in a six-heat challenge match, with Greenwood taking his total of wins to seven out of seven on the night, while also having the distinction of recording the fastest time of 75.0 seconds. Bristol's loss at the hands of Nottingham made the match at Belle Vue two nights later all the more important but, responding positively, the Bulldogs held their collective nerve and stormed to a brilliant 52-31 victory over the Merseysiders. Leading by example, a back-to-form Roy Dook weighed in with 11 points and was backed by Rogers (8), Shepherd (8) and Bill Maddern (8) as Bristol maintained their position at the head of the league table.

Another crucial league encounter then saw Bristol face Birmingham in the 'live broadcast' meeting at Knowle Stadium on 10 September. However, the boys in orange and black proved too strong for their rivals from the Midlands, running out 48-34 winners. Bearing in mind that Birmingham had won on their previous visit, it made this performance all the more remarkable. A crowd of 9,400 turned out to see their heroes riding at the top of their form, with Bill Maddern (9), Harry Shepherd (8), Bill Rogers (8) and Reg Vigor (7) all influential in a solid team effort. Apart from Tiger Hart (9), Steve Langton (9), Malcolm Craven (8) and Les Bowden (4), the other visiting riders could only muster a single point apiece. Popular Bristol junior Reg Lambourne won heat four, thanks to the efforts of Shepherd in holding off the challenges of Danny Lee and Bob Lovell. Following heat seven, with Bristol leading 25-16, the match went 'on air' for twenty minutes. During that time, Vigor won heat ten in the fastest time of the night, 70.0 seconds, and there was a nasty crash two races later involving Roy Dook and Lee. Thankfully, the popular Bulldog escaped without injury, although Lee suffered a badly sprained leg and was carried off on a stretcher. There was further good news for the Bulldogs on 14 September when Nottingham severely jolted Southampton's Championship tilt, defeating the Saints 45-38 at Trent Lane.

On 15 September, Bristol journeyed to Birmingham for their final Provincial Trophy match and forced a 54-54 draw in a gripping encounter. The 302-yard Hall Green circuit served up some terrific action, with Bill Rogers (16) and Harry Shepherd (13) topping the Bristol scoring. Serving the homesters best were Bob Lovell (16), Malcolm Craven (12) and Steve Langton (11), but it was an evening to forget for skipper Tiger Hart, who fell in each of his first four rides. Flying Aussie Rogers was the fastest man on the night, timed at 75.6 seconds in heat eight. This was pretty quick when you consider that heat one was won in 81.6 seconds and times had fluctuated considerably in between. That draw meant Bristol had to be content with second position in the final National Provincial Trophy table, finishing a single point behind Nottingham.

When Bristol met Norwich at Knowle Stadium on 17 September, their goal was simple – to win the match and virtually make certain of claiming the Provincial League Championship. Having lost the title the previous season on race-points difference, the Bulldogs were really charged up and set about piling up as big a score as possible. Roared on by a somewhat disappointing attendance of 8,200, they romped to a thumping 60-23 success over a poor Stars side, who were severely weakened by the absence of Wal Morton. Novice Jack Clementson replaced Morton but collided with teammate Alan Smith in his first outing (heat three), causing both to hit the deck. Bill Maddern and Roy Dook went on to gratefully accept a 5-0 victory and, by the mid-point of the match, Bristol had stormed into a 32-9 lead. Norwich captain Dick Wise collected his side's only race win in heat twelve and, with Bill Birtwell finishing third, the visitors also claimed their one and only advantage of the meeting. For the Bulldogs, Reg Vigor and Bill Rogers charged to full maximums with the rest of the side packing the points thus: Maddern 9; Dook 8; Harry Shepherd 7; George Saunders 7. Even Reg Lambourne collected 5 points, with fellow reserve Reg Gore being the only non-scorer. Wise finished as the leading man for the Stars on the night, scoring a meagre 6 points. Ronnie Greene's programme notes made mention of an upcoming challenge match v. the great Wembley side, to be staged at Knowle on 5 October, when admission prices would be slightly altered as follows: 1s and 2s (adults); 6d and 1s (children).

On 24 September, there was a welcome break from the Bulldogs' hectic schedule when Knowle played host to a grand challenge match between America and Australia. Despite inclement weather conditions, a crowd of 14,300 witnessed the Aussie boys run up a marvellous victory by 64.5 points to 43.5. American Jack Milne clocked the fastest time of the night, 68.0 seconds, when outpacing Lionel Van Praag in the opening race, although the Australian did manage to avenge the loss in heat ten. Milne also suffered two defeats at the hands of Bluey Wilkinson in heats four and thirteen. In fact, Wilkinson's only dropped point of the evening came when teammate Bill Rogers headed him in heat eleven. The tightest finish of the match occurred in heat eight, when Ron Johnson and Pete Colman dead-heated for third place. Former Bulldog Eric Collins performed well, collecting 13 points for the Kangaroos and would almost certainly have done even better but for a fall in heat five. Full result: Australia 64.5 (Wilkinson 17; Van Praag 17; Collins 13; Rogers 8; Johnson 4.5; Ernie Evans 4; Bill Maddern 1) America 43.5 (Milne 15; Wilbur Lamoreaux 11; Byrd McKinney 10; Colman 3.5; Manuel Trujillo 2; Earl Farrand 1; Shorty Campbell 1).

Tragedy unfortunately struck on 27 September, when twenty-two-year-old Reg Vigor died following a racing crash at Wimbledon. Due to injury problems at Plough Lane, the youngster was representing the Dons in a National League match against Harringay and duly took his place at the start of heat two. Visiting rider Jack Ormston was leading Eric Collins, while Harringay's other representative Dick Smythe battled with Vigor for third place. Vigor appeared to catch his footrest in the safety fence wire and, along with his machine, he somersaulted for some twenty yards down the track. A long delay ensued before he was taken away on a stretcher and, at the close of the meeting, it was announced that he was still unconscious, although no bones were broken. Regrettably, he died three days later in the Nelson Hospital, Merton. Vigor had been one of the finds of the season and the Dons' management had every confidence that he would develop into a real star, having come to the fore as a grass-tracker at California-in-England, near Wokingham. Following impressive trials at Wimbledon, he was loaned out to Bristol and had done extremely well for the Bulldogs, totalling 103 points from the sixteen matches he had appeared in. Ironically, he lived with his mother and sisters, very close to the track on which he was to suffer his ultimately fatal crash.

September ended well for Southampton in the chase for the Championship, with home wins over Birmingham (59-25) and Belle Vue Merseysiders (53-30). The two Saints' victories kept the pressure on Bristol and meant the Hampshire outfit could still mathematically overhaul them at the top of the table, although their chances were slim. Southampton's match against the Merseysiders, held on 29 September, was followed by a nine-heat challenge v. the Bulldogs. This resulted in a 34-20 win for the home side, Harry Shepherd posting Bristol's solitary race win when taking the flag in heat seven. Frank Goulden recorded a three-ride maximum for the Saints, while Syd Griffiths recorded 7. Bill Rogers was the leading Bulldog with 6 points in what was the side's final away action of the season.

On 1 October all eyes were focussed on Knowle, as the Bulldogs entertained Birmingham in a match that would determine the outcome of the Championship. There was a sombre note, however, with the programme containing a tribute to Reg Vigor, whom Ronnie Greene described as 'a perfect gentleman'. Prior to the racing, the riders and 9,500 supporters all stood in silent tribute to the brilliant youngster. Despite the sadness of the occasion, the Bulldogs went on to record a 50.5-33.5 victory against their visitors, who never really offered any kind of threat to the Champions elect. The Bristol boys produced a succession of wins, crossing the line first in eleven of the fourteen heats. Superb team riding gave them a 15-3 lead after heat three, although they were helped by a tapes exclusion suffered by Tiger Hart in the second race. Harry Shepherd tumbled in heat four, but young Reg Gore stormed past Danny Lee to win, while the home captain remounted to collect a point. The Bulldogs led 38-16 after heat nine, having provided each and every race winner, before Hart finally took the flag for the visitors. Steve Langton secured another Birmingham success in the penultimate race, which also featured a dead-heat for second position between George Saunders and Lionel Stanger. With the match and the league title in the bag, Bristol afforded the visitors the luxury of a last-heat maximum, courtesy of Lee and Malcolm Craven. Looking at the scorers, Bill Rogers carded another maximum, while Roy Dook scored 10 points and Shepherd accumulated 8 on an historic night for the homesters. Meanwhile, Langton was best for the visitors, scoring a hard-earned 8 points. After the meeting, Mr A.J.M. Ivison of the Auto-Cycle Union presented the League Championship trophy to Mrs Ronnie Greene, wife of the Bristol supremo and a director of Bristol Motor Sports Ltd. Mrs Greene passed the silverware on to club skipper Harry Shepherd, who proudly paraded around the track with his triumphant teammates.

On 5 October, the world-famous Wembley side visited Knowle in a grand challenge match. Not surprisingly, their class shone through as they strolled to a 65-43 victory. Ginger Lees led the Lions with an impeccable 18-point maximum, while the rest of his colleagues contributed thus: Lionel Van Praag 14; Tommy Price 11; Cliff Parkinson 10; Eric Gregory 8; Wally Lloyd 4; Les Bowden 0. The Bulldogs were again best served by Bill Rogers, who scored 11 points, while Bill Maddern tallied 10, but the rest of the side found the pace a little too hot. Superstar Lees was at the time the rider with the highest transfer fee on his head, having been signed by Wembley from Belle Vue in 1935 for a massive £1,000.

The final track action of the year saw Bristol entertain old rivals Southampton in a twelve-heat challenge match on 8 October. The Bulldogs brought the curtain down on a wonderful season in front of another huge attendance in what was the fifty-eighth meeting at the stadium since the return of the sport the previous year. Bristol won the match with relative ease, 45-27, despite being behind for the first four races, with Harry Shepherd and Bill Maddern topping the scorechart on 11 points apiece. For the visitors, Frank Goulden suffered a fall, but won his other three outings for a 9-point haul. The second half of the programme was described as 'Crazy Night', and included riders and supporters racing on donkeys, a cycling championship and a mixture of comical events. A collection was made for the mother of Reg Vigor throughout the meeting and raised over £91, an amount that took the total raised since the youngster's untimely death to £195. It was also revealed that nearly 300,000 supporters had gone through the turnstiles at Knowle during the course of the season, which for 32 meetings averaged out at well over 9,000.

Following what had been a hugely successful campaign, the Bristol followers requested that the side move into the First Division, and application was duly made to the Control Board. A strong point in the club's favour was obviously the average size of attendances at Knowle Stadium.

Excluding the expunged league fixtures against Leicester, the Bulldogs completed a total of forty-eight meetings (twenty National Provincial League, ten National Provincial Trophy, four National Trophy, four Coronation Cup and ten challenge). Bill Rogers was the top rider of the year, scoring 447.5 points from forty-six meetings for a match average of 9.73. Fittingly, skipper Harry Shepherd was the only team member to remain ever-present and he was second in the statistical stakes with 402 points from his forty-eight matches, while Roy Dook totalled 312.5 points from forty-one meetings.

1937 STATISTICS

(Bristol's score shown first unless otherwise stated)

NATIONAL PROVINCIAL LEAGUE

Opponents	Home	Away
Birmingham	W48-34	W44-39
	W50.5-33.5	W45-38
Leicester	W68-15	W57-23
	Not staged	Not staged
Liverpool/Belle Vue II	W58-25	W55-29
	W59-24	W52-31
Norwich	W64-18	W54-27
	W60-23	L39-44
Nottingham	W49-31	L40-42
	W48-35	L35-45
Southampton	W45-36	L38-46
	W55-28	L31-52

MATCH AVERAGES

Rider	Matches	Points	Average
Bill Rogers	20	179	8.95
Reg Vigor	6	51	8.50
Harry Shepherd	20	167	8.35
Roy Dook	19	153.5	8.08
Rol Stobart	11	84.5	7.68
Fred Leavis	13	84	6.46
Bill Maddern	19	85	4.47
George Saunders	17	75.5	4.44
Jack Dalton	6	23	3.83
Bill Longley	2	7	3.50
Reg Hay	1	3	3.00
Reg Gore	4	11	2.75
Reg Lambourne	11	29	2.64
Harry Bowler	2	4	2.00
Johnnie Millett	3	6	2.00
Harold Bain	3	5	1.67
Fred Lewis	3	2	0.67

NOTE: Match averages do not include expunged fixtures v. Leicester.

NATIONAL PROVINCIAL LEAGUE TABLE

Team	Matches	Won	Drawn	Lost	For	Against	Pts
Bristol	20	15	0	5	969.5	680.5	30
Southampton	20	13	0	7	892	771	26
Nottingham	20	11	0	9	892	758	22
Liverpool/Belle Vue II	20	8	0	12	774	883	16
Norwich	20	8	0	12	707	941	16
Birmingham	20	5	0	15	729.5	930.5	10

NOTE: Leicester resigned after six matches, with their record expunged from the league table; Liverpool transferred their home fixtures to Belle Vue in mid-season.

NATIONAL PROVINCIAL TROPHY

Opponents	Home	Away
Birmingham	L50-58	D54-54
Liverpool/Belle Vue II	W67-41	W62-43
Norwich	W72-34	W62-45
Nottingham	W60-47	L40-68
Southampton	W54-50	L48-59

MATCH AVERAGES

Rider	Matches	Points	Average
Bill Rogers	10	137	13.70
Harry Shepherd	10	110	11.00
Rol Stobart	4	40	10.00
Roy Dook	6	57	9.50
Fred Leavis	9	81	9.00
Reg Vigor	6	35	5.83
George Saunders	10	56	5.60
Bill Maddern	10	46	4.60
Reg Lambourne	6	6	1.00
Fred Lewis	2	1	0.50

NOTE: Match averages do not include reserve appearances when a rider took no rides.

SPEEDWAY IN BRISTOL 1928-1949

NATIONAL PROVINCIAL TROPHY TABLE

Team	Matches	Won	Drawn	Lost	For	Against	Pts
Nottingham	10	7	0	3	612	458	14
Bristol	10	6	1	3	569	499	13
Southampton	10	6	0	4	590	473	12
Liverpool/Belle Vue II	10	4	0	6	498	569	8
Birmingham	10	3	1	6	459	612	7
Norwich	10	3	0	7	474	591	6

DAILY MAIL NATIONAL TROPHY

Opponents	Home	Away	Aggregate
Nottingham	W48-36	L37-46	W85-82
Southampton	L41-42	L32-51	L73-93

MATCH AVERAGES

Rider	Matches	Points	Average
Harry Shepherd	4	32	8.00
Roy Dook	4	31	7.75
Bill Rogers	4	27	6.75
Fred Leavis	4	21	5.25
Rol Stobart	4	18	4.50
George Saunders	3	11	3.67
Reg Gore	1	3	3.00
Bill Maddern	4	10	2.50
Reg Hay	1	2	2.00
Jack Dalton	2	3	1.50
Harold Bain	1	0	0.00

CORONATION CUP

Opponents	Home	Away	Aggregate
Norwich	W53-29	W47-35	W100-64
Nottingham	W47-37	L29-55	L76-92

MATCH AVERAGES

Rider	Matches	Points	Average
Bill Rogers	4	34.5	8.63
Roy Dook	4	34	8.50
Harry Shepherd	4	27	6.75
Fred Leavis	3	16.5	5.50
George Saunders	4	21	5.25
Bill Maddern	2	10	5.00
Reg Lambourne	2	8	4.00
Reg Vigor	2	8	4.00
Reg Gore	2	7	3.50
Reg Hay	1	3	3.00
Jack Dalton	2	5	2.50
Fred Lewis	1	2	2.00

CHALLENGE

Opponents	Home	Away
All America	(1) L34.5-37.5	–
All America	(2) L32-40	–
New Cross	W46-35	–
Southampton	W45-27	L20-34
Wembley	L43-65	–
West Ham	L36-72	–
West Ham Res.	W60-23	–
Wimbledon	L33-39	L36-48

MATCH AVERAGES

Rider	Matches	Points	Average
Bill Rogers	8	70	8.75
Eric Collins	2	17	8.50
Rol Stobart	4	29	7.25
Harry Shepherd	10	66	6.60
Ron Johnson	2	12	6.00
Johnnie Millett	1	6	6.00
Fred Leavis	6	31.5	5.25
Bill Maddern	8	38	4.75
Roy Dook	8	37	4.63

Harold Bain	2	9	4.50
Reg Vigor	2	9	4.50
Reg Lambourne	4	16	4.00
Reg Gore	1	3	3.00
George Saunders	6	15	2.50
Ron Howes	1	2	2.00
Fred Lewis	2	4	2.00
Jack Dalton	2	1	0.50

NOTE: Match averages do not include reserve appearances when a rider took no rides.

MINI-MATCH

Opponents	Home	Away
West Ham Hawks	–	L11-12

MATCH AVERAGES

Rider	Matches	Points	Average
George Saunders	1	5	5.00
Roy Dook	1	4	4.00
Fred Leavis	1	2	2.00
George Pepper	1	0	0.00
Rol Stobart	1	0	0.00

1938

Following Bristol's tremendously successful season in 1937, both on and off the track, the Speedway Control Board, at a meeting on 3 March, decided to promote the club to the National League. On 8 April, the 1938 season duly kicked off with an individual meeting entitled the Opening Cup. Ronnie Greene was very upbeat in his programme notes, stating, 'We proved to the sporting world that London was not the be all and end all of speedway racing. Bristol became known for what it is –

one of the finest speedways in the country. We entered for, and won the Provincial League Championship. Now we have come to the parting of the ways. So far as Bristol is concerned the Second Division is no more. The thing for which we have worked and planned has come to pass. BRISTOL IS IN THE FIRST DIVISION.' Later in his piece, Greene went on to say, 'As you know, it was only a few weeks ago that the opportunity occurred for us to enter the senior division. Hackney withdrew and we have taken their place. All negotiations were made through the ACU Control Board, who allocated to Bristol those two famous riders Cordy Milne (world number three) and Morian Hansen (world number twelve). Owing to the fact that so many riders are abroad, we will be unable to introduce all members of the team at tonight's meeting but, to cut a long story short, we will have at our disposal last year's Bristol stalwarts Bill Rogers, Harry Shepherd, Roy Dook, Rol Stobart and Bill Maddern. From Hackney, in addition to Milne and Hansen, we secured the famous Australian Vic Duggan and probably Bill Clibbett. I say probably in the case of Clibbett, because there is a big likelihood that he may retire from racing altogether. But if he does ride, he will be with Bristol.'

When Cordy Milne was signed, he took over the club captaincy, as former skipper Harry Shepherd immediately went to the management and suggested that the American should succeed him for 1938. This was typical of Shepherd's sporting nature, and the Bristol fans welcomed the subsequent announcement that he was to be Milne's vice-captain.

The opening meeting itself was witnessed by a crowd of 15,437 enthusiasts and produced some brilliant racing from a star-studded field of sixteen riders. The evening was a great triumph for West Ham ace Arthur Atkinson, who took the magnificent trophy and scorched to a new track record, not once, but twice! The flying Lancastrian clocked 67.4 seconds in his first ride (heat two), before lowering that record still further to an incredible 66.8 seconds in his next outing, three races later. The meeting was run over sixteen qualifying heats, with the top four scorers going into a grand final. Atkinson strolled into the deciding race with 11 points, where he was joined by three riders who each totalled 9, namely Wimbledon's Geoff Pymar, West Ham's Eric Chitty and Joe Francis of New Cross. Atkinson took an early lead in the final before going on to comfortably win from Francis and Chitty in 68.2 seconds. Going back to the qualifying heats, Wimbledon's Benny Kaufman rode particularly well in heat thirteen, inflicting the only defeat of the meeting on Atkinson. In spite of this, the man from the USA could only tally 7 points. Full result: (Qualifying scores) Atkinson 11; Pymar 9; Chitty 9; Francis 9; Tommy Croombs 8; George Wilks 8; Kaufman 7; George Newton 7; Goldie Restall 6; Harry Shepherd 4; Stan Greatrex 4; Tommy Price 3; Roy Dook 2; Nobby Key 2; Rol Stobart 2; Reg Lambourne 2. Final: 1st Atkinson; 2nd Francis; 3rd Chitty; 4th Pymar.

A week later, on Good Friday, 15 April, Bristol entertained New Cross in an eighteen-heat challenge match and 17,499 fans from all over the West Country flocked to Knowle Stadium for a first look at the new Bulldogs' line-up. The original 'Great Dane' Morian Hansen didn't disappoint, riding brilliantly to collect 13 points, while Buffalo-born Cordy Milne tallied 12 and also posted the fastest time of the night when clocked at 68.2 seconds in heat five. Bristol's new American star fairly thrilled the crowd with his sensational white-line style of riding, as well as his 'bronco' starting technique. The meeting started in spectacular fashion, with Joe Francis and George Newton colliding on the first bend in the opening race. Francis was carried off on a stretcher with a bad leg injury, but Newton recovered to win the re-run. Heat nine saw Milne and Hansen secure a 5-1 over Bill Longley to reduce the visitors' lead to 28-26, only for Newton and Jack Milne to immediately reply with a New Cross maximum in the race that followed. The Milne brothers came together in heat fifteen, with the visiting sibling emerging on top and showing just why he had scooped the World Championship at Wembley the previous September. Unfortunately the Bulldogs lacked the necessary strength in depth and finally went down to a 62-43 defeat. The victorious London outfit were superbly led by 17 points from Jack Milne, while George Newton weighed in with 15. As previously mentioned, the World Champion's only defeat came at the hands of Newton in heat ten, meaning he would have been credited with a paid maximum in the modern era but, at the time, bonus points simply did not exist!

Easter Monday, 18 April, saw Bristol join forces with New Cross in a challenge match v. a combined Wimbledon and West Ham side at the superbly appointed Plough Lane Stadium. A huge attendance saw the two composite teams battle out a thrilling 48-48 draw on the 343-yard circuit. The Wimbledon/West Ham combination was well served by maximum man Arthur Atkinson (12), with strong support supplied by

Geoff Pymar (9), Eric Chitty (9) and Benny Kaufman (9). Meanwhile, the New Cross/Bristol select was ably led by Jack Milne (11), Cordy Milne (10) and Stan Greatrex (8), with their remaining points scored thus: Ron Johnson 5; Morian Hansen 4; Goldie Restall 4; Bill Clibbett 4; George Newton 2. There were reasons for some of the rather indifferent performances, with Newton taking three falls during the match, while Johnson suffered from machine problems and a sore arm following a recent vaccination.

There was another challenge match for the Knowle faithful on 19 April, when the Bulldogs played host to North America and only just came out on top in a tight match, by 43 points to 41. The crowd of 9,231 witnessed some superb racing, with Jack Milne romping to a 12-point full-house for the visitors, while Benny Kaufman plundered 11. Looking at Bristol's scorechart, Cordy Milne was the top man with 11 points, suffering his only defeat at the hands of his brother in the opening race. Heat two saw Morian Hansen fall at the pits bend before remounting and passing both Ray Duggan and Bob Sparkes to grab second place behind Kaufman. Later on, in heat eight, Hansen was unlucky not to beat Kaufman when his engine blew. The scores stood at 33 points apiece after heat eleven, but a marvellous effort from Cordy Milne and Harry Shepherd produced a 4-2 over Goldie Restall to put the Bulldogs marginally ahead. This was an advantage they managed to hold until the end of the match, although Vic Duggan gave everyone heart failure when he almost fell while leading the final race, before recovering to take the flag. After the main match, Cordy Milne set a new track record for two laps (with rolling start), clocking 32.0 seconds. The programme for the meeting stated that membership of the supporters' club had already reached 8,000 for the season. They still had a long way to go to match West Ham though, for the Hammers' membership stood at an astonishing 30,000!

On 22 April, the Bulldogs opened their league campaign with a 47-36 victory over Harringay at a wet Knowle in front of 10,528 spectators. This represented a tremendous start to senior league racing, and was achieved despite the fact that both Bill Clibbett and Rol Stobart were unable to ride. Heat one featured a remarkable ride from Australian Bill Maddern, who had only just returned to Britain from his native country. The legendary Jack Parker fell on the first turn, with Cordy Milne losing a lot of ground in avoiding the stricken rider. That allowed Bill Pitcher to streak clear, with Maddern in hot pursuit for over three laps, until the final bend, when the pressing Bulldog daringly cut inside to defeat his rival by inches. Alec Statham clocked 68.2 seconds in heats two and eleven, and this proved to be the fastest time of the night. Heat three brought a nasty spill for Les Wotton, but thankfully he wasn't seriously injured and duly completed the meeting. Norman Parker had problems in heat six and rode off the track, leaving Morian Hansen and Vic Duggan to gain a 4-2 over Wotton. Two races later, Hansen and Roy Dook collected a 5-0 after problems befell both visitors, Statham taking a fall and Will Lowther dropping out through motor problems. That left Bristol leading 28-19 and they had no trouble in sharing five of the remaining heats while gaining a 4-2 in the other to run out comfortable winners. Both Hansen and Milne finished with 10 points each, while the Tigers were best served by Jack Parker (9), who won all his remaining rides following his opening-heat spill.

Ronnie Greene's programme notes encouraged the Bristol fans to join in the chorus of the Bulldogs' signature tune 'Marching Along Together', which went like this:

Marching along together,
Singing all along the line,
What do we care for the weather,
We'll be there in rain or shine,
Ready for war and kisses,
Ready to love and fight.

We roll along with a cheery song,
Lightening every mile,
We pack our troubles in our kit bags,
And that is why we smile,
Marching along together,
Happy just to be side by side.

The following night Bristol ventured to Green Lanes in London for the return fixture with Harringay. To everyone's utter amazement, the Bulldogs completed a quick-fire double with a 42-41 victory on the 336-yard circuit. Riding with great confidence, Cordy Milne overtook and beat Jack Parker in heat one and, with Bill Maddern in third place, Bristol took an early lead. Despite struggling with a damaged groin muscle following his fall in heat eight the previous evening, Alec Statham took his place in the meeting, but it was to prove a bad decision. In heat two he led Morian Hansen, but pulled up in agony and subsequently had to be removed on a stretcher. That allowed Hansen to secure the Bulldogs' second race win of the evening, and there was yet more misfortune for the home camp in the very next race. Les Wotton and Norman Parker were sat on a 5-1, when the former's machine spluttered to a halt yards from the line, allowing Bill Rogers through to grab second position, while Wotton coasted across the line in third spot. Reg Lambourne came through from the back in the next heat, and was shepherded home by Milne to give Bristol maximum points and a 14-9 lead. Although Lambourne's winning time of 78.0 seconds was the slowest of the night, it spoke volumes for Milne's team-riding tactics. Race wins followed for Harry Shepherd (heat six), Milne (heats seven and ten) and Hansen (heat eight), as the Bulldogs built up a lead of 11 points, before the homesters started an ultimately unsuccessful revival. Milne, with 11 points, and Hansen (10) led the way for the triumphant men in orange and black, while the somewhat unlucky Tigers were held together by Jack Parker (11).

Bristol came back to earth with a thud on 29 April, however, when the Lions of Wembley stole away from Knowle with a 47-37 victory under their belts. It was a brave effort from the Bulldogs, but they were up against the brilliant pairing of maximum man Lionel Van Praag (12) and Frank Charles (11), who won half of the fourteen heats between them. For Bristol, Cordy Milne won two heats in his 9-point total, while Morian Hansen ran two lasts before winning his third and fourth outings. It was an enjoyable meeting though, and another large attendance of some 13,000 thoroughly enjoyed witnessing some of the world's best riders on their own patch.

The next dose of National League activity took the Bulldogs to West Ham on 3 May, but it was a bad night, as they crashed to a 55-29 defeat on the 440-yard Custom House raceway. Bristol failed to gain a single heat advantage and provided the race winner on just three occasions, with Cordy Milne and Morian Hansen heading their scoring on 8 points apiece. The Hammers meanwhile, were solid throughout, with five of the side scoring 8 points or more, thus: Tommy Croombs 11; Tiger Stevenson 9; Arthur Atkinson 9; Eric Chitty 9; Bluey Wilkinson 8. The fastest recorded time was 81.0 seconds, being clocked by both

Wilkinson, in heat five, and Hansen, in heat eight; interestingly, this was converted into a speed figure of 44.44mph.

Back at Knowle on 6 May, Belle Vue provided the opposition for a gripping league encounter, which eventually ended in a single-point defeat for the homesters, 41–40. The Aces were indebted to Frank Varey and Bill Kitchen, both of whom scorched to maximums and totalled 24 of their side's 41 points. Cordy Milne led the Bulldogs' scoring, but was restricted to just 8 points thanks to the brilliance of Belle Vue's big two. Another huge attendance of 11,600 witnessed Bristol in trouble from the off as the Aces moved 10-2 ahead after just two races. Heat three saw the visiting pair of Bob Harrison and Wally Hull crash out, while Bill Clibbett pulled up with engine problems, leaving Bill Rogers to coast home alone for a 3-0 advantage. The Bulldogs battled gamely following that, but never quite got on terms and, although a last-heat 5-1 from Bill Maddern and Rogers brought them to within a point, the result was slightly flattering.

The next night, Bristol travelled to Manchester for the return fixture v. the Aces and, although the homesters moved to the top of the league table with a 49-35 victory, the Bristol boys acquitted themselves well at the 418-yard circuit. The meeting was marred by a crash involving home captain Eric Langton heat four, which saw the popular rider suffer damage to his right ankle, forcing him to withdraw from the remainder of the match. Frank Varey completed another fine maximum for the Manchester outfit, it actually being his fifth in a row at Hyde Road since the start of the 1938 campaign. He received solid support from Oliver Langton (9), Bill Kitchen (9) and Bob Harrison (8), while Bill Clibbett topped the Bristol scoring on 9.

On 13 May, Wimbledon were the welcome visitors to Knowle for National League action, with the sides fighting out a thrilling 41–41 draw. The crowd of 9,700 witnessed keen racing with fast times throughout and once again it was the popular Bulldogs skipper Cordy Milne who caught the eye, winning all four of his heats in polished style. In the opening race he inflicted the only defeat of the night on Wilbur Lamoreaux in a super-quick 68.6 seconds, although his time was later bettered by 0.2 of a second when Morian Hansen clocked 68.4 in heat eight. Bristol trailed 37-34 after heat twelve but then enjoyed a large slice of luck when the Dons pair of Geoff Pymar and Wilf Plant both fell, handing Bill Rogers and Harry Shepherd a gift 5-0. That turned the score around completely, putting the Bulldogs 39-37 ahead, only for Norman Evans and Nobby Key to claim a 4-2 over Vic Duggan in the final race to tie the meeting. After the match, Cordy Milne set a new record for two laps (with clutch start), when he scorched around in 34.2 seconds.

Bristol hit the road again on 16 May, when they ventured to Plough Lane for another go at the Dons. Things started badly though, with Cordy Milne suffering from mechanical gremlins in heat one and Morian Hansen falling at the start of the second race. Milne notched the Bulldogs' first win in heat five, but they only collected a further two race victories, courtesy of Bill Rogers in heat six and again by Milne in heat nine, before going down by 53 points to 31. Solid-scoring Wimbledon were spearheaded by maximum man Wilbur Lamoreaux (12) and his American compatriot Benny Kaufman (10), while Cordy Milne and Rogers topped the Bristol scorechart with 8 points apiece. To make matters worse for the dejected Bulldogs, it was revealed after the meeting that Bill Maddern had been fined by the steward for turning up late.

At Knowle on 20 May, an 11,000 gate saw star-packed New Cross steal away with a comfortable 46-38 success, thanks in particular to the fine efforts of Jack Milne (11), Ron Johnson (10) and George Newton (9). The most outstanding feature of the evening occurred in heat nine, when Bill Clibbett somehow managed to beat the great Jack Milne. Subdued scoring in the home camp saw four riders end as joint top scorer with just 6 points apiece, namely Cordy Milne, Vic Duggan, Morian Hansen and Clibbett.

The Old Kent Road beckoned on 25 May when Bristol travelled to the tiny 262-yard racing strip known affectionately throughout the speedway world as the 'Frying Pan'. New Cross had little difficulty in taming the West Country boys, running out winners by 51 points to 33 and on only three occasions did a Bristol rider cross the line first. The big two of Cordy Milne and Morian Hansen suffered with numerous problems, resulting in low returns of just 3 points apiece. Topping the scoring, Bill Rogers fully deserved his 9 points, but he could do nothing to stop Jack Milne from storming to another full-house. Not even the rain, which fell in torrents prior to the start, could hold back the flying home star. Due to the conditions, the early heats were quite sluggish but, by the end of the second-half event, Milne had clocked 59.6 seconds. Even so, that was still some way short of George Newton's track record of 58.0 seconds for the mini-track.

After staging sixty-six consecutive meetings since reopening in 1936, it was with great disappointment that the eagerly awaited National League clash *v.* West Ham was rained off at Knowle on 27 May. 'HRH' in a later programme stated, 'It was impossible to even suggest racing, but we must not blame the condition of the track too severely, because the storm that broke over our section of Knowle forty-five minutes before racing was due to start was one of the heaviest downpours I have ever witnessed.'

On 1 June, Southampton defeated New Cross 47-33 in an English Trophy fixture, staged amid high winds and occasional heavy showers. In the second half of the programme, a nine-heat challenge match pitched the Saints against Bristol and resulted in a 27-26 victory for the visiting Bulldogs. A back-to-form Cordy Milne led the Bristol scoring with a three-ride maximum, while Syd Griffiths finished on top of the Southampton pile with 7 points from his three outings.

A couple of evenings later, Belle Vue made their second trip of the year to Knowle for an ACU Cup tie. The Aces had actually held the trophy since the tournament's inception in 1934, but they were to suffer a crushing defeat. Indeed, a Bristol rider finished first in sixteen of the eighteen heats as they hammered out a 74-34 victory. Cordy Milne led the inspired homesters with 17.5 points from six rides, receiving solid support from Bill Rogers (13), Bill Clibbett (10.5) and Vic Duggan (10). Milne's dropped half-point was at the hands of teammate Bill Clibbett, when they dead-heated in heat thirteen. However, he didn't appear too bothered and proved it by equalling Arthur Atkinson's track record of 66.8 seconds in the final race of the match. In stark contrast to the home lads, Belle Vue were in a state of disarray, emphasised by the fact that skipper Frank Varey failed to score in four of his five heats. Meanwhile, in recording both of the Aces' heat wins, Bill Kitchen was the only visitor to do himself any justice on the way to a tally of 11 points. The only downside of a terrific night for the Bulldogs was a somewhat disappointing attendance of just 7,500. The programme stated that Bill Maddern was going through a temporary bad spell, with the reason attributed to his habit of arriving late at virtually every meeting. On one race day, he apparently overturned his car at Calne, Wiltshire, but didn't telephone the stadium to let anyone know what had happened until 7.50 p.m. Despite being fined several times, the Aussie was still not arriving on time and was warned that he was running out of chances.

The Bulldogs were totally overwhelmed by Belle Vue in the return leg of their ACU Cup tie at Hyde Road on 4 June. The fired-up homesters avenged their defeat and more, running out winners by 78 points to 30. Bristol were totally outclassed on the night, although their cause wasn't helped by Bill Maddern's usual late arrival. Only Cordy Milne offered any real resistance to the onslaught, gathering 10 points from his six outings, while the rampant Aces were best served by Frank Varey (17), Bill Kitchen (14), Bob Harrison (14), Oliver Langton (11) and Walter Hull (10). Varey's only dropped point occurred in heat eight, when he was beaten to the line by teammate Harrison. A home rider took the chequered flag on seventeen occasions, with the Bulldogs' solitary race win coming from Milne in the penultimate heat.

At Knowle on 7 June, an improved attendance of 8,750 witnessed the Bulldogs face Wimbledon in a challenge match for the *Speedway News* Cup. A vociferous crowd enjoyed close, thrilling racing throughout, with Bristol coming out on top to take the trophy by a single point, 42-41. They were led as usual, by brilliant white-line exponent Cordy Milne, whose four starts yielded 9 points and an engine failure. For the Dons, Wally Lloyd (11) topped the scorechart, while former Bulldog Eric Collins had a disappointing night and could only muster a lowly 4 points, his performance including an exclusion following a fall in heat one. In his programme notes, Ronnie Greene spoke about the all-star Wembley side due to visit Bristol on 10 June, and made special mention of Frank Charles, thus: 'The speedway world was astonished when it heard that Wembley had paid £1,000 for Frank Charles, but they were lucky to get him at that price, for quite recently I have offered as much for riders nothing like so good as Charles, only to be met with a point-blank refusal.'

The previously mentioned match against Wembley was an ACU Cup encounter, and a thunderstorm greeted the illustrious visitors, with the start of the meeting delayed for fifteen minutes before the track was declared fit to race on. The Lions quickly adjusted to the greasy conditions and showed extreme control to earn a marvellous 64-44 victory. Apart from Cordy Milne, the Bristol boys struggled to get to grips with the track surface and they were an easily beaten side. Milne underlined his undoubted talent though, storming to five straight wins before coming up against Frank Charles and Lionel Van Praag in the final heat. Charles got away at the start, with Van Praag tucked in behind and a Wembley

5-1 looked highly likely. After two laps, however, Milne stormed past Van Praag and was mighty close to overhauling Charles at the finish. Even so, a total of 17 points against such quality opposition was a great achievement, especially when a look down the Bristol scorechart revealed that Bill Rogers, Morian Hansen and Harry Shepherd were next in line on just 5 points apiece! Wembley, on the other hand, possessed three riders in double figures, namely Frank Charles (15), Lionel Van Praag (12) and Cliff Parkinson (10). The adverse weather obviously affected the crowd level, with just 6,500 paying customers passing through the Knowle turnstiles.

On 16 June, Bristol made their first-ever visit to Wembley Stadium for more ACU Cup action against the Lions. Unsurprisingly, the Bulldogs were beaten, although the margin of defeat wasn't as great as it had been at Knowle. With both Cordy Milne (13) and Morian Hansen (12) riding well, Bristol managed to restrict Wembley to a 61-47 victory, and even managed to record three maximum heat wins. Heat eight was eventful, as Lionel Van Praag wobbled from the start and went on to the grass. His red disqualification light came on but the Australian carried on riding, only for the black flag and his helmet colour to be waved next time around. Utter confusion reigned supreme, as all the riders then stopped and wondered what exactly was going on. Hansen quickly realised and started racing again, with Milne and George Wilks soon following suit. Amid a chorus of booing, Hansen went on to win by half a lap from his teammate in a time of 85.0 seconds – some way short of the track record for the 378-yard circuit, which stood at 73.6 seconds. Main men on the night for the homesters were Tommy Price and Van Praag, who each bagged 14 points.

Twenty-four hours later there was more ACU Cup activity as Bristol entertained Wimbledon for the second time in ten days. A crowd of 9,000 saw some of the most exciting racing ever witnessed at Knowle and, considering the Bulldogs were 10 points in arrears after heat six, they did exceptionally well to go down by just a couple of points in the end, 55-53. In fact, Bristol did get the score back to 51 points apiece with one race to go, but Wilbur Lamoreaux clinched the vital win from an ever-pressing Cordy Milne, while Wally Lloyd claimed the match-winning point ahead of Bill Clibbett. As usual, the Bulldogs' leading performer on the night was Cordy Milne (16), although the American did receive some backing from Bill Clibbett, who notched 10. The Dons, meanwhile, were led by Lamoreaux, who plundered 15 points, while

Wally Lloyd tallied 14. With a foot in both camps, Ronnie Greene decided to hand over the Bristol team manager's duties to Fred Mockford for the evening but, as he stated in his programme notes, 'How I am going to walk around among you without at times rushing over to the pits and slating poor old Fred and the officials, I fail to understand; at any rate I feel my actions will give satisfaction to you all!'

On 22 June, Bristol paid their second visit of the month to Southampton for another challenge match. In what formed the second part of a double-header, the fourteen-heat affair took place after the Saints had defeated Norwich 35-18 in a replayed National Trophy tie, with the Hampshire side again emerging triumphant, albeit by the slender margin of 43 points to 41. The Bristol boys did well, keeping the scores close throughout, and the sides were level at 39-39 going into the final heat, only for Frank Goulden and Bert Jones to secure a 4-2 over Vic Duggan. The defeat was a bitter blow for the many travelling supporters in attendance, especially after the efforts of Cordy Milne in recording a classy 12-point maximum. He received little support, however, with Bill Maddern next on the list with a meagre return of 6 points. The Saints were a much more compact outfit, headed by Frank Goulden's 11 points, while Bert Jones netted 9.

On 24 June, a break from the cut-and-thrust of team racing saw a World Championship qualifying round on the Knowle agenda. Before a gate of 10,000, sixteen top stars battled it out over twenty heats with Bristol captain Cordy Milne taking all the accolades with a superb 15-point maximum. Two of Milne's race wins were particularly worthy of special mention. Heat six saw him account for Lionel Van Praag's only defeat of the night. Then, in heat ten, he had to work hard to beat George Wilks, finally succeeding with a marvellous *outside* pass on the last lap, his winning time of 67.8 seconds being the fastest of the night. Full result: Milne 15; Van Praag 14; Wilks 12; Geoff Pymar 11; Eric Gregory 9; Jimmy Gibb 8; Vic Duggan 8; Les Wotton 8; Doug Wells 7; Morian Hansen 7; Frank Varey 5; Bill Rogers 5; Bill Clibbett 2; Eric Collins 2; Bill Maddern 1; Frank Goulden 1.

The Bulldogs journeyed to Wimbledon for more ACU Cup activity on 27 June, but it was a night to forget as they slumped to a 73-35 defeat. The one-sided affair gave the Dons a chance to produce some exhibition riding to entertain a large crowd. The best Bristol could offer on the night was 10 points from Vic Duggan, while the usually reliable

Cordy Milne suffered three falls when trying to make fast starts, before ending the evening with just 4 points to his name. The powerhouse homesters were led by an impeccable 18-point maximum from Geoff Pymar, with Benny Kaufman (15), Wilbur Lamoreaux (14) and Wally Lloyd (10) all scoring solidly in support.

West Ham were the next side to visit Bristol on 1 July, when *Daily Mail* National Trophy fare was on offer for the regular patrons. Unfortunately, the Hammers inflicted another defeat on the beleaguered Bulldogs, the 56-50 reverse being the seventh home loss of the season, as the men in orange and black continued to struggle with the pace of the higher division. The attendance of 8,500 saw the lead change hands five times, and no fewer than eleven maximum heat wins were recorded during the match. Visiting star Bluey Wilkinson was involved in an horrific crash in heat nine when chasing after Cordy Milne. The Australian ran into the safety fence and was thrown right over the top although, fortuitously, he didn't receive a scratch and went on to win his final two outings. With Bristol trailing 53-41 after heat sixteen, a fairly heavy defeat looked on the cards, but they fought back to gain a 4-2 and a 5-1 from the last two races, reducing the deficit to 6 points at the close. Looking at the completed scorechart, Cordy Milne was back at his best with 15 points, while Vic Duggan yielded a superb tally of 14. The West Ham side, however, was packed with several big hitters, namely Arthur Atkinson (12), Tiger Stevenson (11), Bluey Wilkinson (10), Tommy Croombs (9) and Charlie Spinks (9).

Needless to say, the return leg at Custom House on 5 July was a foregone conclusion, with Johnnie Hoskins' Hammers charging to a 72-35 success. Led brilliantly by Bluey Wilkinson's 17 points, West Ham coasted through to the semi-final stage courtesy of a 128-85 victory on aggregate. Apart from Cordy Milne (13), the remainder of the Bulldogs were at sixes and sevens, suffering four falls and a disqualification during the match. Milne was in fact the only man to take a point off Wilkinson, when leading the way home in heat nine: this win was achieved in by far the fastest time of the evening, 79.6 seconds, which equated to an average speed of 45.23mph.

After a run of seven successive defeats, it was with great relief to most in the gate of 8,600 that the Bulldogs managed to put one over on old rivals Southampton in a challenge match at Knowle on 8 July. Having lost at Banister Court by just 2 points, Bristol were determined to avenge the defeat and rode magnificently to record a 64-20 victory. A home man crossed the line first in each and every race, with a massive ten maximums being recorded during the course of the fourteen heats. Cordy Milne won all four of his starts for a 12-point haul, as indeed he had done in the corresponding fixture at Southampton, and he was well supported by Morian Hansen (11), Bill Rogers (11), Bill Clibbett (10) and Vic Duggan (9). Meanwhile, for the bedraggled Saints, Frank Goulden headed the scoring with just 6 points.

Neither the riders from Bristol not West Ham would forget St Swithin's Day, which fell on 15 July. The Hammers travelled to Knowle for a National League match but, with Bristol holding a 13-4 lead after heat three, proceedings were abandoned with the track flooded in parts following heavy rain, which had fallen since the start time. It was the second occasion that rain had affected the clash, having completely washed out the first attempt to run the fixture on 27 May. The decision was the right one though, as Bluey Wilkinson had fallen in the opening race, while Bronco Dixon and Tiger Stevenson had crashed together in heat two. For the record, the points were scored thus: (Bristol) Vic Duggan 3; Morian Hansen 3; Cordy Milne 2; Bill Rogers 2; Bill Clibbett 2; Bill Maddern 1; (West Ham) Charlie Spinks 3; Jimmy Gibb 1. In his programme notes, Ronnie Greene stated, 'We are now halfway through our first season in the First Division. At this stage, I think it would be a good idea if we paused a moment and considered what effect our promotion has had upon Bristol and speedway racing generally. As a Bristol man myself, I am convinced that my best policy will be to adopt a policy of absolute frankness. Getting mixed up with the senior clubs has been an interesting experience. But it has been an experience that has benefited the London clubs more than Bristol.'

A week later, on 22 July, they tried again at Knowle Stadium, with a league fixture v. Wimbledon. However, the 9,300 spectators saw yet another defeat, with the Bulldogs going down by 44 points to 40. The London outfit owed much of their success to Wilbur Lamoreaux, who went through the card unbeaten to total 12 points. The top-end support for 'Lammy' came from Benny Kaufman (10) and Geoff Pymar (8), while Bristol were spearheaded by Cordy Milne and Vic Duggan, who compiled 10 points apiece. For much of the fixture it looked as though Bristol would win only their third league match of the season but, despite holding a 35-31 advantage after heat eleven, it wasn't to be.

The visitors scorched to 5-1s in heats twelve and thirteen to end the Bulldogs' hopes, with the final race ending all square. Winning times were fast throughout the meeting, with Lamoreaux clocking 67.4 seconds in heat one and Morian Hansen equalling the time in heat eight, while Benny Kaufman was timed at 67.6 seconds in heat six. The result left Bristol firmly rooted to the foot of the First Division standings with just 5 points, four of which had been gained from the first two official matches of the campaign, against Harringay!

It was to the aforementioned London venue that Bristol journeyed on 23 July when, despite a valiant effort, they went down 45-39 in another league match. The Bulldogs took the lead with a 5-1 in heat two, but they were unable to hold on and, though the scores were close throughout, the Tigers always held the upper hand. Jack Parker led their scoring with an unbeaten 12 points while Les Wotton accumulated 11. For the Bulldogs, Cordy Milne headed the way with 11 points, while Vic Duggan continued to impress in scoring 9. After the main match, a six-heat challenge was staged between London and America, with the tourists having little difficulty in running up a 26-10 victory as Cordy Milne grabbed 8 points and his brother notched 7.

It was a case of going into the Lions' den on 28 July, when the under-fire Bulldogs made the trip to Wembley for another league thrashing. There wasn't much to report, save for the one-way traffic supplied by the Wembley men, who were led by Lionel Van Praag's dozen points from four starts, while Frank Charles and Malcolm Craven each carded tallies of 9. For Bristol, only Cordy Milne and Vic Duggan supplied any real resistance, each totalling 8 points. The second half of the programme featured a competition for the *Daily Sketch* International All-Star Scratch Race Trophy. Sixteen of the world's best speedsters were on show, with the races being held over just three laps. There was only one qualifying heat for each rider, with the first two going into the semi-finals, and so on again into the grand final. With its sudden-death nature, there were plenty of shock eliminations, with Cordy Milne, Frank Charles, Benny Kaufman, Les Wotton, Morian Hansen, George Wilks, Eric Langton and Wally Kilmister all going out at the first hurdle. The semi-finals saw Lionel Van Praag, Jimmy Gibb, Arthur Atkinson and Wilbur Lamoreaux take early baths, leaving Bluey Wilkinson to win the final from Bill Kitchen, Jack Milne and George Newton.

On 29 July, the Bulldogs entertained Wembley at Knowle. However, as had fast become the norm, it was a field day for the visitors, who easily won by 50 points to 32. The result left Bristol with the unenviable record of having won just two league matches from a total of fourteen ridden. Cordy Milne was outstanding in defeat, scorching to a full 12 points, while Vic Duggan again impressed with 10. However, the rest of the side were simply dreadful, with just 10 points spread between six riders! For the imposing visitors, Malcolm Craven raced to 10 points, while Lionel Van Praag collected 9. Disappointingly though, the attendance to see the mighty Wembley slipped to 8,500.

On 5 August, Knowle played host to another qualifying round of the World Championship and a much-improved crowd of 10,500 arrived to witness a blood-and-guts event involving sixteen of the very best riders in the sport. The meeting featured an unusual occurrence when Tommy Price mistook a photographer's flash and roared through the tapes. The steward showed a great deal of sympathy for the rider, however, and allowed him to participate in the restart. Bulldogs skipper Cordy Milne produced a tremendous performance, notching 14 points to win the meeting ahead of Bluey Wilkinson and Jack Parker, who tied for second place. Full result: Milne 14; Wilkinson 12; Parker 12; Tommy Croombs 11; George Newton 10; Eric Langton 10; Bill Kitchen 9; Geoff Pymar 8; Vic Duggan 7; Les Wotton 6; Frank Varey 5; Wally Lloyd 5; Jimmy Gibb 5; Morian Hansen 3; Tommy Price 3; Bert Spencer 0. The meeting programme explained that the field of sixteen riders would share prize-money totalling £260, of which each rider received £1 per start, while £4 10s was paid for a race win, £3 for second place and £1 10s for third place. In layman's terms, it meant that anyone scoring maximum points could earn £27, an amount that would be regarded as a small fortune at the time.

The following day, Bristol sent the equivalent of a reserve side on the long haul up to Edinburgh for a nine-heat challenge match at Marine Gardens, in the lovely Portobello area of the city. There was no Cordy Milne, Morian Hansen, Bill Clibbett or Vic Duggan but, even so, a crowd of some 4,000 turned out to see the Bulldogs adapt well to the 440-yard circuit, before running out winners by 28 points to 26. Bill Rogers and Roy Dook led the way with 8 points apiece, while Ernie Price topped the Edinburgh scoring with an identical total. Additional attractions in the second half saw Oliver Hart defeat Harry Shepherd in the Captains' Match Race before Dook took victory in his heat and subsequently the final of the Scottish Gold Helmet.

Back at Knowle on 12 August, an official international match was staged between two composite sides, one including riders from England and Australia, the other comprising speedsters from the USA and Canada. The meeting was packed with thrills, as the USA/Canada combination took victory by a single-point, 54-53, in front of a 13,000 audience. The meeting began in sensational fashion, with Lionel Van Praag and Arthur Atkinson both coming through from the back to pass Jack Milne, giving the England/Australia team a big 5-1. Wilbur Lamoreaux led heat three from the gate, and was eventually joined by a battling Benny Kaufman, who somehow displaced Bluey Wilkinson. The brilliant Aussie gained some revenge for that defeat in heat five, however, when he held off Cordy Milne to win in the fastest time of the night, 67.6 seconds. Lamoreaux posted another win in heat nine and, with Kaufman finishing behind Bill Kitchen, the USA/Canada side drew level at 27-27. Jack Milne and Jimmy Gibb then grabbed a maximum in heat ten, but only after Van Praag had unluckily pulled out with engine problems. Lammy lost his unbeaten record in heat fifteen when he rode onto the grass in order to avoid the fallen Arthur Atkinson. In a grandstand finish, heat seventeen saw Van Praag and Atkinson gain a 4-2 over Cordy Milne, thereby setting up a last-heat decider, with England/Australia leading by a single point at 51-50. In the vital heat, Lamoreaux defeated Kitchen, while the race for the final point went to Kaufman ahead of Ron Johnson, giving victory to the USA/Canada side. Full result: England/Australia 53 (Kitchen 14; Van Praag 13; Wilkinson 12; Atkinson 6; Vic Duggan 6; Les Wotton 1; Johnson 1; Frank Varey 0) USA/Canada 54 (Jack Milne 15; Lamoreaux 15; Cordy Milne 13; Kaufman 7; Gibb 4; George Pepper 0; Goldie Restall 0).

Another week passed before Belle Vue visited Bristol for a National League encounter on 19 August. Surprisingly, the Bulldogs rode with much greater solidity to record only their third league success of a difficult campaign in front of 8,100 diehard supporters. Cordy Milne, Vic Duggan and Bill Clibbett each chipped in with 9 points, as Bristol rode to a super 45-38 success. Although Bill Kitchen won all four of his rides for the Aces, his only support came from Eric Langton with 11 points. However, the Manchester side didn't have to wait long to avenge their defeat, as the following night they thumped the Bulldogs 54-30 at Hyde Road. The Belle Vue heat-leaders were really on song, with both Bill Kitchen and Frank Varey romping to 12-point maximums, while Eric

Langton tallied 11. Between the three of them, they won eleven of the fourteen heats, with colleagues Jack Hargreaves (twice) and Ernie Price taking the flag in the other three heats. In a quick return to their poor form, the best Bristol could do on the night was Cordy Milne's four second-place finishes.

On 26 August, the Bulldogs ended the month on a better note when they managed to scrape a narrow 42-41 victory over Harringay at Knowle Stadium. An attendance of some 9,000 witnessed a titanic struggle from start to finish, as the homesters dug deep to eke out the win. The match went to a last-heat decider with Bristol leading 39-38, only for the race to be stopped after Norman Parker had fallen and been pinned under his machine. The re-run was won at a canter by the excluded rider's brother Jack but, with Bill Rogers and Harry Shepherd unchallenged in the minor scoring positions, they comfortably secured a much-needed victory. Cordy Milne was instrumental in the success, racing to another full 12-point score, while Vic Duggan plundered 11. Jack Parker also carded 11 points for the Tigers, but received scant support from the rest of his side. Ronnie Greene didn't mince words in his programme notes, with his obvious annoyance aimed at Bill Maddern. Picking up his comments, he stated, 'He was an hour late for a match at Belle Vue. Once, he arrived at West Ham after the twelfth heat had been decided, and another time he was late for his first ride at Wembley. You will agree that this is not good enough. Frankly, I cannot understand Bill.' Later in his column, he stated: 'We have given Bill numerous opportunities to mend his ways, and now I feel that in fairness to the team, our only alternative is to suspend him for the time being.'

In the World Championship Final at Wembley on Thursday 1 September, West Ham's Bluey Wilkinson took the coveted title ahead of Jack Milne and Wilbur Lamoreaux in front of 93,000 screaming spectators. Top Bulldog Cordy Milne, who had finished third the previous year, had to be content with a drop to sixth position, but it was still a great achievement amongst a particularly strong field. On the night though, he just couldn't get going properly and only managed two race wins in his 8-point tally. Interestingly, Wilkinson's prize-money for lifting the title was a massive £350, which, at the time, would have more than paid for a large detached house with a garden.

Bristol finally staged their twice rain-affected league meeting v. West Ham on 2 September. Amazingly, they put on a great show to win their third consecutive match at Knowle by 44 points to 39. Frustratingly though, the attendance to witness the World Champion's first meeting since taking the crown was just 9,000, although Bluey Wilkinson certainly didn't disappoint those who were present. He equalled the track record of 66.8 seconds in heat one, before going on to record an immaculate 12-point maximum. Nevertheless, it was Bristol's night with Cordy Milne (11), Vic Duggan (10) and Bill Rogers (9) all playing a major role in the win. Heat six turned into a farce when Bronco Dixon fell at the first turn, with the warning lights subsequently flashing on in order to stop the race. However, when the riders did shut off and start touring around for a re-run, they were instructed to carry on, apart from Bill Clibbett, who was disqualified for boring. The race therefore continued on, with Rogers eventually winning from Tommy Croombs in a remarkably slow time of 105.2 seconds. No one was happy with the steward's handling of the race and West Ham supremo Johnnie Hoskins later lodged a protest with the ACU over the happenings. In the match programme, Ronnie Greene revealed that he had received an approach from one of the London tracks for the fast-rising Aussie Vic Duggan. Not surprisingly, Greene refused to consider the offer, preferring of course, to keep the rider exactly where he was.

Bristol ventured to the Old Kent Road for their second away league match v. New Cross on 7 September. This was indeed a tough proposition, as the Rangers were sitting pretty on top of the National League table. In fact, going into the meeting, just one more win for the homesters would guarantee them the Championship. After a shared opening race, New Cross gained a 5-0 in heat two and from then on there was no looking back, as they cruised to a 48-34 victory over the league's basement club. Leading the way for the new Champions were Jack Milne (11), Ron Johnson (10) and Bill Longley (9), while Cordy Milne with 8 points was Bristol's leading performer. Jack Milne's only dropped point was to teammate Clem Mitchell in heat ten, when the American cleverly shepherded his partner home.

The return fixture against New Cross attracted a crowd of 9,150 on 9 September, when the Bulldogs gained a momentous 52-31 victory over the League Champions. As usual, Cordy Milne was Bristol's star man, roaring to a four-ride maximum, as well as equalling the track record of 66.8 seconds in heat one when putting one over his brother. For once, Bristol had three men in double figures, with Milne receiving great support from Vic Duggan and Bill Rogers, each of whom registered 11 points. On a poor night for the Rangers, Jack Milne (10) and George Newton (8) recorded all but 13 of their side's 31 points. After the main match, both Cordy and Jack Milne made separate attempts on the one-lap (flying start) track record, which stood at 16.2 seconds and was held by the aforementioned Newton. Amazingly, both scorched around in exactly the same time to establish a new record of 15.8 seconds. The programme for the meeting featured a forthright letter from Mr R.A. Pitt, which stated, 'I should like first of all to ask you, what is wrong with the support of speedway racing in Bristol? I say quite plainly that West Country people as a whole are the most unsporty set in England. You in Bristol, as well as in Bath and the surrounding districts are guilty of the accusation, which is not directed against the supporters' club of the Bristol Speedway. There are many here who will deny this statement, but let me first give you an instance. At the end of last season, Ronnie asked you if Bristol went into the First Division, would you give him the support that you do now, even though it may mean that the Bulldogs may be like Wimbledon, who won only two matches? Up went your hands and loud were your cheers for Bristol to go among the "Big Seven", but you haven't kept your word. I happen to know that this 1938 season is costing the Bristol management more than twice as much to give you the best possible racing, and yet you are not appreciating it. Football is near at hand and you go to see your pet team win. If they get a series of losing matches, you stay away and say to yourself, "Oh, I'm not following a side that can't win at home," and this applies to the Bristol team. Just when Cordy and his side need your B-R-I-S-T-O-L war cry, you let him down. There's not another track in England where racing is finer than that seen at this stadium and it's very rare that a "procession" is seen in races. You are saying to yourself that this article is just newspaper talk, but I will let you into a secret. Speedway reporting is not my job and neither do I get paid for doing it. It is because I am fond of thrills that I come here every Friday. Now supporters, especially back-sliders, please give the Bristol management a square deal, and if the Bristol speedway-loving public, by increased support can prove the above statement is wrong, I shall be the first to congratulate them.'

The Bulldogs' had to wait a week for their next track action, when several of the side participated in the prestigious West of England Championship at Knowle on 16 September. In front of a 10,400 gate, the meeting featured a massive field of twenty-one riders, with each taking four rides and the top four scorers going into a grand final. After twenty action-packed heats, both Milnes, along with Benny Kaufman and Lionel Van Praag were the big four to make it through. Jack Milne duly took the final from his sibling, while Kaufman grabbed third spot ahead of Van Praag. It was something of a surprise that World Champion Bluey Wilkinson failed to qualify for the final despite winning his first two rides. However, Van Praag beat him in heat fifteen and he then ran an uncharacteristic last in heat eighteen behind Cordy Milne, George Newton and Wilbur Lamoreaux. Full result: (Qualifying scores) J. Milne 12; C. Milne 11; Kaufman 10; Van Praag 8; Arthur Atkinson 8; Wilkinson 8; Lamoreaux 8; Eric Collins 7; Vic Duggan 7; Newton 7; Geoff Pymar 5; Tommy Price 5; Bill Maddern 4; Harry Shepherd 4; Bill Clibbett 4; Wally Lloyd 3.5; Morian Hansen 3; Reg Lambourne 2.5; Jack Parker 2; Roy Dook 1; Alec Statham 0. Final: 1st J. Milne; 2nd C. Milne; 3rd Kaufman; 4th Van Praag. The half-point occurred when Lloyd and Lambourne dead-heated for third place in heat twenty.

Custom House Stadium beckoned on 20 September, as the Bulldogs returned to league action against West Ham and the homesters took the opportunity of jumping into second place in the league standings, comfortably winning 54-30. Cordy Milne made a mess of the start in heat one and ran a bad last behind Bluey Wilkinson, Jimmy Gibb and Harry Shepherd. After that, however, he recovered his composure to win his other three rides to once again top the Bristol scoring. For the happy Hammers, Wilkinson went through the card in fine style, while Charlie Spinks' efforts yielded 10 points. After the match, Wilkinson defeated Jack Milne 2-0 in the £25 Match Race Challenge. Unique to the London raceway was a fascination with average speeds, with Wilkinson being the fastest rider of the night when clocked at 45.86mph in the second match race against Milne.

On 23 September West Ham made the journey in the opposite direction for Bristol's final home league fixture of what had been a very difficult season. A crowd of 10,400 turned up to witness a match that was close throughout but that finally saw the Bulldogs go down by 44.5 points to 39.5. West Ham had three stars in Tommy Croombs (11), Bluey Wilkinson (10) and Arthur Atkinson (9), while Bristol's leading lights were Cordy Milne (11) and Morian Hansen (8). The match started in breathtaking fashion, with Cordy Milne and Harry Shepherd combining to keep Wilkinson at bay with four laps of perfect team-riding. Ironically,

Milne's only defeat came at the hands of Wilkinson in the final heat, when the World Champion stormed home in 67.4 seconds – the fastest time of the meeting. Heat two was also worthy of a mention, as Vic Duggan collided with Charlie Spinks and both men came down. The closely following Croombs was unable to avoid the melee and also fell, while Hansen shot through a gap, only to over-slide and tumble as well. With no one left running, the steward had no alternative but to stop the race and order a re-run, which was duly won by Croombs. After the meeting, American Putt Mossman rode from the top of the grandstand down a long plank spanning the enclosure and track, before zooming through a wall of blazing timber on the infield. This was obviously a taster of things to come on 7 October, when Mossman was scheduled to present his American Rodeo and Circus.

The Bulldogs were back at Ronnie Greene's other track, Wimbledon, for a league encounter on 26 September, when a fighting display saw them eventually go down by 47 points to 35. The match formed the second part of a double-header, which had earlier seen the Dons defeat Harringay 48-35. Despite being run on a very heavy circuit following torrential rainfall, Wilbur Lamoreaux had an outstanding night, recording full maximums in both matches. Wally Lloyd provided great support for Lammy in the match v. Bristol, scoring 10 points, while Cordy Milne, as usual, headed the Bulldogs' scoring with a tally of 11. Due to the poor conditions, winning times became very slow towards the end of the second fixture, emphasised when Geoff Pymar clocked 79.0 seconds in heat twelve – some 10 seconds outside the track record.

Billed as 'Crazy Night', Knowle staged a composite meeting on 30 September featuring the Supporters' Club Trophy, as well as midget car racing, a donkey derby and various other fun events. On a rain-soaked circuit, Cordy Milne, riding from scratch, won the main event, beating Bill Clibbett, Morian Hansen and Bill Maddern in the final. With so many things to cram in on the night, there were only two qualifying heats before the grand final, but there was no more deserving winner than the American, bearing in mind his tremendous efforts throughout the entire season. On a busy evening, the junior title was won by Fred Lewis, who defeated Reg Lambourne, Reg Gore and Harry Shepherd in the final. Later on, a team from London beat their Coventry counterparts 14-10 over four heats of midget car racing, before Harry Shepherd, on Hyperion, and Morian Hansen, on Bung Ho, dead-heated in the donkey derby final. In the race-day programme, news via the supporters' club expressed disappointment that membership had fallen from the level they had enjoyed the previous season, despite the fact that Ronnie Greene had brought First Division racing to the track. Mr Greene's closing notes on the season were rather low key, save to thank all the riders and the fans who had stuck by the team. He did, however, especially thank all the members of staff who had done so much work behind the scenes during the year.

On 6 October, Bristol completed their campaign with a third trip to Wembley, but they regrettably went out on the end of a 54-28 thrashing. As with the meeting at Wimbledon the previous week, the Bulldogs found themselves as the second part of a double-header. Ironically the Dons featured in the first match but, despite Wilbur Lamoreaux's maximum, they went down to a 45-39 defeat. In the fixture against Bristol, the Lions were spearheaded by Lionel Van Praag, who won all four of his starts, while young whizz-kid Malcolm Craven accrued 11 points. Inevitably, Craven's only defeat was suffered when he came up against the ever-reliable Cordy Milne, who closed the season with another 10-point haul for the Bulldogs. The result meant that Bristol had achieved only six wins and a solitary draw over the league programme, as they finished 8 points adrift of Harringay at the foot of the table.

Although not billed as a speedway meeting, Putt Mossman's American Rodeo and Circus Night at Knowle on 7 October was afforded the usual Bristol Speedway programme, albeit containing less pages than usual. The meeting featured one-lap time trials, won by Frank Robinson in 16.5 seconds, midget car racing, match races, various stunts, egg juggling and balloon shooting. There was also the 50 Guineas Solid Gold Cup, run over four laps from a rolling start, which was won by Mossman himself in 69.0 seconds flat.

Looking at the statistics for the year, the Bulldogs completed forty fixtures (twenty-four National League, two National Trophy, six ACU Cup and eight challenge). Cordy Milne was easily the club's leading rider, scoring a quite remarkable 404.5 points from thirty-nine appearances for a match average of 10.37. Vic Duggan improved as the season wore on and did extremely well to accumulate 235 points from thirty-eight matches, while Morian Hansen finished third in the scoring stakes with 211 points from one meeting less, although it would probably be fair to say this was a lower than expected return from the Dane. Despite the general disappointment over crowd figures, a total of over 250,000 people actually went through the turnstiles at Knowle Stadium during the year, which averaged out at around the 10,500 mark.

There was a big scare in Bristol towards the end of November when news broke that Cordy Milne had been killed while riding in his homeland. This led to the local press enduring a busy time while they dealt with the hundreds of telephone calls from worried Bulldogs fans. Where the story emanated from nobody knew, but there was no truth in it whatsoever, since Milne was alive and well in Australia.

1938 STATISTICS

(Bristol's score shown first unless otherwise stated)

NATIONAL LEAGUE DIVISION ONE

Opponents	Home	Away
Belle Vue	L40-41	L35-49
	W45-38	L30-54
Harringay	W47-36	W42-41
	W42-41	L39-45
New Cross	L38-46	L33-51
	W52-31	L34-48
Wembley	L37-47	L27-57
	L32-50	L28-54
West Ham	W44-39	L29-55
	L39.5-44.5	L30-54
Wimbledon	D41-41	L31-53
	L40-44	L35-47

MATCH AVERAGES

Rider	Matches	Points	Average
Cordy Milne	24	224	9.33
Vic Duggan	24	152.5	6.35
Morian Hansen	22	119	5.41
Bill Clibbett	22	117	5.32
Bill Rogers	20	103	5.15
Harry Shepherd	24	77	3.21

Bill Maddern	19	46	2.42
Roy Dook	16	33	2.06
Reg Lambourne	14	17	1.21
Rol Stobart	3	2	0.67
Reg Gore	1	0	0.00

NOTE: Match averages do not include reserve appearances when a rider took no rides.

NATIONAL LEAGUE DIVISION ONE TABLE

Team	Matches	Won	Drawn	Lost	For	Against	Pts
New Cross	24	15	1	8	1,072	925	31
West Ham	24	13	1	10	1,050.5	939.5	27
Wembley	24	13	1	10	1,043	953	27
Wimbledon	24	12	3	9	1,005	996	27
Belle Vue	24	11	0	13	949	1,052	22
Harringay	24	10	1	13	980	1,018	21
Bristol	24	6	1	17	890.5	1,106.5	13

DAILY MAIL NATIONAL TROPHY

Opponents	Home	Away	Aggregate
West Ham	L50-56	L35-72	L85-128

MATCH AVERAGES

Rider	Matches	Points	Average
Cordy Milne	2	28	14.00
Vic Duggan	2	16	8.00
Harry Shepherd	2	10	5.00
Roy Dook	2	9	4.50
Bill Rogers	2	8	4.00
Morian Hansen	2	6	3.00
Bill Maddern	2	5	2.50
Bill Clibbett	1	2	2.00
Reg Lambourne	1	1	1.00

ACU CUP (GROUP ONE)

Opponents	Home	Away
Belle Vue	W74-34	L30-78
Wembley	L44-64	L47-61
Wimbledon	L53-55	L35-73

MATCH AVERAGES

Rider	Matches	Points	Average
Cordy Milne	6	77.5	12.92
Bill Rogers	6	44	7.33
Morian Hansen	6	38	6.33
Bill Clibbett	6	37.5	6.25
Vic Duggan	6	35	5.83
Bill Maddern	6	18	3.00
Harry Shepherd	6	17	2.83
Roy Dook	6	16	2.67

ACU (GROUP ONE) TABLE

Team	Matches	Won	Drawn	Lost	For	Against	Pts
Wimbledon	6	4	1	1	355	292	11
Wembley	6	3	1	2	335	310	8
Belle Vue	6	3	0	3	320	326	6
Bristol	6	1	0	5	283	365	2

NOTE: 3 points were awarded for an away win and 2 points for an away draw.

CHALLENGE

Opponents	Home	Away
Edinburgh	–	W28-26
New Cross	L43-62	–
North America	W43-41	–
Southampton	–	(1) W27-26
Southampton	W64-20	(2) L41-43
Wimbledon/West Ham	–	D48-48
Wimbledon	W42-41	–

MATCH AVERAGES

Rider	Matches	Points	Average
Cordy Milne	7	75	10.71
Morian Hansen	7	48	6.86
Bill Rogers	5	33	6.60
Bill Clibbett	7	37.5	5.36
Vic Duggan	6	31.5	5.25
Harry Shepherd	6	30	5.00
Bill Maddern	4	18	4.50
Roy Dook	5	18	3.60
Ray Duggan	3	8	2.67
Rol Stobart	2	5	2.50
Fred Lewis	2	2	1.00
Ron Howes	1	0	0.00

1939

After their disastrous season in the top flight, it came as no surprise when it was announced in March 1939 that Bristol were to compete in the National League Second Division. Former Wimbledon rider Ron Howes was to team up with old favourites Harry Shepherd, Roy Dook, Reg Lambourne and Reg Gore, while early rumours about the signing of former Bulldog Ernie Evans or West Ham's Bronco Dixon proved premature. Another possible signing, Les Bowden, formerly with Wembley and Birmingham, also failed to materialise, the rider deciding to retire owing to business commitments and his health. Australian Jack Bibby, however, was signed, and the ex-Lea Bridge, Hackney and Plymouth rider was to prove a more than useful addition to the Bristol ranks. Former Birmingham speedsters Bob Lovell and Jeff Lloyd were also brought in to bolster the side following the closure of the Hall Green circuit. Understandably, Shepherd was reappointed club captain; a move that was universally popular with riders and supporters alike. At the start of April, alterations were made to the Bristol track, with a gang of workmen completely relaying the racing strip. Thousands of tons of earth were also put down on the popular side of the stadium in order to create banking and give the fans a better view of the action. Meanwhile, the race night was changed from Friday to Tuesday, giving the Bristol management more time to prepare the riders' machines for away matches.

The first track action for the Bristol boys took place at Wimbledon on 7 April, when a four-man team took part in a two-heat mini-match *v.* the Dons' reserves. This was staged after the main Wimbledon side had beaten a New Cross/Norwich combination 54-30 in a challenge fixture. The mini-match resulted in a 7-5 victory for the home side, with Harry Shepherd (3), Ron Howes (2), Jeff Lloyd (0) and Eric French (0) being the Bulldogs representatives who took just one ride apiece. Interestingly, former Bristol rider Fred Leavis represented the Wimbledon outfit, winning his only ride.

In mid-April, young Australian Bill Melluish arrived in Britain hoping to make his name. He soon found himself in the thick of the action, making his debut for the Bulldogs in their first full-team match at Crystal Palace on 22 April. This was Bristol's first ever visit to the superbly appointed Sydenham venue and its 449-yard circuit. It was also the first official fixture to be staged at the venue since Crystal Palace had participated in the National League of 1933, although occasional open-licence meetings had been held in the intervening years. As it was, the Bulldogs got their season off to a flying start, winning the English Speedway Trophy fixture by 46 points to 33. This was after the home duo of Keith Harvey and Leslie Trim had claimed a 4-2 over Harry Shepherd in heat one. Following a shared heat two, when Roy Dook beat Ernie Pawson and Harold Saunders, Bristol took command of the match with a series of race advantages. The first of these was gained in heat three, when Crystal Palace were dealt a double blow. Firstly, Mick Mitchell was excluded for breaking the tapes and then George Liddle crashed, leaving Bob Lovell and Reg Lambourne to collect a gift 5-0 success. Steadily, the Bulldogs accumulated the points thereafter to lead 43-28 after twelve races. Then, in heat thirteen, home representative Alf Markham was disqualified for jumping the start. That left Jack Bibby to head Mitchell, while Bill Melluish pulled up with motor problems. Unluckily, Bibby then suffered with mechanical gremlins, handing Mitchell the lead but, on lap three, the Crystal Palace man shed a chain, allowing the Aussie to coast home first in 92.6 seconds – some 11 seconds outside Tiger Stevenson's track record. The farcical heat thirteen therefore resulted in a 3-0 advantage for Bristol and, although Crystal Palace gained a last-heat 5-0 after Melluish had fallen and Lambourne had suffered engine failure, it made little difference to the final result. Bibby completed a 12-point maximum for the victorious Bulldogs, being well supported by Shepherd (11), Dook (8) and Lovell (8), while the leading light in the home camp was Harvey (11).

The season at Knowle began on 25 April, when Crystal Palace travelled to the West Country for the return English Speedway Trophy match. The Bulldogs simply carried on from their wonderful performance three days earlier, surging to a 51-32 victory before an opening-night crowd of some 7,000. Skipper Harry Shepherd was the star of the show, winning all four of his outings, although he had to work hard in heat ten to complete his maximum, coming through to pass Ernie Pawson on the third lap. Bristol riders won ten of the fourteen heats, with Roy Dook (10) and Bob Lovell (10) looking particularly impressive. Young Australian Norman Lindsay came down in heat two but later recovered to post his first race win in British racing when defeating teammate Dook and Crystal Palace's Alf Markham in heat eleven. For the out-of-sorts visitors, Keith Harvey finished with a creditable 9 points and the South African went on to prove his tally was no fluke by winning the Golden Helmet event from Lovell, Dook and Shepherd. Meanwhile, a special three-lap match race saw 1938 Bulldog Morian Hansen defeat Shepherd in 52.4 seconds, with the Dane's winning time recorded as the track record for the distance.

The programme for the opening meeting at Knowle showed a marked change, for Bristol had adopted the larger format preferred by Wimbledon, with a cover price of 3d. In it, the race-day magazine stated that Messrs Greene and Mockford, together with new general manager Dicky Maybrook, had been superintending the track improvements at the stadium and hoped that all the hard work would produce faster winning times and more hectic racing. Under the heading of 'Ronnie Greene Calling', the Bristol promoter commented, 'Last year should have been a great one for us, it failed to be because apparently many hundreds of supporters did not survive the acid test of seeing their favourites beaten frequently, despite their promises that they would back up my efforts to give them First Division racing. No man, or company, can run a speed-way just for the love of it; that would require a limitless banking account. None was more disappointed than I at the meagre support of last year;

however, that is a thing of the past as, with the opening of another season, hope begins anew. How near to losing your favourite pastime, is known only to a few of those behind the scenes. We were obliged to resign from the First Division for very important reasons. First of all, I knew I should be losing certain riders. Bill Rogers, for instance, has finished for good. The retirement of Bill Clibbett was another setback for, to have a reasonable chance, our team needed strengthening, not depleting. To add to our troubles, good riders cannot be bought for love or money; and the First Division is no training ground for new talent. Raising a team for the Second Division has been a big problem, the demand for riders having been made much more intense by the opening of new tracks, and particularly by the decision of Bluey Wilkinson to promote at Sheffield. This factor caused Ernie Evans to change his mind and go north to his old club, rather than come to Bristol. In a similar manner Bronco Dixon will oppose us, instead of riding for us. Despite all this, I have managed to get together an enthusiastic set of riders who I feel sure will re-establish Bristol on the speedway map, once they have settled down and become used to each other.'

On 28 April, the Bulldogs ventured up to Cleveland Park, Middlesbrough for their first league match of the campaign, only to end up on the wrong end of a 64-20 roasting. Every member of the Bristol side struggled, emphasised by the fact that Roy Dook top-scored with just 5 points. For the Bears, both Will Lowther and Bob Wells netted 12-point maximums, while George Greenwood totalled 9 after being excluded from his first ride for a tapes offence. On what was a field night for the homesters, Wilf Plant also plundered 9 points.

Back home at Knowle on 2 May it was a chance to regroup after the thrashing at Middlesbrough, but it all went horribly wrong as Hackney ran riot, winning an English Speedway Trophy meeting by an astonishing 59 points to 22. To lose by a margin of 37 points represented Bristol's worst-ever defeat at Knowle – worse even than the 72-36 defeat at the hands of West Ham on 16 July 1937. The triumphant Wolves merited their victory though, winning twelve of the fourteen heats and collecting seven maximum advantages along the way. The visitors took the lead in the opening race, and it wasn't until heat seven that a Bristol man won a race, courtesy of team captain Harry Shepherd. For the woeful Bulldogs, Melbourne-born Norman Lindsay provided their only other race winner when taking heat eleven ahead of Archie Windmill. Even when Ken Brett was excluded for exceeding the time allowance, the Bristol riders contrived to mess things up when Lindsay and newcomer George Craig collided with each other, allowing Stan Dell to post an unchallenged 3-0 success in a very slow 78.0 seconds. As could have been expected, the scoring in the home camp was poor, with Shepherd topping the chart on just 6 points. For Hackney, Frank Hodgson won all four of his rides, while Jim Baylais (11) and Doug Wells (10) added solid support. The second half saw Hodgson defeat Baylais, Wells and Windmill in the Golden Helmet event, when he clocked the fastest time of the meeting, 67.8 seconds.

It was with great trepidation then, that the Bristol boys made the trip to the Wolves' den for the corresponding fixture on 6 May. Not surprisingly, they went down 56-25, albeit with a slightly better performance than they had shown at Knowle. Hackney skipper Frank Hodgson set the ball rolling in heat one, storming home in 72.1 seconds to establish a new track record for the 340-yard circuit. Thereafter, the meeting was littered with falls, mainly from the beleaguered Bulldogs, as Hackney steadily built up their score and ran out easy winners. Hodgson netted 10 points but would have had a full dozen had he not lost count of the laps in heat four. The home captain actually slowed down at the end of lap three, letting both Tiger Hart and Norman Lindsay past, before realising his error. Stan Dell also recorded 10 points for the happy Hackney boys, while Jeff Lloyd notched a creditable 8 for Bristol.

Returning to Knowle on 9 May, the Bulldogs so wanted to put their miseries behind them, but it wasn't to be as Norwich collected a 43.5-40.5 victory in another English Speedway Trophy encounter. This, however, was generally a much better performance from Bristol, in particular Birmingham-born Jeff Lloyd, who sparkled brightest for the second successive match with 8 points. Next in line on the chart were Norman Lindsay (7), Harry Shepherd (6) and Jack Bibby (6). Two former Bulldogs, meanwhile, led the Stars' scoring, with Wal Morton's efforts yielding 11 points, while Bert Spencer grabbed 9. Heat seven provided a dead-heat for second place, when Reg Lambourne and Dick Wise couldn't be separated at the finish. The Bulldogs' chances of claiming a win disappeared in heat thirteen when Lloyd fell while sat in a 5-1 position behind partner Ron Howes. His fall allowed Wise and Paul Goodchild to share the race, and a last-heat split of the points gave the Stars their victory, Alan Smith taking the flag ahead of Bibby and Lambourne.

128

1. New Zealander Stewie St George thrilled the crowd with a demonstration of his broadsiding skills prior to the first meeting at Knowle Stadium on 25 August 1928.

2. Bath's Len Parker was the undisputed master of Knowle in the initial period of activity, winning an amazing sixty-one titles between 1928 and 1930.

3. *Above left:* Ted Bravery was a regular performer at Knowle in 1929 and 1930, before being identified with a number of teams prior to the outbreak of the Second World War, including Wimbledon, Stamford Bridge, Plymouth, West Ham, Cardiff, Nottingham, Hackney Wick, Sheffield and Stoke.

4. *Above right:* Famous Irish female rider Fay Taylour appeared at the Knowle raceway on 13 August 1929. She was also known for driving cars and midget racing in an illustrious career.

5. *Left:* Legendary promoter Ronnie Greene, who managed the Bulldogs' affairs during their first spell of league action from 1936 to 1939.

6. *Opposite above:* Bristol Bulldogs 1936. From left to right, back row: Bill Rogers, Ronnie Greene (speedway manager), Roy Dook (on bike), Mike Erskine, Bert Spencer. Front row: Fred Leavis, Ron Howes, Eric Collins, Ernie Evans, Henry Collins, Harry Shepherd.

7. *Above left:* Roy Dook was Bristol's skipper in their very first league fixture at Nottingham on 28 April 1936. The London-born rider went on to make sixty-one league appearances for the club before the Second World War.

8. *Above right:* Australian Eric Collins made his debut for Bristol in the away match at Nottingham on 28 April 1936. He proved a tower of strength that season, heading the side's league scoring with 126 points from fifteen matches.

9. *Above left:* Londoner Harry Shepherd represented the Bulldogs in seventy-three league matches from 1936 to 1939, scoring a total of 439 points in the process.

10 *Above right:* Another Aussie to represent Bristol was the spectacular Bill Rogers, who made fifty-five league appearances between 1936 and 1938.

11. The Bristol and Belle Vue teams line up under a blaze of light at Knowle Stadium prior to a challenge match on 22 September 1936.

12. Bill Maddern hailed from Adelaide, South Australia and made his debut for the Bulldogs on 9 April 1937 in a challenge match against West Ham Reserves at Knowle Stadium. He was actually christened Thornton Alexander Maddern and, in two years with Bristol, his thirty-eight league appearances yielded 131 points.

13. *Above left:* American Cordy Milne, who captained the Bulldogs upon their elevation to the First Division in 1938. The brilliant white-line rider also topped the side's scoring with 224 points from twenty-four league matches.

14. *Above right:* The original 'Great Dane' Morian Hansen made his debut for the Bulldogs in a challenge match against New Cross at Knowle Stadium on 15 April 1938. He went on to net 119 points from twenty-two league appearances in what was his only year with the club.

15. *Left:* Brilliant Australian rider Vic Duggan also first appeared for the Bulldogs on 15 April 1938 at Knowle in the challenge fixture against New Cross. He went on to ride for Wimbledon in 1939, before representing Harringay with distinction from 1947 to 1950.

16. Locally born Bill Clibbett entertained the Bristol supporters in 1938 and 1939 with his superb leg-trailing style. Long before representing his home-town team, he had actually ridden in the first meeting at Knowle Stadium on 25 August 1928.

17. Jeff Lloyd joined the Bulldogs in 1939 and again represented the side during their open-licence season in 1946. Aside from racing for Bristol, he also appeared for several other teams, including his home-town club Birmingham, as well as Wembley Reserves, Newcastle, New Cross and Harringay.

18. *Opposite above left:* Swindon-born Roger Wise made his debut for the Bulldogs in a challenge fixture against Birmingham at Knowle on 2 August 1946. He was very popular with the supporters and went on to make 155 league appearances for the club.

19. *Opposite above right:* Mike Beddoe also first appeared for Bristol in the challenge match against Birmingham on 2 August 1946. He bravely overcame a serious foot injury sustained at Fleetwood on 11 May 1948 to total 126 league appearances for the club.

20. *Opposite below:* The Bulldogs pose for the camera prior to a challenge match against Sheffield at Knowle Stadium on 23 August 1946. From left to right, back row: Reg Witcomb (co-promoter), Ron Howes, Jeff Lloyd, Frank Lawrence, Bob Steel (co-promoter), Roger Wise, Roy Dook. Front row, kneeling: Jack Mountford, Percy Brine, Billy Hole, Reg Lambourne, Mike Beddoe.

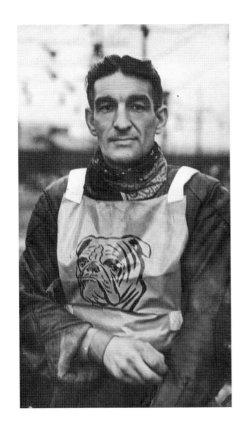

21. Billy Hole hailed from Bath and, after making his debut for the Bulldogs in the match against Sheffield on 23 August 1946, he went on to establish the club record for both appearances and points. In the league alone he appeared in 220 matches, scoring 1,609 points, whereas overall his record rose to 391 appearances and 2,937 points.

22. *Right:* Jack Mountford came from Salisbury and first sported a Bristol race jacket in a challenge match against The Rest at Knowle Stadium on 30 August 1946. He was to remain with the Bulldogs until the end of 1952, making a total of 201 league appearances.

23. *Below:* Tiger Stevenson ran a highly successful training school at Knowle during the winter of 1946/47. Pictured are a group of youngsters listening intently to the former West Ham and England rider during one of his sessions.

24. *Left:* Eric Salmon made his debut for the Bulldogs in a league encounter at Middlesbrough on 10 April 1947. The Bath-born rider went on to make 204 league appearances for the club, before injury curtailed his career in 1953.

25. *Below:* Lanky Fred Tuck linked with the Bulldogs in 1947, making his club debut in a league fixture at Newcastle on 7 July that year. The Londoner was to make a total of ninety-one league appearances in the club's colours prior to his retirement in 1950.

26. Comedy double act Laurel and Hardy visited Knowle for a British Speedway Cup encounter against Wigan on 18 July 1947. They are pictured with their wives on the centre green during the interval.

27. Bristol Bulldogs 1948. From left to right, back row: Cyril Quick, Jack Mountford, Roger Wise, Eric Salmon, Bill Hamblin (team manager), Johnny Hole, Reg Witcomb (promoter). Front row: Nobby Stock, Billy Hole (on bike), Fred Tuck.

28. *Opposite above:* Johnny Hole followed in the footsteps of his older brother Billy, making his debut for the Bulldogs in a challenge match against Southampton & Hastings at Knowle on 19 March 1948. He went on to make 203 league appearances for the club, recording 795 points along the way.

29. *Opposite below:* A superb action shot from the National League Second Division fixture between Bristol and Ashfield at Knowle Stadium on 13 May 1949. Rol Stobart narrowly leads from Eric Salmon and Ken Le Breton, while Roger Wise attempts to dive through from fourth place.

30. A typical race-day scene from a packed Knowle Stadium as the riders blast from the start.

It was an unlucky 13 May for the battle-scarred Bulldogs, as they crashed to a hefty 60-24 loss in the return English Speedway Trophy encounter with Norwich at The Firs Stadium. The homesters revelled on their sweeping 425-yard racing strip and the Bristol boys were well and truly blitzed. On only two occasions did a visitor win a race, Roy Dook in heat six and Jack Bibby in heat fourteen. Wal Morton scorched to a classy 12-point maximum for the rampant Stars, while Bert Spencer (11), Wilf Jay (9) and Dick Wise (9) all weighed in heavily. The best visitor on the night was Dook, who also registered 9 points.

Tuesday 16 May was one for the record books at Knowle Stadium, as the Bulldogs took out all their frustrations on a hapless Crystal Palace side in the National Trophy. The men in orange and black literally ran riot, winning by a staggering 83 points to 22. A Bristol rider crossed the line first in each and every heat, while maximums were recorded in no fewer than fourteen races. The Bulldogs were bolstered by the inclusion of Bill Clibbett, who obviously found it difficult to watch from the sidelines and made a quick return to the saddle following his pre-season retirement. He was clearly happy to be back too, and celebrated by scorching to a 15-point maximum. He wasn't the highest scorer though, that honour instead going to Jeff Lloyd (16), while Harry Shepherd (14), Roy Dook (10), Jack Bibby (10) and Ron Howes (10) all made significant contributions. For Crystal Palace, Mick Mitchell (4), George Gower (4) and Charlie Challis (4) were the most productive team members on an evening of total embarrassment for the London outfit. To add insult to injury, the visitors' black night was compounded in heat nine, when Mitchell and teammate Ernie Pawson collided, with the latter subsequently taken to hospital having fractured a leg.

One week later on 23 May, Hackney returned to Knowle for a Second Division fixture and Bristol produced a very different performance from the one displayed when the Wolves had visited three weeks beforehand. Still riding on the crest of a wave after thumping Crystal Palace, the Bulldogs rode brilliantly to secure a 48-35 victory. Bill Clibbett had no trouble in winning all four of his rides and was ably supported by Aussie Jack Bibby's 9 points. As had been the case on their last visit, Hackney were best served by Frank Hodgson and Jim Baylais, both of whom plundered 11 points. An interesting programme article, run all season long, was specifically aimed at car and motorcycle owners. It stated that each driver/rider displaying a Bristol Speedway pennant would be presented with a free programme. With pennants available at 6d and 9d, this represented a very good incentive for those with their own transport.

It was with great expectation that the Bulldogs made the trip to Crystal Palace on Saturday 27 May for an afternoon start in the second leg of the National Trophy tie. Their high spirits were not misplaced, since they cantered to a comfortable 65-35 victory over a side that had fast become 'whipping boys'. Apart from Bristol running up a series of 5-1s, the meeting was decidedly uneventful save for heat six, when Bill Clibbett's clutch dragged him into the tapes and caused him to stall. The starting tapes were subsequently released and the three remaining riders toured round for a lap, expecting the race to be restarted. However, they eventually realised that they were meant to be racing and put in another four faster laps. When it emerged that five laps had been completed, the steward declared the race void with a 0-0 score, before promptly moving straight on to heat seven! The main point scorers of the match were: (Crystal Palace) Keith Harvey 9; (Bristol) Roy Dook 12; Bill Melluish 12; Harry Shepherd 11; Jack Bibby 10. Young Melluish's performance was remarkable, as he showed a real turn of speed, romping to victory in each of his first three rides.

Following the afternoon match at Sydenham, the Bulldogs travelled across London for an 8.15 p.m. start at Hackney in a Second Division encounter. The strain of participating in two meetings on the same day obviously showed, as Bristol went down to a 53-29 defeat at the Waterden Road circuit. Things started badly for the jaded visitors, with several falls, including a spectacular spill for Bill Clibbett in heat six. The Wolves gained what was their fourth maximum in heat seven, increasing their lead to 31-10, and a thrashing looked on the cards. Thankfully, the Bulldogs dug deep and fared much better in the second half of the match and it is a matter of conjecture as to what might have happened had they not ridden two matches on the day. Jim Baylais recorded a faultless maximum for the homesters, while Tiger Hart (11), Frank Hodgson (10) and Stan Dell (9) supplied more than adequate backing. The best Bristol could manage was 5 points apiece from Harry Shepherd and Clibbett. After the match, former Bulldog Vic Duggan defeated home star Hodgson in a match race, clocking a winning time of 76.35 seconds.

Bristol entertained Newcastle in a league fixture on 30 May, with the Geordie side paying a first-ever visit to Knowle. A mediocre crowd witnessed the Bulldogs suffer defeat by 44 points to 39, as

George Pepper inspired the visitors with an outstanding four-ride full-house, while former Bristol favourite Rol Stobart weighed in with 11 points. The home team's problem on the night stemmed from a lack of top-end firepower, as they only supplied five race winners, compared with Newcastle's total of nine. In spite of their difficulties, they plugged away throughout and trailed by just a single point, 39-38, going into the last heat. Unfortunately luck wasn't on their side, however, as Roy Dook took a tumble and Ron Howes was unable to prevent Kid Curtis and Maurice Stobart from gaining a 5-1. Bill Clibbett headed the Bulldogs' scorecard on 9 points, with Harry Shepherd being the next best contributor on 7. In light of the loss, it was ironic that Ronnie Greene's programme column should state, 'Building a team capable of winning matches has proved a bigger task than I ever dreamt of when making up my mind to give Bristol Second Division racing, after it became apparent that I no longer had a side of the required strength for the First Division. I don't mind admitting that during the early weeks of this season, I often became fed up with the whole thing.'

On 6 June, a World Championship qualifying round was held at Knowle, featuring plenty of thrills and spills. A major disappointment for the home fans occurred when Bill Clibbett injured his left leg when trying to avoid the fallen George Craig. That was the first of five falls that Craig suffered during the course of the evening, the worst of which occurred in heat seventeen, when he and Ray Duggan were in collision. Duggan was pinned to the track, but thankfully survived relatively unscathed following treatment in the ambulance room. Harringay's Dick Harris eventually won the meeting with 14 points, while Bristol's Jeff Lloyd occupied second position on 11. Full result: Harris 14; Lloyd 11; Harry Shepherd 10; Nobby Key 10; Crusty Pye 10; Roy Dook 8; Norman Lindsay 8; Reg Lambourne 8; Duggan 8; Frank Dolan 8; Ron Howes 7; Jack Bibby 2; Crocky Rawding 2; Reg Gore 1; Clibbett 0; Craig 0.

It was revealed in the speedway press that Bristol had made an application to the Control Board to have their race night changed back to Friday. This was seen as being a popular move in an effort to get more people through the turnstiles, as Tuesday evenings had proved an abject failure.

In the meantime, Bristol's next meeting took them to The Firs for a league match against Norwich on 10 June. Following a brace of shared heats, the Stars took the lead with a 5-1 in heat three and managed to remain in front for the duration, finally winning by 47 points to 37. Norwich skipper Bert Spencer rode to an untroubled maximum, while teammate Wilf Jay notched 10 points. For the Bulldogs, Roy Dook gave an excellent showing to register 11 points, while skipper Harry Shepherd tallied 8. Dook's only defeat came at the hands of Spencer in heat ten, while his win from the back against Jay in heat six was particularly noteworthy.

Middlesbrough were the next team to visit Bristol, arriving for a league encounter on 13 June. Ronnie Greene was none too happy in his programme notes, commenting, 'Does speedway promoting in the provinces get a man down? I say it does, and apparently I am not the only victim. Middlesbrough, our visitors tonight, have been putting up performances as good as any recorded in the Second Division, yet two weeks ago, small attendances were responsible for a special meeting of the directors, who had to make up their minds whether it was worthwhile continuing.' He went on to state, 'The position here is very similar, and equally disappointing. I have given the public the best racing possible in the circumstances, and I don't think any of you can grumble or complain that racing during the last few weeks has been lacking in thrills. But apart from the 5,000 odd "die-hards", no one seems interested in one of the most fascinating of modern sports.'

The meeting v. Middlesbrough was to result in a win for the Bulldogs, albeit by the narrowest of margins, 43-41, following a night of close and exciting racing. The victory looked highly unlikely for almost all of the contest, as the visitors had taken the lead in heat two and still led 40-38 after heat thirteen. However, the last race saw Jeff Lloyd and Jack Bibby grab a match-winning 5-1 over Tommy Bateman and Wilf Plant after both Bears had fallen while in challenging positions, the latter eventually remounting to claim the final point of the meeting. Earlier, heat eleven had seen Bateman take the chequered flag but, immediately after the race, Ronnie Greene, along with the ACU steward and Bears' skipper George Greenwood, inspected the white line at the pits bend and following a short discussion, Bateman was disqualified for briefly crossing on to the centre. Jeff Lloyd was Bristol's top scorer with 10 points, while Greenwood scorched to an immaculate maximum for Middlesbrough. Later in the programme, Jeff Lloyd set a new track record for three laps in the Whitchurch Hurricane event, clocking 51.8 seconds to better Morian Hansen's time of 25 April. Within an hour of the match the Middlesbrough directors had decided that enough was enough and withdrew from the league. Ronnie Greene wasted no time in making a bid to sign either George Greenwood or Will Lowther, but unfortunately, neither prospective move came to fruition.

For the third time in only eight weeks, the Bulldogs made the journey to Crystal Palace on 17 June, with National League fare on the agenda. As on the previous two occasions, the visit proved successful, with the Bristol boys comfortably winning by 46 points to 37. Perhaps unsurprisingly, the home side were the division's basement club and, although the result represented an improved effort compared with their other matches against the Bulldogs, a number of falls and costly mechanical failures certainly didn't help their cause. Indeed, the usually reliable Keith Harvey fell in his first outing and lost a chain in his last race, thus restricting his score to only 5 points. Mick Mitchell twice fell and Vic Weir had a fall and a retirement in his four starts, although he won his other two rides. Bob Lovell, who had started the season with Bristol, turned out to be the home side's top man, carding 9 points. Meanwhile, Ron Clarke, a newcomer to the London side, looked fairly ordinary in scoring 4 points, but went on to win the Sylvan Scratch event in the second half, beating established names like Weir, Mitchell and Lovell on the way. Despite the home side's problems, the Bulldogs merited their victory, thanks largely to star performances from Jeff Lloyd (10), Roy Dook (9) and Norman Lindsay (8).

Having beaten the team occupying the cellar position, five days later Bristol travelled up to Hanley Stadium to face second-from-bottom Stoke. However, if they thought it was going to be a stroll in the park, they were quickly brought down to earth with a bump, losing 55-28 on the 350-yard Sun Street circuit. Literally speaking, the Bulldogs were overwhelmed and only supplied a race winner on two occasions, in heat nine through Harry Shepherd and in heat fourteen when Jack Bibby made it home ahead. Alan Butler stormed to 11 points for the Potteries outfit, being beaten only by teammate Fred Tuck in heat eight. Butler in fact set a new track record in heat two, thundering home in 77.2 seconds to eclipse the previous best established by Stoke captain Ted Bravery. On a bad night for the Bulldogs, Shepherd was the team's leading contributor, his four rides yielding 8 points.

Bristol's next action was a league fixture *v.* Norwich on 23 June, when Friday night racing returned to Knowle Stadium. Against a side weakened by injuries, the Bulldogs produced a stunning display to thrash the Stars by 63 points to 18. The visitors were hampered when they lost Dick Wise with concussion after a crash in heat seven, and two races later they were dealt another cruel blow when Bert Spencer was rendered out of action after tangling with teammate Alec Lewis. For the rampant Bulldogs, Bill Clibbett scorched to a 12-point maximum, with solid support offered by Roy Dook (10), Jeff Lloyd (9.5), Harry Shepherd (9) and Jack Bibby (8.5). The half-point occurred in the final heat, when Bibby and Lloyd diced with each other for the duration, and couldn't be separated as they crossed the line in a blur. On a dismal night for Norwich, Wilf Jay topped their scoring with a meagre tally of 6 points.

In a break from league racing, Bristol ventured up to Sheffield for a potentially difficult National Trophy semi-final tie on 29 June. Unfortunately, the Bulldogs found it difficult adapting to the super-fast 390-yard Owlerton bowl and were thumped 75-32. George Craig was Bristol's sole race winner in heat fourteen, as the home side accumulated ten 5-1s, including an opening salvo that saw them establish a 20-4 lead after heat four. No fewer than five home riders finished in double figures, namely Ernie Evans (15), Stan Williams (14), Ossie Powell (12), Bronco Dixon (12) and Paddy Mills (11). For the sorry Bulldogs, Harry Shepherd was the leading points scorer, recording a lowly 7 points from six starts.

The second leg of the National Trophy tie was staged the following evening at Knowle and, although Bristol performed better than they had at Owlerton, the powerhouse Tigers had little problem in posting a 59-46 victory to cruise through by an aggregate score of 134-78. After heat seven, Bristol held a slight lead at 22-19, only for Sheffield to register a 5-1 and take the lead through Ernie Evans and Stan Williams. Although Bristol hit back with a maximum of their own courtesy of Harry Shepherd and Bill Clibbett, a 5-0 from Bronco Dixon and Williams in heat ten put the Tigers in the ascendancy; this after both Jack Bibby and Norman Lindsay had failed to finish. Evans went on to complete an outstanding 18-point maximum, while Williams totalled 15 points from his six starts. For Bristol, in what was another awful performance, the best they could offer was 10 points apiece from Jeff Lloyd and Shepherd.

Following the earlier demise of Middlesbrough, it was announced at the start of July that Crystal Palace had resigned due to falling attendances. Despite having over 1,100 members in their supporters' club, the management felt that the sport hadn't sufficiently caught on with local folk. Most meetings at the Sydenham venue had been run at a loss, with as much as £100 going adrift at some. The results for both Middlesbrough and Crystal Palace were therefore expunged from the league table.

The Bulldogs faced the long haul up to Newcastle for league business on 3 July and found the Brough Park circuit to their liking. Indeed, after heat five, they were only a point adrift of the homesters at 15-14 in arrears. However, Norman Hargreaves and Maurice Stobart then raced to a maximum advantage over Norman Lindsay to begin a run of three 5-1s, which effectively killed off the Bristol challenge. Former Bulldog Rol Stobart led the Newcastle charge with 11 points, as they ran out comfortable 46-36 victors in the end. A hard-riding Harry Shepherd was Bristol's most effective rider on the night, his 10 points including excellent victories over both Rol and Maurice Stobart, before he took the second-half Brough Scratch Race final from George Pepper. There was controversy surrounding this meeting though, as the Newcastle line-up included George Gower, who had been a member of the Crystal Palace side. Gower rode at reserve, in place of the injured Billy Lamont and, according to the Newcastle management, this change had received approval from the authorities. Bristol later attempted to claim the league points on the grounds that Gower was still a Crystal Palace rider, waiting to be allocated by the Control Board, but their appeal was unsuccessful.

The return league match v. Newcastle was held at Knowle Stadium on 7 July, but it was another bad night for the Bulldogs as they slipped to a 43-40 reverse. This was Bristol's fifth home defeat of the season and the second occasion that Newcastle had come down and done the business. The match was close throughout and went to a last-heat decider with the Bulldogs trailing by a single point, 39-38, only for Jack Bibby to rear and fall. With his exclusion, Bristol were resigned to defeat and this was confirmed when Kid Curtis won the re-run from Jeff Lloyd and Norman Hargreaves. Newcastle deserved their success though, with both George Pepper and Rol Stobart romping to superb 12-point maximums. Skipper Harry Shepherd was again the most effective Bulldog on show, scoring 10 points. The second half saw Pepper win the Golden Helmet event from Maurice Stobart, Lloyd and Curtis, while Eric Chitty defeated Morian Hansen 2-1 in a special match race series.

In a welcome break from the rigours of league racing, Bristol staged a Test match between England and the Dominions on 14 July. In spite of heavy rain before the start, a crowd of 6,000 turned out to witness the all-star Dominions canter to a 63-44 victory. Try as England did, they were unable to contend with the powerful spearhead contained within the opposition. Indeed, Eric Collins and Eric Chitty blitzed through the card to record six-ride maximums, while George Pepper sped to 17 points. So dominant were the Dominions that their riders crossed the line ahead in all but one of the eighteen heats. Former Bristol rider Collins fairly revelled in the heavy conditions, flying around in the opening heat to clock 67.2 seconds, his time being the year's fastest at Bristol. Turning to England, their solitary race win came from Frank Hodgson in heat twelve, on his way to a tally of 11 points. Full result: Dominions 63 (Collins 18; Chitty 18; Pepper 17; Ernie Evans 4; Goldie Restall 4; Jack Bibby 2; Norman Lindsay 0) England 44 (Hodgson 11; Jim Baylais 11; Harry Shepherd 6.5; Bill Clibbett 6.5; Stan Williams 5; Jeff Lloyd 4; Ron Howes 0).

Back to league action the following night, the Bulldogs went down fighting at Hackney, finally losing 45-39. The West Country boys actually led 16-14 after heat five, but three maximums in the next four races put the Londoners in command. Bristol did claw their way back to within 6 points after a maximum from Roy Dook and Jeff Lloyd in heat eleven, but a 5-1 from the home duo of Nobby Stock and Jim Baylais ended their brave challenge. For the Wolves, Frank Hodgson posted 11 points, while George Saunders registered an impressive 10. Meanwhile, Lloyd and Ron Howes accumulated 7 points apiece to head a set of middle-figure scoring for the Bulldogs.

Bristol slumped to another defeat in their next match at Knowle on 21 July, when Norwich stole away with a narrow 42-41 success. Amid pouring rain, a smallish crowd witnessed exciting racing, with thrills galore on the greasy track surface. The Bulldogs looked to have the meeting under control when they led 21-15 after heat six, only for Wilf Jay and Alan Smith to wallop in a 5-1. Although Bristol gained a 4-2 advantage in heat eight, a maximum in the next race from Bert Spencer and Fred Strecker brought the scores level at 27-27. A re-run heat ten saw Jack Bibby win from Keith Harvey, the two being the only finishers after Harry Shepherd had crashed out at the first time of asking. Jay and Smith then combined for a further Stars' maximum and, with the next two races evenly split, the visitors took a 40-37 lead into the final heat. With a 5-1 required for a Bristol victory, Jeff Lloyd raised the supporters' hopes by streaking ahead, but with Strecker just holding second place from a battling Bibby, it was Norwich who clinched the win. Bill Clibbett headed the Bristol scoring with 8 points, but once again there wasn't a rider in the side who could string together race wins, as had been the case throughout much of the season. The victorious Stars, meanwhile, were led by 9 points each from Smith and Jay, while Spencer grabbed 8. A second-half match-race series saw Les Wotton defeat Benny Kaufman 2-0. In his programme notes, Ronnie Greene welcomed Vic Weir, who had been allotted to the Bulldogs following the closure of Crystal Palace.

League leaders Newcastle beckoned on 24 July, as the Bulldogs faced the long journey up to Brough Park for the second time in three weeks. Not unexpectedly, the home lads coasted to a 52-29 victory and, from a Bristol point of view, the result was a great disappointment, since they had gained 36 points on their previous visit. Still, they were up against the best side in the league and as such the Geordie side were full of confidence. Their heat leaders were quite awesome, with George Pepper and Kid Curtis recording fine maximums, while Rol Stobart's efforts yielded 11 points. Pepper in fact established a new track record in the opening race, clocking 74.0 seconds – a time he subsequently equalled in heat four. Ron Howes topped a disappointing Bristol scorechart with 8 points, while Vic Weir netted just 2 points on his club debut.

Regrettably, in June, Stoke had become the third team to pull out of the Second Division, blaming the fact that 3,000 people took a cheap excursion from the Potteries every Saturday up to Manchester in order to watch speedway at Belle Vue. It was with some irony then that Belle Vue Reserves took over the results and outstanding fixtures of the Stoke team. So it was that the Belle Vue outfit arrived at Knowle on 28 July and, having lost seven matches on the trot, it was with great relief that Bristol managed to pull off a 43-40 win. That was after Belle Vue had gone into the last heat leading 39-38, only for Jack Bibby and Jeff Lloyd to secure a 5-1 over Jack Gordon and Stan Lemon. The Australian's heat-fourteen victory was all the more remarkable, considering his bike had been damaged in a recent bomb explosion at King's Cross Station. After the match, Belle Vue protested that Bibby had broken the tapes at the start of the crucial last heat. However, the meeting steward insisted that the tapes had in fact snapped as the gate had risen. Top points-scorers on the night for Bristol were Lloyd (9) and Bill Clibbett (8), while Belle Vue Reserves were best served by Tommy Bateman (11) and Ted Bravery (8).

Ronnie Greene commented in the programme about the precarious nature of promoting a speedway track, stating, 'The novelty seems to wear off quickly and then difficulties arise. A couple of home reverses and attendances flop to an alarming extent. Sometimes the weather is also to blame but, all the time, the promoter has to find the money to keep things going, and when he can no longer run his track as a business proposition, there is no alternative but to close down.' Mr Greene obviously had great sympathy with the situations that had arisen at Middlesbrough, Crystal Palace and Stoke during the year.

On 4 August, Bristol suffered only their second rained-off meeting in four years as an attractive league fixture v. Sheffield fell victim to adverse weather. There was better luck on 11 August when the Bulldogs entertained Hackney in a Second Division match, with Ronnie Greene taking the opportunity to comment on the previous week's postponement in his programme notes. He stated, 'Last Friday came as a disappointment and, as I might have foreseen, caused quite a stir among the hundreds of you who came into the stadium after hearing the news. I was told "the track is rideable... this is possible... that is possible", to which I replied that the decision was made for the best interests of everybody. We could have delayed announcing the decision and taken your money, only to return it if less than six races had been decided.' Back to the match against Hackney, and the Bulldogs registered another much-needed victory by 42 points to 39, thanks to some solid scoring throughout. With 6 points apiece, reserves George Craig and Norman Lindsay were the real match-winners, although steady Jeff Lloyd weighed in with an excellent tally of 10. Lindsay recorded two fine wins in heats four and thirteen, while Craig won his first league race of the season at Knowle, beating Archie Windmill and Stan Dell in heat eleven. It's impossible to overstate what a great performance this was from Bristol, for they actually trailed 9-2 after heat two, and later found themselves in arrears prior to heat thirteen. However, a 5-1 from Lindsay and Ron Howes turned things around before Lloyd took the flag in the final heat to win the match. Despite this, Hackney boasted the two brightest stars of the meeting in Jim Baylais, who scorched to an unbeaten 12 points, and Frank Hodgson, who netted 11. Lloyd was the only rider to defeat Hodgson, when heading him home in heat nine. After the main match, Baylais took victory in the Golden Helmet event, with Hodgson filling the runner-up spot ahead of Lloyd and Roy Dook.

With Union Cup action on the agenda, Norwich visited Knowle for the fourth time in the season on 18 August. The competition was split into two groups, with Bristol, Norwich and Hackney partaking in the southern section, while Newcastle, Glasgow, Edinburgh, Belle Vue Reserves and Sheffield contested the larger northern group. Having lost two of their previous home matches against the Norfolk side, Bristol were in no mood for complacency and they again had their reserves to thank for a 44-39 victory. As with their last home match v. Hackney, a total of 12 points was gleaned from the reserve pairing, with Ron Howes accounting for 7, while Norman Lindsay scored 5. Bill Clibbett was the star man though, only being beaten by Alan Smith in heat one on his way to 11 points. However, it was a bad night for George Craig, as he fell in heat two, tumbled again in heat five, was excluded for exceeding the time allowance in heat eleven and fell once more in heat thirteen. Norwich were best served on the night by Smith and Bert Spencer, each of whom recorded 9 points. The programme made mention of the World Final, scheduled to take place on 7 September, for which a return coach fare from Bristol to Paddington would cost 5s 3d, while admission to Wembley Stadium was 3s 6d for numbered and reserved seats, and 2s for unreserved seats. Regrettably, the prestigious event was to be cancelled four days before it was due to be staged, due to the declaration of the Second World War.

Bristol rode at Hackney in their second and, as it turned out, last Union Cup fixture on 19 August. Regrettably, it was an evening of very little to enthuse over as the Wolves gained a comfortable 51-33 victory. Aside from Jeff Lloyd's 11 points, this was another indifferent showing from the Bulldogs. The Brummie was a one-man band, being beaten only by maximum man Frank Hodgson in heat seven. Indeed, both Jim Baylais and Tiger Hart would also have recorded maximums but for Lloyd, who saw off the former in heat three and then the latter in heat eleven.

On 23 August the Bulldogs travelled down to Southampton to face Hackney once again in a nine-heat challenge match. This took place after the Banister Court circuit had played host to the South of England Championship, which was won by former Bulldog Cordy Milne ahead of Syd Griffiths and Benny Kaufman, after Frank Goulden had tumbled out on the first bend of the grand final. In a busy schedule, a track record attempt saw Milne equal the circuit's best-ever time of 64.8 seconds, previously recorded by Goulden. The challenge match proved a keenly contested affair, with Hackney emerging as victors by 28 points to 25. Doug Wells topped the Wolves' scoring with 8 points, while Roy Dook also tallied 8 to lead the way for Bristol.

In what turned out to be the last pre-war meeting at Knowle Stadium, the Bulldogs performed admirably to defeat Sheffield 47-37 in a league match on 25 August. The Bristol boys rode as a solid unit, with Bill Clibbett amassing 10 points, while Jeff Lloyd and George Craig both accumulated 8. This was, without doubt, Craig's finest meeting of the season and it was such a shame that he was about to lose what would have been his best racing years because of the Second World War. Turning to the Tigers, Ernie Evans swept to a superb 12-point maximum, while Stan Williams (11) and Bronco Dixon (9) also scored well. The trio received little in the way of support though, totalling all but 5 of their side's 37 points between them. In what was the last race at the venue before the outbreak of war, Ernie Evans won the Knowle Scratch Race final, defeating Clibbett, Williams and Mick Mitchell in 70.2 seconds. The Bristol promoter ended his programme column thus: 'See you all again next week at 8.15 p.m., yours, Ronnie W. Greene.' Perhaps he was being optimistic; unfortunately, there wasn't to be another meeting at Knowle until 19 July 1946.

The Bulldogs' final pre-war meeting took place at Belle Vue on Wednesday 30 August, when they ventured up to Hyde Road for a semi-final encounter in the Provincial Trophy. In a match staged over sixteen heats, the Bristol boys were well and truly thrashed, going down by 66 points to 29. The Aces stormed to eight maximum heat victories, while the under-fire Bulldogs could manage just one race winner all night, when George Craig took the flag in heat six. That also proved to be their only heat advantage of the night, with Jack Bibby following Craig across the line for a 5-1. Prior to that, in heat four, Harry Shepherd, after finishing second, was disqualified for forcing Jack Gordon onto the grass verge. Spearheading the powerful Belle Vue side was the unbeaten Ernie Price (15), while three of his colleagues also reached double figures, namely Tommy Bateman (14), Alan Butler (13) and Ted Bravery (10). For Bristol, on an evening best forgotten, their leading performer was Bibby with 8 points.

With the season ending prematurely, it provided an opportunity for reflection but, on the whole, it wasn't a good year for the Bulldogs, who had only won five out of fourteen league matches, not to mention just two out of six in the English Speedway Trophy. Although the racing at

Knowle was always close and exciting, the attendance figures slumped to an average of around 5,000, compared with 10,500 the previous year.

Rounding up who scored what over the season, with the exclusion of league matches that were expunged *v.* Crystal Palace and Middlesbrough, skipper Harry Shepherd was top man with a total of 189 points from the twenty-eight meetings the team completed for a match average of 6.75. The highly impressive Jeff Lloyd recorded 168.5 points from twenty-five matches, finishing marginally below Shepherd on a 6.74 figure. Meanwhile, Roy Dook appeared in all twenty-eight matches and accumulated 164 points.

1939 STATISTICS

(Bristol's score shown first unless otherwise stated)

NATIONAL LEAGUE DIVISION TWO

Opponents	Home	Away
Belle Vue Reserves	W43-40	Not staged
	Not staged	Not staged
Crystal Palace	Not staged	W46-37
	Not staged	Not staged
Hackney	W48-35	L29-53
	W42-39	L39-45
Middlesbrough	W43-41	L20-64
	Not staged	Not staged
Newcastle	L39-44	L36-46
	L40-43	L29-52
Norwich	W63-18	L37-47
	L41-42	Not staged
Sheffield	W47-37	Not staged
	Not staged	Not staged
Stoke	Not staged	L28-55
	Not staged	Not staged

MATCH AVERAGES

Rider	Matches	Points	Average
Bill Clibbett	10	73	7.30
Harry Shepherd	14	93	6.64

Jeff Lloyd	13	83.5	6.42
Roy Dook	14	74	5.29
Jack Bibby	14	70.5	5.04
Ron Howes	14	69	4.93
Norman Lindsay	14	53	3.79
Reg Gore	1	3	3.00
Norman Wolsey	1	3	3.00
George Craig	12	33	2.75
Vic Weir	1	2	2.00
Reg Lambourne	1	2	2.00
Bill Melluish	2	2	1.00
Bob Lovell	1	0	0.00

NOTE: Match averages do not include expunged meetings *v.* Crystal Palace and Middlesbrough.

NATIONAL LEAGUE DIVISION TWO TABLE

Team	Matches	Won	Drawn	Lost	For	Against	Pts
Newcastle	15	10	0	5	675	574	20
Hackney	13	7	0	6	567	512	14
Sheffield	8	6	0	2	361	302	12
Norwich	12	6	0	6	501	493	12
Bristol	14	5	0	9	561	596	10
Belle Vue Reserves	14	4	0	10	490	678	8

NOTE: Table as at the outbreak of the Second World War; Crystal Palace and Middlesbrough resigned in mid-season, with their records expunged from the final league table; Stoke's fixtures were taken over by Belle Vue Reserves in mid-season.

DAILY MAIL NATIONAL TROPHY

Opponents	Home	Away	Aggregate
Crystal Palace	W83-22	W65-35	W148-57
Sheffield	L46-59	L32-75	L78-134

MATCH AVERAGES

Rider	Matches	Points	Average
Bill Melluish	1	12	12.00

Harry Shepherd	4	42	10.50
Jeff Lloyd	4	39	9.75
Bill Clibbett	4	32	8.00
Roy Dook	4	31	7.75
Jack Bibby	4	27	6.75
Norman Lindsay	4	19	4.75
Ron Howes	3	15	5.00
George Craig	3	8	2.67
Reg Gore	1	1	1.00

ENGLISH SPEEDWAY TROPHY (SOUTHERN SECTION)

Opponents	Home	Away
Crystal Palace	W51-32	W46-33
Hackney	L22-59	L25-56
Norwich	L40.5-43.5	L24-60

MATCH AVERAGES

Rider	Matches	Points	Average
Roy Dook	6	39	6.50
Harry Shepherd	6	38	6.33
Jeff Lloyd	4	20	5.00
Jack Bibby	6	29	4.83
Bob Lovell	4	18	4.50
Norman Lindsay	5	21	4.20
Reg Lambourne	5	19.5	3.90
Ron Howes	5	15	3.00
Reg Gore	1	2	2.00
Bill Melluish	2	3	1.50
George Craig	4	4	1.00

ENGLISH SPEEDWAY TROPHY (SOUTHERN SECTION) TABLE

Team	Matches	Won	Drawn	Lost	For	Against	Pts
Norwich	6	5	0	1	278.5	222.5	10
Hackney	6	4	0	2	315	182	8
Bristol	6	2	0	4	208.5	283.5	4
Crystal Palace	6	1	0	5	190	304	2

SPEEDWAY IN BRISTOL 1928-1949

UNION CUP (SOUTHERN SECTION)

Opponents	Home	Away
Hackney	Not staged	L33-51
Norwich	W44-39	Not staged

MATCH AVERAGES

Rider	Matches	Points	Average
Jeff Lloyd	2	20	10.00
Bill Clibbett	2	13	6.50
Jack Bibby	2	10	5.00
Harry Shepherd	2	10	5.00
Ron Howes	2	9	4.50
Norman Lindsay	2	7	3.50
Roy Dook	2	6	3.00
George Craig	2	2	1.00

UNION CUP (SOUTHERN SECTION) TABLE

Team	Matches	Won	Drawn	Lost	For	Against	Pts
Hackney	3	2	0	1	116.5	134.5	4
Norwich	3	1	0	2	140.5	109.5	2
Bristol	2	1	0	1	77	90	2

NOTE: Table as at the outbreak of the Second World War.

PROVINCIAL TROPHY

Opponents	Home	Away	Aggregate
Belle Vue Reserves	Not staged	L29-66	–

MATCH AVERAGES

Rider	Matches	Points	Average
Jack Bibby	1	8	8.00
George Craig	1	6	6.00
Roy Dook	1	6	6.00

Bill Clibbett	1	4	4.00
Jeff Lloyd	1	3	3.00
Harry Shepherd	1	1	1.00
Vic Weir	1	1	1.00
Ron Howes	1	0	0.00

CHALLENGE

Opponents	Home	Away
Hackney	–	W28-25

NOTE: Match ridden at Southampton.

MATCH AVERAGES

Rider	Matches	Points	Average
Roy Dook	1	8	8.00
Bill Clibbett	1	5	5.00
Harry Shepherd	1	5	5.00
Jack Bibby	1	4	4.00
Jeff Lloyd	1	3	3.00
Vic Weir	1	3	3.00

MINI-MATCH

Opponents	Home	Away
Wimbledon Reserves	–	L5-7

MATCH AVERAGES

Rider	Matches	Points	Average
Harry Shepherd	1	3	3.00
Ron Howes	1	2	2.00
Jeff Lloyd	1	0	0.00
Eric French	1	0	0.00

1946

Despite hostilities having ended, it still came as something of a surprise when an article in *Speedway and Ice News* mentioned a possible revival of the shale sport at Knowle in its issue dated 23 May 1946. The feature appeared on the 'Cracks from the Tracks' page and stated that it was more than just idle rumour, as the directors of the stadium had apparently already made preliminary arrangements. A resumption of the sport hinged on the supply of electricity for the lighting system, although work had already started on the relaying of the track.

Mr L.P. Allan, managing director of the stadium, commented thus in the local press: 'Whenever speedway is mentioned, I get deluged with letters. Although there are so many controls and regulations, we will do what we can to get it started, because we know how keen Bristol people are.' The article also stated that an application for a permit to install lighting had been forwarded to the Board of Trade in London, and as Wimbledon had seen their recent application granted, there was no reason to suppose that Bristol's would not also receive the green light.

It was subsequently revealed in the local press that the new promoters of the sport at Knowle Stadium would be Bob Steel and Reg Witcomb. The management duo had visited London for talks with established promoters Ronnie Greene, Stan Greatrex and Arthur Atkinson, who had all pledged their support and help with making riders available to appear at Knowle. While in the capital, on 25 June, the Bristol promoters watched West Ham defeat Wembley 50-46 in an ACU Cup encounter, which was played out before a massive crowd of some 61,000 spectators. The new management team subsequently made contact with many other promoters, all of whom were very positive and helpful with the availability of riders to grace the Bristol circuit.

With everything moving along nicely, it was announced that the supporters' club was to be restarted, and that the membership fee of *2s 6d* would cover both the 1946 and 1947 seasons. All members received a special badge depicting the club's Bulldog mascot and, as an added bonus, any supporters spotted wearing their badge by club officials away from the stadium would receive a free admission pass.

On 6 July, Speedway Control Board manager Dicky Southouse made an inspection of the circuit and it was hoped to start Friday evening meetings later that same month. Initially, it was planned to confine the events to local juniors in the hope of finding sufficient talent to enter a team into league racing the following season. *Speedway and Ice News* made mention of this, but went on to question whether racing of this kind would suit West Country folk, as they had previously been used to a much higher standard prior to the Second World War.

So it was that the great day arrived and Bristol Speedway was reborn on Friday 19 July, when a Junior Best Pairs event was held. There were a couple of links with the past, with two former Knowle riders working in an official capacity, namely Vic Anstice, who was the timekeeper, and Bill Hamblin, who performed the duties as start-line marshal. Meanwhile, joint-manager Reg Witcomb took up his other role throughout the meeting, that of clerk of the course. Despite inclement weather, a crowd of 10,000 flocked back to the 290-yard raceway and thoroughly enjoyed the thrill of it all as they witnessed Newcastle's Jeff Lloyd and Syd Littlewood take victory in the event. Lloyd, a former Bulldog of course, rode to three superlative wins, while twice shepherding home his partner, thus going through the card unbeaten by an opponent. Between them, Lloyd and Littlewood notched 23 points, but there was a tie for second place between the two New Cross pairings of Frank Lawrence and Mick Mitchell, and Eric French and Les Webbon, who accumulated 18 points apiece. Full result: Lloyd (13) and Littlewood (10) 23; Lawrence (11) Mitchell (7) 18; French (14) and Webbon (4) 18; Cyril Anderson (12) and Jack Cooley (5) 17; Roger Wise (9) and George Gower (6) 15; Percy Brine (7) and Jack White (5) 12; Roy Dook (7) and Laurie Packer (1) 8; Buck Whitby (4) and Ron Howes (2) 6; Broncho Slade (reserve) 2. In the programme notes, Messrs Witcomb and Steel revealed that the stadium directors had given them the go-ahead just three weeks previously, and that they intended to take the Bulldogs to even greater heights than those reached before. They also stated that meetings would start at 7 p.m. and, as the nights lengthened, possibly earlier, owing to the fact that the application to install lighting hadn't yet received approval.

The Bristol bosses had been so impressed with the performance of Jeff Lloyd in the opener that they immediately took steps to arrange for him to skipper the Bulldogs in their subsequent Friday night challenge matches. Renowned as a fast starter, Lloyd was the brother of Belle Vue man Wally. In addition, Roger Wise had also caught the eye, with the promotion making all the necessary arrangements to sign the popular grass-tracker as one of the first riders to sport the Bristol colours in the new era.

Prior to any team meetings, however, the second meeting at Knowle was a Novice Championship on 26 July. Rain did its utmost to ruin the event, with the promotion receiving endless telephone calls throughout the day from supporters eager to find out if the action would go ahead or not. Despite the inclement weather, there had been terrific news for the Bristol promoters earlier in the day, when permits for the installation of track lighting arrived in the morning post. As it was, the weather brightened in mid-afternoon and the tapes went up at the scheduled start time. The highlight of the evening was a special match-race challenge between Australian Test star Ron Johnson and Canadian Eric Chitty. The 9,000 spectators in attendance saw Johnson at his best, as he demonstrated his mastery of the inside line to win the first two heats, before Chitty gained some consolation from an academic third race. The Novice Championship provided plenty of thrills, as the thirteen competitors raced over a thirteen-heat format, with the four highest scorers contesting a grand final. Birmingham rider Jimmy Wright eventually won the event, while Bristol's newest recruit Roger Wise took the runner-up spot after unluckily suffering a puncture on the second lap when holding the lead. They proved to be the only two finishers, however, as Dave Anderson and Dick Tolley were both forced to pull up through mechanical problems. Full result: (qualifying scores) Wright 11; Tolley 11; Wise 10; Anderson 8; Jack White 7; Bruce Semmens 7; Frank Taylor 5; Doug Bell 5; Stan Lanfear 4; Dick Howard 4; Oz Osbourne 2; Broncho Slade 2; Buddy King 0; Bill Osborne (reserve) DNR; Mike Beddoe (reserve) DNR; (Final) 1st Wright; 2nd Wise; Anderson (ret); Tolley (ret).

Bristol held their first team fixture of the new era on 2 August, when they faced Northern League side Birmingham in a challenge match. With Bob Steel taking the position of team manager, it is worth noting the Bulldogs' line-up for the historic meeting: 1. Jeff Lloyd; 2. Stan Lanfear; 3. Bert Spencer; 4. Roger Wise; 5. Roy Dook; 6. Ron Howes; 7.

Percy Brine; 8. Mike Beddoe. The fans were obviously glad to see their team back on track, for a gate of 12,000 was recorded, and those present weren't disappointed either, as the Bulldogs surged to a 62-45 victory. It could so easily have been a night of embarrassment for the Bristol promotion though, as the machines belonging to the Birmingham riders had not arrived by the 7 p.m. start time. The bikes were sent down on coaches, along with the Brummies' supporters, but the drivers just couldn't find their way to the stadium. Racing eventually got underway half an hour late and thankfully there was plenty of tremendous action for the crowd to enthuse over. The delayed start only served to emphasise the need for lighting to be installed though, with the meeting eventually completed in semi-darkness. Lloyd and Spencer led the Bristol scoring with 15 points apiece, while Wise and Howes each yielded 8. For the visitors, Bill Longley led the way with 13 points, while Stan Dell provided the only real backing with a tally of 10. The meeting also featured five falls, but each time the riders involved were able to remount and continue in the race.

In their programme notes, the promoters' page entitled 'What's What' stated that several letters had been received from supporters asking why local grass-track riders were not being invited to ride in meetings. Messrs Witcomb and Steel went on to explain that all the grass-track boys were, in fact, practising at Knowle on Monday nights in order to get the hang of cinder racing, and as soon as their performance justified it they would be given an opportunity on race evenings. As good as their word, the promoters had indeed given a chance to grass-tracker Mike Beddoe in the match against Birmingham, and the lad did reasonably well too, netting 2 points. Incidentally, the Monday night training sessions were held under the supervision of former Bulldog Bill Clibbett, who was only too happy to give the novices the benefit of his experience.

The fourth meeting of the year was run in appalling conditions on 9 August, when Bristol took on Newcastle. However, torrential rain failed to dampen the enthusiasm of an 11,000-strong crowd, which stood in the open for two hours and, despite being thoroughly drenched to the skin, they still cheered the Bulldogs throughout a pulsating match that ended in a 41-41 draw. Once again Jeff Lloyd was the star of the show, riding to an unbeaten 12-point return from his four starts; unfortunately though, he was riding for his parent club Newcastle! Norman Evans gave good support with 10 points, while Bristol were best served by Frank Lawrence (11) and Stan Lanfear (7). New Cross rider Lawrence was, in fact, a late stand-in for Norwich's Bert Spencer, who didn't make the journey to Bristol due to a lack of competitive equipment. The match looked like going away from the Bulldogs as they trailed 39-32 with just two races remaining, but a 5-0 from Stan Lanfear and Roger Wise in heat thirteen brought the homesters right back into the match. A 4-2 then followed from Percy Brine and Roy Dook in the final race, with Syd Littlewood providing the filling in between. One spectacular incident during the meeting saw Roy Dook swerve over the white line and only just miss an ambulance man as he careered across the centre green. When later asked why this had occurred, Dook explained that his twist grip had become so slippery in the wet that his hand had slipped off temporarily and caused him to lose control. As a side attraction to the team event, New Cross star Ron Johnson took part in a match-race series against West Ham's Malcolm Craven, which resulted in a 2-1 success for the Scottish-born Australian. Craven took the first race, with Johnson hitting back to win the second, before a titanic decider saw both men engage in a wheel-to-wheel battle that the New Cross maestro finally won by the narrowest of margins. In the often informative 'What's What' column in the match programme, it was revealed that some supporters had confused the Speedway Supporters' Club with the Knowle Sports Club and the Knowle Greyhound Club. The piece went on to stress that both the Knowle Sports Club and the Knowle Greyhound Club were two quite separate licensed organisations, and to become a member of each meant applying at the general stadium office. However, if membership was granted, the facilities provided by either club would be available to the member at both greyhound and speedway meetings.

The Bulldogs were again on track at Knowle on 16 August, when Middlesbrough were the visitors for another challenge match. In a compelling meeting, the homesters ran out narrow winners by 56 points to 52, with the immaculate Jeff Lloyd, back in Bristol colours, romping to an amazing 18-point maximum. Providing Lloyd with great support, Frank Lawrence recorded 14 points, while Reg Lambourne plundered 8. Meanwhile, although it wasn't quite sufficient for them to take victory, the visitors' scorechart included three riders in double figures, their main men being Frank Hodgson (12), Wilf Plant (11) and Fred 'Kid' Curtis (10). As a measure of how well the Monday night training sessions were going, the meeting also included two junior scratch races, which pitted

Bulldogs reserves Mike Beddoe and Percy Brine against the up-and-coming pairing of Billy Hole and Jack Mountford. Amazingly, Hole won both races, with Mountford finishing as runner-up in the first, while Brine was second in the other heat. Hole later admitted in the *Evening World Speedway Annual* that he had been scared to death prior to that first ride in front of an audience of 11,000. He stated: 'I felt terribly alone and nervous, and my one fear was the crowd – would they like me?... would they cheer me?... could I impress them?... and these questions were turning over and over in my mind.'

A competition was launched that required entrants to design a coat of arms illustrating the different sports held at the stadium, as well as those proposed for the future. The winning design would therefore have to include greyhound racing, speedway, ice skating and boxing. The prize for the best entry was £25, with five runners-up prizes of two guineas.

Sheffield arrived in town for the next challenge match on 23 August and promptly stole away with a 58-50 victory under their belts. Twelve thousand supporters witnessed five riders finish with tallies of 8 points or over for the visitors, while the Bulldogs didn't have the necessary strength in depth to cope. Indeed, with 16 points apiece, only Jeff Lloyd and Frank Lawrence offered any resistance to the Sheffield big guns of Tommy Bateman (12), Jim Boyd (11), Tommy Allott (9), Stan Williams (8) and former Bulldog Jack Bibby (8). Following his two junior race successes of the previous week, Billy Hole was thrust into the Bristol side for the match although, understandably, he failed to score from his two starts. Continuing with the policy of encouraging the youngsters, the match *v.* Sheffield included a further two junior heats, which saw Jack Mountford triumph in both, defeating Mike Beddoe in the first and Percy Brine in the second. In their programme notes, Reg Witcomb and Bob Steel explained that following the preliminary trials of their first batch of novices, they had signed Mike Beddoe, Ben Collins, Billy Hole, Stan Lanfear and Jack Mountford for further training throughout the close season. The management duo went on to state, 'While we continue to bring on these boys, we intend to give trials to a new batch of novices, with the object of finding new talent. We understand that the managements of other tracks are paying keen attention to our trials, realising that there is some fine talent to be found in the West Country but, rest assured, we will have them signed on before anyone else has a chance.'

With new lighting in position, the next meeting, on 30 August, was scheduled for a 7.30 p.m. start time, when an interesting match was anticipated against a star-studded side riding under the banner of 'The Rest'. Frank Hodgson captained the illustrious visitors, with the remainder of the team made up by Kid Curtis, Norman Evans, Bill Gilbert, Roy Craighead, Charlie Spinks, Jack Gordon and Buck Whitby. The best way of describing the action from this meeting is to quote from the report in *Speedway and Ice News*, which stated: 'And yet another water spectacle for the Bristol fans. Seven thousand of them stood for seventy minutes on Friday 30 August, to see the Bristol challenge match against The Rest. The rain emptied down; it lashed the crowd; it waterlogged the track; it saturated everyone and everything, but the match went on, thanks to the gallant staff and mechanics – plus the courage and skill of the riders. But after ten races, with enclosures holding flood water, the track resembling a sea of cinder mud and the crowd yelling delightedly as the heats were contested in tropical weather, the ACU steward in control had no alternative but to call a halt.' At the time of the abandonment, The Rest were leading by 36 points to 24, with Jeff Lloyd unbeaten from four outings for the Bulldogs. With the sheer amount of rain an obvious cause for concern, Lloyd was later quoted as saying: 'Everytime I was at the starting line, I prayed that I should be first away, otherwise it was hopeless.' Unfortunately, no other Bristol rider reached double figures, with the next best being Percy Brine on a meagre 4 points. Despite the weather, it was a momentous occasion for Jack Mountford as he made his Bulldogs' debut, marking the event with a 1-point return. For the visitors, Curtis led the way with 10 points, while their skipper Hodgson tallied 7. In the race-day programme, supporters' club secretary Miss Jean Pomphrey explained that the target figure of 5,000 members had not yet been reached, and encouraged the fans to invite their friends to join. Miss Pomphrey also stated that many people had enquired about pennants and, while the management were trying to replenish their stocks, the main difficulty had been obtaining the rods that allowed them to be secured to vehicles.

The eighth meeting of the year at Knowle saw the Bulldogs face Norwich on 6 September. On a track that was again saturated by rain, the Bristol boys were yards faster than their opponents and swept to a huge 76-30 victory. In general, the Norwich riders failed to master the conditions, with only Bert Spencer (12) and Harry Pike (10) showing any real spirit. Making his first appearance for the Bulldogs, Jack Cooley scorched to 15 points and, but for an overslide in heat fifteen, he would have gone through the card for a six-ride full-house. Backing Cooley all the way, Bristol boasted several other high scorers in Jeff Lloyd (12), Wilf Plant (12), Frank Lawrence (11) and Reg Lambourne (10). Norwich rider Paddy Mills had a nasty accident on his way to the meeting when his car skidded, left the road, jumped a fence and ploughed 30 yards into a field, finishing up with the body smashed in and the chassis broken in half. Yet, despite the severe shaking, the rider still somehow made it to the track, albeit for a couple of point-less rides. In their informative programme notes, the promoters admitted that they had been wondering for some time what had happened to the popular Bristol rider George Craig. Well, they had received a letter from Craig himself, in which he explained that he had just been released from the Army and was dead keen to resume his speedway career.

Next up for the Bristol boys was another challenge match against Newcastle on 13 September, and this was to prove one of the finest meetings ever seen at Knowle. The 11,000 spectators witnessed a see-saw match which the visitors managed to win by the narrowest of margins, 55-53. Having amassed 15 points the previous week, Jack Cooley was beset with problems throughout the meeting, suffering a spill, a dodgy motor and no luck at all on the way to just 3 points. Meanwhile, Jeff Lloyd raced to an outstanding 18-point maximum but, unfortunately, he wasn't sporting Bristol colours, since he was again representing his parent club Newcastle. Norman Evans picked up 10 points for the Geordie side, while Doug McLachlan also carded 10. The best Bulldog on the night was Frank Hodgson, who weighed in with 16 points, while Wilf Plant and Roger Wise totalled 8 apiece. A little further down the line, Billy Hole rode to an impressive 6-point tally and was cleverly shepherded to a fine victory by Ron Howes in heat four, as the home duo collected a 5-1 over Leo Lungo. However, showing that he could also do it without any assistance, in Hole's second ride Howes was left at the gate, and the youngster went on to secure a fine victory on his own, again over Lungo. Interestingly, also appearing for Newcastle was Alec Grant, who was a most useful performer, despite the fact that he had actually lost the sight of one eye. The main match was interspersed with junior races, two of which featured the return to track action of George Craig, who understandably looked a little rusty first time out, but went on to win his second outing. The winner of the coat-of-arms competition was announced in the match programme, with Mr C.L. Gulliver (membership no. 461) of 48 Cotham Road, Bristol 6, receiving the winner's prize of £25 for his excellent design.

On 20 September Sheffield returned to Knowle Stadium for the second time in a month and Bristol avenged their previous defeat, running out comfortable 62-45 winners on the usual rain-soaked track. The wet weather severely affected the crowd, with a smaller attendance of some 5,000 present to witness what turned out to be a keenly fought contest. Although the homesters won the match, it was the visitors who boasted the undoubted rider of the night in Jim Boyd, who beat Jeff Lloyd, Frank Lawrence and Wilf Plant on his way to a 16-point total. He received scant support, however, with former Bristol rider Jack Bibby second in line on the Sheffield scorechart with just 8 points. For Bristol, Lloyd led the way once more with 14 points, while Plant totalled 13 and Norman Evans grabbed 10. Boyd didn't have it all his own way though, as Lloyd got the better of their duel in heat eight, the Bulldogs' skipper leaving it until the last bend before cutting inside with a terrific burst of speed and just winning the race to the line. There was a spectacular spill in heat nine, when both Billy Hole and Dick Geary came down after their machines had locked together on the first bend. Both riders escaped serious injury and although Hole suffered a knock to the leg he was able to resume racing later in the meeting. In their programme notes, the promoters were as honest as ever, admitting they were fully aware that neither the announcing nor the public address system was as good as it ought to be. Messrs Witcomb and Steel went on to state that they were making desperate efforts to obtain the services of a suitable person for this type of job. In the meantime, they hoped the public would bear with them while they experimented with different announcers and equipment. As it happened, a new announcer stepped into the breach that very night; his name was G. McLeod and he was a resident of nearby Whitchurch. 'Mac' as he was affectionately known, proved to be just the man for the job, with a very distinctive and informative delivery.

Middlesbrough made their second journey of the year to Bristol on 27 September, and it was sweet revenge for the visitors who had lost on their previous trip, as they ran out winners by 56 points to 52. The meeting was packed with action and the large gathering of fans were kept on their toes throughout. Going into the last race, Middlesbrough

154

were leading 52-50 and the match could have swung either way, but a win from Frank Hodgson and a fighting third place from Geoff Godwin secured victory for the visitors. Regrettably, Jeff Lloyd missed the meeting after suffering a broken collarbone in a crash at Newcastle four nights previously, so track specialist Jim Boyd was drafted in and he didn't disappoint, scorching to a marvellous 17-point tally. George Craig returned to the Bristol side and rode with great vigour to rack up 8 points, but the only real support for him and Boyd came from Norman Evans, who also scored 8. For the triumphant Middlesbrough team, skipper Frank Hodgson romped to 17 points, with Geoff Godwin scoring 12 and Jack Hodgson 10. Regular Bristol team member Roger Wise missed the meeting, but he had a good excuse, as he was covering himself in glory in speedway's sister sport, winning the Belgian International Grass-track Championship at Bervier. As usual, the programme of events featured several junior heats, and as well as Billy Hole, Mike Beddoe and Ben Collins, there were three newcomers who appeared for the first time in these races, namely Jock Grierson, Len Tupling and Eddie 'Crusty' Pye. In the race-day programme, the 'What's What' column posed the question: 'What did you think of the announcing and loudspeaker last Friday? We thought it was much better. You let us know when it was wrong, so let us know now if you think it's OK.' Lastly, the promotion mentioned that, at the final meeting of the season, supporters' club members would be admitted to the 1s 9d enclosure free of charge upon production of their membership cards.

Bristol's next fixture saw them face the challenge of a composite side entitled Northern League Stars on Friday 4 October. Despite the visiting team including the likes of brothers Frank and Jack Hodgson, as well as Norman Evans, Percy Brine and Wal Morton, the Bulldogs gave an inspired performance to win handsomely by 74 points to 34. Frank Hodgson got the lot (18) for the beleaguered visitors, but he received measly support, with his colleagues only totalling 16 points between them. Turning to the homesters, five men hammered home double-figure returns, namely Wilf Plant (14), Frank Lawrence (13), Jim Boyd (11), Roger Wise (10) and George Craig (10). A bizarre heat sixteen saw Craig fall, yet he still managed to finish in second place. The race featured just one opposition rider, due to the disqualification of Jack Hodgson for breaking the tapes. The re-run saw Craig come down in a heap before remounting and passing Percy Brine on the final lap to follow Jim Boyd home for a Bristol maximum.

The promoters' programme notes explained that they had hoped their final meeting, scheduled for 25 October, would feature a fourteen-heat team match followed by an hour of comedy events. However, the ACU had granted permission for them to stage something of far greater importance in the shape of the Northern Riders' Championship. The winner of the prestigious event would be presented with a cheque for £40 and a silver trophy, while the runner-up would receive £15 and the third-placed man £5. In their column, Messrs Witcomb and Steel also mentioned that they were going off to London in order to meet up with many of the other promoters to discuss the possibility of forming a Southern League for the 1947 season. The Bristol bosses were keen on this idea, as it would reduce travelling and make it possible to lay on coaches for the supporters. They also commented that several fans had complained as they had been unable to hear the announcements of race results due to the noise of the rattles and cheering around them. A system was subsequently introduced whereby a bell would be rung before each announcement, so that the noisier supporters would then hopefully quieten down. Talking of the tannoy, it had long since become evident that the favourite tune played during the short open licence season was the attractive dance number entitled 'May I?'

Having previously visited Knowle on 2 August, Birmingham made a return trip on 11 October for what was the thirteenth meeting of Bristol's comeback season. The Bulldogs had triumphed in the first encounter by 17 points and the only question regarding the second match centred on the margin they would win by. As it was, the Bristol boys recorded no less than fourteen race winners from the eighteen heats, as they scorched to a huge 74-34 success. The visitors were literally swamped and only former home favourite Roy Dook offered any resistance in notching 10 points. Wilf Plant, who recorded a quite brilliant 17-point tally, headed the rampant Bulldogs' scorechart, while Frank Lawrence weighed in with 16 and the highly promising Jack Mountford tallied 11. Much sympathy was felt for the Brummies, however, since they had been rocked by the death of popular thirty-three-year-old Canadian Charlie Appleby in a track crash at Newcastle just four nights previously. The riders made a collection during the interval, raising a total of £183 2s 4d, which went to the dependents of the late Birmingham rider. The usual junior races were included in the programme of events and these featured Ben Collins, Dennis Bond, Vic Brinkworth, Eric Salmon, Mike Beddoe and

Percy Brine. In their programme notes, the promotional duo mentioned the eventful heat sixteen of the previous week's encounter against the Northern League Stars. Quoting from the programme, they stated, 'Everybody took a rather poor view of the riding of George Craig in heat sixteen, but don't be too hard in your judgement. George came to us afterwards and was most apologetic, saying that after laying off for so many years, his lack of practice and keenness to prove himself better than ever, unintentionally caused him to ride wildly. Consequently we are giving him another opportunity but, if ever we are of the opinion that a rider intentionally rides dangerously, we should not continue his bookings in the interest of good speedway racing.'

In the issue of *Speedway and Ice News* dated 17 October, it was revealed that, early in November, young Bristol riders would find a training school in operation at Knowle, with the instructor in charge being none other than legendary track ace Tiger Stevenson. The idea behind the venture was to train promising youngsters for the southern tracks at Bristol, while Stevenson would run a similar operation at Birmingham for the benefit of the northern circuits.

On 18 October, Bristol staged their final team match of the campaign, which featured the third visit of Sheffield. The Bulldogs continued in their dominant vein at Knowle, handing out a 74-33 pasting to the Yorkshire side. It was the third meeting in a row in which Bristol had reached a 74-point total, with the Northern League Stars and Birmingham being the previous recipients of such hidings. Jeff Lloyd returned to the saddle after recovering from his collarbone injury and piled up a magnificent 17 points. Meanwhile, Wilf Plant scored 15, with Frank Lawrence notching 11 and Roger Wise 10. For the visitors, only Jim Boyd put up any resistance with a hard-earned 15 points. One amusing incident in the meeting occurred when George Craig unexpectedly tumbled off while heading teammate Jeff Lloyd and, when later asked what had happened, the rider jokingly explained, 'I thought I saw sixpence on the ground!'

So to 25 October and the prestigious Northern Riders' Championship Final at Knowle Stadium. The Bristol promoters went to town on this one and produced a superb twenty-four-page souvenir programme, which included a number of features, including photographs and pen pictures of all sixteen competitors, plus the three reserves. A record attendance for speedway at the stadium turned up for the meeting, with 20,000 folk packed in to see the racing long before the scheduled start time. The meeting, which was run along the same lines as the Wembley-staged British Riders' Championship, threw up plenty of tremendous racing, but it was Bill Longley of Odsal who emerged triumphant with a faultless 15-point maximum. Second place went to Middlesbrough star man Frank Hodgson, while the ever-popular Jeff Lloyd finished third. Full result: Longley 15; Hodgson 13; Lloyd 12; Norman Evans 11; Jim Boyd 10; Wilf Plant 9; Will Lowther 8; Wal Morton 8; Kid Curtis 6; Roger Wise 6; Frank Lawrence 5; Paddy Mills 4; Wilf Jay 4; George Craig 3; Phil 'Tiger' Hart 2; Jack Mountford (reserve) 2; Stan Dell 1; Mike Beddoe (reserve) 1; Billy Hole (reserve) DNR. The main event was followed by the Junior Trophy, which saw Mike Beddoe take the spoils of victory ahead of Eric Salmon. In the 'What's What' column, Messrs Witcomb and Steel revealed that the good folk of Bristol had seen ninety-three riders going through their paces in the fifteen meetings that had been staged. They went on to sincerely thank all the other promoters for enabling them to get speedway restarted in mid-season by consenting to all the riders, including many former Bulldogs, appearing at Knowle in the various challenge matches. These helpful promoters included Alice Hart (Belle Vue and Sheffield), Ian Hoskins (Glasgow), Ronnie Greene (Wimbledon), Dicky Wise (Norwich), J.B. McCreton (Middlesbrough), Les Marshall (Birmingham), Phyllis McQuillen (manageress of Newcastle), Fred Mockford (New Cross), Stan Greatrex and Arthur Atkinson (West Ham), Alec Jackson (Wembley) and Johnnie Hoskins (Odsal). Not wanting to miss anyone out, the promoters went on to thank all the staff for the various off-track jobs that helped to keep the speedway ticking over.

End-of-season facts and figures revealed that, despite the cold and wet weather that was prevalent at virtually every meeting, a total of 160,000 supporters had poured through the Knowle Stadium turnstiles for the fifteen meetings. Putting this into perspective, a total of 6,623,587 people went to speedway meetings throughout Britain in 1946, with gate receipts exceeding over £1 million. So, any early reservations as to the viability of bringing the sport back to Bristol had been well and truly dispelled. On track, Jeff Lloyd proved to be the top Bulldog, notching a total of 104 points from just 7 meetings. Frank Lawrence was second in the scoring stakes, weighing in with exactly 100 points, while Wilf Plant was next in line on the 84-point mark.

Upon the close of the season, Tiger Stevenson began his training school in order to give opportunities to young English boys. Following adverts in the press and public announcements, there was no shortage of lads that came forward for tuition. Within a fortnight, Stevenson had received 1,200 letters, and that figure soon rose to 1,400, but rather wisely he decided to concentrate on just 100 youngsters. Initially, the sessions were held at Birmingham on Fridays and Saturdays, with Bristol being used on Mondays. However, after a while this was altered to Saturdays at Birmingham, with the activities at Bristol being held on Mondays and Tuesdays. The school was held right through the winter months from November until March, and the lads always turned up despite travelling difficulties and the often-atrocious weather conditions. On many occasions the youngsters were greeted with a track that was covered in frost and snow but, full of enthusiasm, they even swept the snow from the track and still rode on in their search for fame and glory!

1946 STATISTICS

(Bristol's score shown first unless otherwise stated)

CHALLENGE

Opponents	Home
Birmingham	(1) W62-45
Birmingham	(2) W74-34
Middlesbrough	(1) W56-52
Middlesbrough	(2) L52-56
Northern League Stars	W74-34
Newcastle	(1) D41-41
Newcastle	(2) L53-55
Norwich	W76-30
Sheffield	(1) L50-58
Sheffield	(2) W62-45
Sheffield	(3) W74-33
The Rest	L24-36

MATCH AVERAGES

Rider	Matches	Points	Average
Frank Hodgson	1	16	16.00

Bert Spencer	1	15	15.00
Jeff Lloyd	7	104	14.86
Jim Boyd	2	28	14.00
Frank Lawrence	8	100	12.50
Wilf Plant	7	84	12.00
Jack Cooley	2	18	9.00
Norman Evans	2	18	9.00
George Craig	4	30	7.50
Roger Wise	11	77	7.00
Reg Lambourne	4	25	6.25
Jack Mountford	6	32	5.33
Jack Bibby	1	5	5.00
Roy Dook	3	15	5.00
Ron Howes	8	32	4.00
Mike Beddoe	8	31	3.88
Percy Brine	8	31	3.88
Billy Hole	7	24	3.43
Stan Lanfear	3	9	3.00
Crusty Pye	1	3	3.00
Stan Dell	1	1	1.00
Aussie Powell	1	0	0.00

1947

Tiger Stevenson had continued to run his training school throughout the winter and, by 1947, there were some seventy really promising lads. Stevenson suggested that they bought their own machines and no less than forty did so. The enthusiasm of these boys knew no bounds and they would make the most difficult of journeys by road and rail to attend the training sessions. The efforts of Stevenson proved fruitful and the school was hailed as an outstanding success. From it, valuable riders were allocated to both Bristol and Birmingham, while several others went on to enjoy success elsewhere.

The year saw the publication of the first *Bristol Evening World Speedway Annual*, edited by Bob Hatsell, a journalist who had become synonymous with the sport in the area. This was the first speedway annual ever circulated in the provinces and it proved a tremendous success, selling out within a few weeks of publication. The wonderful little booklet traced Bristol's records right back to 1936, and also looked forward to the season ahead. There was much to enthuse over too, as promoters Reg Witcomb and Bob Steel endeavoured to bring league racing back to Knowle. Speedway was booming and the year saw the introduction of a Third Division for the first time in the sport's history. At one point, it looked like Bristol would be joining the new sphere of racing, but an appeal to the Speedway Control Board eventually saw them allocated a place in the Second Division. The Bulldogs therefore took their place in an eight-team league which also included Birmingham, Glasgow, Newcastle, Norwich, Sheffield, Middlesbrough and Wigan. The make-up of the league schedule meant that teams would face each other four times over the course of the season, twice at home and twice away.

Briefly referring back to the *Bristol Evening World Speedway Annual*, Bob Hatsell mentioned the possibility of a match-race challenge along the lines of 'The Management' *v.* 'The Press'. The promoters were asked to communicate with Mr Hatsell without delay, but it would be fair to assume that they didn't relish the idea!

The Bulldogs' management put together a useful-looking side for the campaign, with the backbone of the squad consisting of Billy Hole, Eric Salmon, Jack Mountford, Mike Beddoe and George Craig, all of whom had appeared the previous year. In addition, promising twenty-eight-year-old Cyril Quick was signed, while other riders brought on board included Frank Evans, Graham Hole (brother of Billy), Charles Bourdon, Ken Monks and Bill Clifton. The promoters were only too aware that they also needed an experienced heat leader to transform the Bulldogs into a first-class side but, as the tapes rose on the season, negotiations to achieve this object were still in progress. Messrs Witcomb and Steel admitted that they had travelled up to Leeds to meet with the other Second Division promoters in order to discuss the matter and they had, in fact, made an offer of well over £1,000 for the services of the popular Jeff Lloyd. They remained hopeful that Newcastle promoter Johnnie Hoskins would do business with them. Meanwhile, there was also the news that several Australian riders were on their way to these shores, and Bristol's management duo were confident they would be able to entice at least one to Knowle.

In the informative 'What's What' column from the Bulldogs' opening programme of the season, the promoters stated that they had also tried to sign several other riders, including Wilf Plant, Jim Boyd, Jack Cooley and Frank Hodgson. They went on to explain that the situation was difficult in the Second Division, due to the fact that there were not enough heat leaders to go around. While there were no disagreements among the division's promoters, they realised that, in order to release a star rider to Bristol, it would leave the track he left without a heat leader.

Prior to the opening meeting at Knowle, Bristol travelled up to Middlesbrough's 335-yard circuit at Cleveland Park for their first league encounter on Thursday 10 April. It was an inauspicious start for the Bulldogs, however, as they went down to a heavy 61-23 loss, as if to emphasise the lack of a quality heat leader. No fewer than five members of the awesome home side completed the meeting with double figures, namely Frank Hodgson (12), Jack Hodgson (10), Wilf Plant (10), Geoff Godwin (10) and Kid Curtis (10). Meanwhile, offering something of a token resistance to the onslaught from the Bears, both Billy Hole and Frank Evans managed to net just 6 points apiece, while Mike Beddoe and Jack Mountford could only muster 4 each.

The following evening, the Bulldogs entertained Birmingham at Knowle in a challenge match that was witnessed by 12,000 speedway-starved supporters. In a closely fought contest, the homesters went down to a 57-49 defeat, despite both Jack Mountford and Mike Beddoe notching brilliant 15-point returns. Unfortunately, with the next riders in the scorechart only claiming 6-point tallies, Billy Hole and Frank Evans, Bristol were no match for the Brummies' all-round strength in depth. Still keen on helping the younger element along, the meeting was interspersed with three junior scratch races, featuring the likes of Bill Bundy, Charlie Bourdon, Graham Hole and Ken Monks.

Strangely, Birmingham were back at Bristol seven days later, on 18 April, for a National League match and, having been given a practice run the previous week, the Midlanders swept to a convincing victory by 49 points to 35. The Bulldogs were strengthened by the inclusion of Roger Wise and George Craig, who had missed the previous two matches, but the team was unfortunately beset with motor troubles throughout the evening. Another gate of 12,000 fans witnessed Eric Salmon crash out while leading heat four, and Mike Beddoe suffered motor problems when he led the way three races later. Beddoe was to prove a most unlucky man on the night, for he also crashed while leading heat ten. Billy Hole topped the Bristol scoring with just 7 points, while Birmingham were well served by

Bob Lovell (10), Tiger Hart (9) and Dick Tolley (9). In their programme notes, the promoters, in response to public demand, declared that they had decided the winning times would be announced for races. Quoting from the article, they went on to say, 'But you must remember that a successful flat-out race usually returns a bad time, whereas when a man gets ahead from the gate and has a solo, although the race loses its spectacularness, the time is invariably good.' Although heat times had not been given since the return of the sport to Knowle, the programme credited Jeff Lloyd with a track record of 66.0 seconds, set in 1946! The programme also gave a brief pen picture on Billy Hole, which stated that he was born in Bath and had begun grass-track and speedway racing in 1946. He was a motor engineer by trade but, during the Second World War, had served in the Air Force.

On 19 April, Bristol travelled up to the Midlands to once again face Birmingham at their 402-yard Alexander Stadium circuit in the Perry Barr district. As had been expected, the Bulldogs found the going tough, losing 53-31. Mike Beddoe collected two good race victories on his way to an impressive 10-point score, while Roger Wise tallied 7. Billy Hole was Bristol's only other race winner, but he could only manage a meagre 4-point total. Meanwhile, Stan Dell and Bob Lovell topped the Brummies' scoring with 12 points each. The meeting was marred by an accident to Birmingham rider and former Bulldog Roy Dook, who hit the safety fence when chasing Beddoe, suffering a broken arm in the process.

Next up, Bristol tackled Norwich in a home league match on 25 April and, in a much better team performance, they went down to a narrow 44-39 defeat. Indeed, the Bulldogs were just 3 points in arrears after heat twelve, only for the Stars to strike a 5-1 courtesy of Paddy Mills and Geoff Revett in the very next race to guarantee victory. Before an 11,000-strong audience, Bristol's plucky display was headed by a 9-point return from Billy Hole. Norwich, meanwhile, boasted two men in double figures, with Bert Spencer notching 11 points while Ted Bravery totalled 10. It was a feast of racing for those present, with a total of twenty-three races on the programme, including a match-race challenge between Les Wotton and Malcolm Craven. This saw Wotton produce a late burst to take the opening race, before Craven pulled up in the second with motor trouble. This made the third race academic, thus reducing the entertainment to twenty-two heats! Also on the programme were a series of senior scratch races featuring Alf Kaines, who had ridden at Southampton prior to the outbreak of the Second World War. The Bristol management were giving him a trial, but he unfortunately failed to impress and wasn't signed on. While on the subject of possible signings, the promoters were investigating several avenues and were still looking at the possibility of signing an Australian. They were prepared to pay the return travel fares involved, but were unable to get an assurance from the Control Board that any such riders would actually be allocated to Bristol. Mike Beddoe was the rider under scrutiny in the match programme, his pen portrait revealing that he was born in Bolton on 23 May 1923. He purchased his first bike for 30s at the age of thirteen and had initially ridden in trials and scrambles in 1940, but it wasn't until 1946 that he made his debut on the grass-track scene and capped his first season by winning the Hereford Trophy. During the Second World War he had worked at the Bristol Aeroplane Company and joined the ARP Dispatch Riders' Service.

The Bulldogs completed the first month of the season with the return fixture against Norwich at The Firs Stadium on 26 April. The home side easily won the match by 58 points to 26, with Bristol being described as 'all at sea' in the report that subsequently appeared in *Speedway News*. In netting 12 points apiece, Bert Spencer and Ted Bravery topped the Stars' scoring, while the leading Bulldog was Mike Beddoe on the 7-point mark.

On 2 May, it was the turn of Middlesbrough to visit Knowle on league business and there was success at last for the Bulldogs with a 47-35 victory. The Bears had numerous problems though, with only one of their reserves actually making it to the track, while Wilf Plant was disqualified after winning heat eleven because his wheels had crossed the white line. However, it was a night for the Bulldogs and they rode out of their skins to defeat the 1946 Second Division Champions with their most inspired performance of the year thus far. With some fine riding, Eric Salmon grabbed 9 points to head Bristol's scoring, while brothers Frank and Jack Hodgson also notched 9 apiece for the visitors.

The ever-popular Jeff Lloyd was back at Knowle for the meeting *v.* Middlesbrough, riding in a special match race against brother Wally. Jeff had made many visits to Bristol during the winter, attending social functions organised by the supporters' club, but this was his first track appearance since the end of the 1946 season. His hopes of a winning return were scuppered though when his sibling took victory in the fast time of 69.2 seconds. The two brothers went on to race in a couple of four-man challenge races, which also included Frank and Jack Hodgson, with Wally winning the first and Jeff taking the flag in the second. Jack Mountford was the rider under the spotlight in the programme, which stated that he had only made his track debut in a trial at Bristol on 22 July the previous year. The article also mentioned that he was happily married to a keen Bulldogs' supporter and lived in a bungalow close to the track.

The Bristol riders then faced a heavy northern schedule that featured three meetings in five days at Wigan, Newcastle and Glasgow. After the euphoria of their first win of the season, the Bulldogs quickly returned to earth with a thud, suffering successive heavy defeats. At Wigan's Poolstock Stadium on 3 May, the homesters won nine of the fourteen heats on their way to a 49-35 victory, with Jack Gordon's 10 points leading the way. With a maximum 12 points, Billy Hole out-scored Gordon and was the main man of the meeting, although he fought a one-man battle with no real support from his colleagues on the tight 321-yard circuit. It was later revealed that Hole had buckled his bike in a crash during the home victory over Middlesbrough, and had worked all night with brother-in-law and teammate Eric Salmon in order to get it fixed before rushing up to Wigan. Two nights later, Newcastle defeated the Bulldogs by 50 points to 34, and it was no surprise to see Jeff Lloyd heading the Diamonds' scorechart with a 12-point haul. On 7 May, the third match of an arduous tour took the Bristol boys up to the White City Stadium in Glasgow, where they lost 48-36 in what was their best performance of the tour. Will Lowther (12) was the Tigers' best man, while 10 points apiece from Mike Beddoe and Jack Mountford was very encouraging indeed for the Bulldogs. Looking briefly at the facts and figures from the five-day excursion, both Beddoe and Hole yielded totals of 24 points, while Jack Mountford tallied 17.

All hopes of Bristol signing Jeff Lloyd evaporated with the news that he had opted to join a London track. After much negotiation, with speculation variously linking Lloyd with Wembley, Wimbledon and Harringay, he eventually joined New Cross after some gentle persuasion from promoter Cecil Smith. The deal to sign Lloyd involved a £1,000 transfer fee, plus the release of 'White Ghost' Ken Le Breton from New Cross to replace him at Newcastle. Interestingly, Lloyd was entitled to a cut of the transfer fee, amounting to 10 per cent of the agreed fee, along with another 2.5 per cent for each year he rode with Newcastle. There was some activity on the transfer market involving Bristol, however, with the news that Reg Witcomb had travelled to West Ham and successfully secured the services of Cyril Anderson.

Wigan were the next visitors to Knowle on 9 May but, in front of 12,000 spectators, the Bulldogs suffered no end of misfortune, going down to a 43-37 defeat. Jack Mountford was top man for Bristol with 11 points, while Dick Geary finished on top of the Warriors' pile, also with 11. The Wigan side included a couple of riders who were familiar to the Bristol public, namely Percy Brine and Reg Lambourne. In their programme notes, Messrs Witcomb and Steel revealed that Johnnie Hoskins had offered them Wal Morton but, as the rider was on the injured list at the time with a broken leg, they were hanging fire before making a definite decision about signing him. Eric Salmon was the latest rider to be featured in the programme, which revealed that he began grass-track racing in 1938 but gave up at the start of the Second World War to join the RAF, serving in England, France and Germany. Salmon subsequently began riding on the cinders during the latter part of 1946, and had continued to practise during the winter with Tiger Stevenson's boys. He lived in Bath and was a motor engineer by trade, being in business with fellow Bulldog Billy Hole, whose sister he was married to.

Glasgow appeared at Bristol a week later on 16 May, and it was a night when the Bulldogs silenced their critics with a staggering 57.5-26.5 victory. Indeed, they provided the race winner on ten occasions and claimed six maximum heat advantages along the way. The meeting also included a dead-heat in the thirteenth race, when Mike Beddoe and Bert Shearer couldn't be separated as they flashed across the line in unison. Eric Salmon, Billy Hole and Jack Mountford all weighed in with 9 points each for the Bulldogs, while the under-fire Tigers were headed by 9 from Will Lowther. Having received approval from the Control Board, thirty-three-year-old Cyril Anderson appeared in the Bristol line-up, but a 5-point return was somewhat disappointing. The shine was taken off the Bulldogs' victory in the second half when Beddoe came off and suffered a broken collarbone, which was to rule him out of action for a month. In the 'What's What' feature in the programme, the promoters revealed they had sent a letter to Glasgow's Ian Hoskins stating that they wished to accept the offer of signing Wal Morton, provided the speedster was passed fit to ride by the medical officer within six weeks. George Craig's pen picture was also included in the programme, revealing that he was born in south-east London on 6 June 1915. He had commenced motorcycling at the age of fifteen and, in August 1938, he witnessed his first speedway meeting at Dagenham's Ripple Road venue. Craig was immediately attracted to the sport and had trials at New Cross, as a result of which he joined Bristol in 1939. His enthusiasm was unbounded and when anyone endeavoured to get him to use a little more discretion, thus avoiding so many falls, his reply was, 'If a bloke's in front of me, my job is to beat him if I can and not watch his back wheel for four laps.' Prior to becoming a full-time rider, Craig had apparently tried his hand at most things, including being an electric welder, timber humper at the docks and a deck hand on a tramp steamer. Married at the beginning of the 1947 season, he had a house at Catford and travelled to Bristol every week for race meetings.

On 22 May the Bristol men, minus Mike Beddoe, made the journey up to Sheffield for their first British Speedway Cup tie, but it wasn't a pleasant experience as they went down to a huge 76-20 defeat. It is interesting to note that, unlike league matches, 3 points were awarded for a win in this competition. Tommy Allott weighed in with 12 points for the Tigers, receiving solid support from Len Williams (11), Jack Bibby (11) Jack White (10) and Tommy Bateman (10). Meanwhile, with a measly 5 points, Cyril Quick was the best Bulldog on show, while Cyril Anderson scored 4. To make matters worse for Bristol, Billy Hole was unfortunate enough to dislocate his shoulder in a track spill and, although it slipped back into place as the St John Ambulance men were removing his leathers, he was advised to stay for treatment at the local hospital.

Sheffield made the trip to Bristol for the return match the following evening, when Billy Hole was forced to watch the proceedings from the pits with his arm in a sling. Already without Mike Beddoe and now minus their inspirational skipper, the Bulldogs stood little chance, but they rallied and only went down to a narrow 50-44 loss, which was outstanding under the circumstances. Bristol's cause was helped when Sheffield's Stan Williams came crashing down in the opening heat and was subsequently rushed off to hospital, ironically with a dislocated shoulder. Despite a nasty accident the previous night at Owlerton, Jack Mountford heroically rode to 10 points, giving great support to Cyril Quick, who produced his best performance thus far in collecting 12 points. The visitors also had two riders in double figures, with Bruce Semmens notching a round dozen, while ex-Bulldog Jack Bibby grabbed 10. Quick continued to thrill the 10,000 gate in the second half, roaring to victory over Tommy Bateman and Semmens in the Senior Scratch final. It was certainly Quick's night, as he was also the featured rider in the programme! The article revealed that he was a native of Taunton in Somerset and was born in January 1919. He had begun grass-track racing in 1937 and had met with considerable success until joining the forces at the outbreak of the Second World War. Quick enjoyed his first taste of speedway at one of the Monday night practice sessions at Knowle in 1946, and continued to train as a pupil in Tiger Stevenson's school. A poor engine had hampered his early-season form in 1947, but the 12-point tally against Sheffield suggested it was only a matter of time before he became a top-line rider. A mechanic by trade, when not attending to his bike he could be found working at a local garage.

In a welcome break from the cut and thrust of league and cup competition, a side billed as Bristol and West Ham took on New Cross at Knowle on 26 May in a challenge match. The homesters were bolstered by the presence of top Hammers Eric Chitty and Malcolm Craven, while they also included Middlesbrough ace Frank Hodgson. Turning to their opponents, the all-star New Cross side was made up as follows: 1. Bill Longley, 2. Frank Lawrence, 3. Jeff Lloyd, 4. Geoff Pymar, 5. Eric French, 6. Mick Mitchell, 7. Ray Moore, 8. Jack Hodgson. The thought of seeing so many leading riders certainly appealed to the public, with 16,000 folk packed into the stadium. However, in the face of such high-quality opposition, it wasn't a shock when the home composite side went down to a 64-44 defeat. The three guests performed well, with Eric Chitty recording 14 points, Frank Hodgson 11 and Malcolm Craven 8. Meanwhile for the Rangers, Bill Longley piled up 15 points and Geoff Pymar yielded 12. The programme advertised goodies that were on sale in the supporters' kiosk including rosettes (1s 9d), photographs (1s), badges (1s 6d), badge bars (6d) and *Bristol Evening World Speedway Annuals* (1s).

There was further transfer speculation in *Speedway News*, which stated that Bristol had reached an agreement to sign Jack Cooley from West Ham. However, just two days after arranging the deal, Cooley damaged his shoulder when appearing for the Hammers against Belle Vue.

Although he was likely to be out of action for a while, the transfer was still expected to go through when the rider regained full fitness.

Bringing the curtain down on the month, the Bulldogs again entertained Glasgow in a British Speedway Cup match on 30 May. Incredibly, this was the Tigers' second trip down to Knowle in a fortnight and, as had happened the first time, Bristol again ran out convincing winners by 59 points to 37. The Bulldogs were still without Mike Beddoe, but Billy Hole made a welcome return to the saddle, scoring 7 points. In a powerful team performance, they were well served by Jack Mountford (12), Cyril Quick (10), Eric Salmon (9), Roger Wise (9) and George Craig (8), while Will Lowther topped the Glasgow scorechart on 11. The performance of Wise was all the more remarkable, as he was riding with a broken bone in his wrist following a crash in his last outing against Sheffield seven days previously at Knowle. Bristol had hoped to unveil Frank Lawrence as their new signing for this match but, although the rider was in attendance, he wasn't permitted to participate as all the necessary paperwork had not been completed.

It was the turn of Roger Wise to go under the spotlight in the programme for the match *v.* Glasgow and this revealed that he had graduated from club trials and scrambles to grass-track racing in 1935, becoming Midland Centre Champion in 1936 and Wessex Champion in 1939. In 1946, Wise won the prestigious International Grass-track Championship at Bervier in Belgium. He also took his first rides on the cinders during 1946 and was transferred from West Ham to Bristol upon the commencement of racing at Knowle Stadium. He was in business with his brother Ken, running a bakers and confectioners in his home town.

On 6 June, the Knowle raceway hosted a qualifying round of the British Riders' Championship, which featured a star-studded cast. Among those on show were Bert Spencer, Tommy Bateman, Bernard 'Bat' Byrnes, Dick Geary, Stan Dell, Paddy Mills and Kid Curtis. A brilliant evening's racing included Spencer winning heat six in the fastest time of the season – 67.4 seconds. Meanwhile, five superlative victories saw Curtis come out on top, with Geary finishing as runner-up on 14 points. Bateman claimed third position courtesy of 13 points, while the best of the local contingent was Jack Mountford, who notched 10 points to finish in fourth spot. The Bristol rider could have finished even higher though, since his double-figure tally was achieved despite encountering a mechanical problem in his very first ride. First prize for the event was a cool £50, which was a lot of money at the time to say the least. Full result: Curtis 15; Geary 14; Bateman 13; Mountford 10; Billy Hole 9; Roger Wise 9; Don Houghton 8; Spencer 7; Mills 7; Eric Salmon 7; Dell 6; Cyril Quick 6; Doug McLachlan 5; Byrnes 2; Frank Evans 2; Laurie Packer 0. The promoters' programme notes mentioned that new turnstiles would be installed in time for the following week's meeting in an effort to cut down on some of the queueing that supporters had to endure. The management duo also brought to everyone's attention a letter from a supporter suggesting that a brand new Excelsior speedway machine should be bought out of the funds of the supporters' club. The idea was that the bike could be used by a member of the team, with Frank Evans being the writer's suggestion. This was because Evans had always tried hard, but often been hampered by the poor standard of his equipment. The promoters thought this was a sound idea, but asked for public opinion on whether or not to spend the funds in this manner and, if so, which rider ought to benefit?

It was back to team business on 7 June as Bristol made the journey up to Wigan for a National Trophy tie. After conceding successive 5-1s in the opening two heats, the Bulldogs slumped to a heavy 73-34 defeat. A crowd of 7,000 spectators witnessed the one-sided affair, which featured a nasty accident involving George Craig in heat seven, when he overcooked a bend and was thrown heavily, with his machine landing on top of him. The race was immediately stopped by the ACU steward, with Craig being subsequently carried from the circuit having suffered a head injury. Amazingly, he reappeared for heat eleven with his head bandaged but, after looking far from steady, he eventually careered off the track and pulled up. The Warriors' scoring was led by Jack Gordon, Percy Brine and Dick Geary, who each weighed in with 14 points, while Roger Wise's score of 11 was sufficient to top the Bristol scoring on a disappointing night.

The return National Trophy encounter was staged at Knowle on 13 June and, although Bristol raced to a 62-45 victory, they headed out of the competition, losing by 22 points on aggregate. The match saw Jack Cooley make his debut appearance for the Bulldogs after recovering from his shoulder injury and he duly won his first race before finishing the night with 5 points to his name. A masterly 16 points saw Roger Wise finish the evening as the best Bulldog, while Dick Geary also plundered a 16-point haul for the visitors. In the 'What's What' feature, Messrs Witcomb and Steel mentioned that they had received numerous letters on the subject of purchasing a machine, and the correspondents were unanimous in agreeing that it should be donated to Frank Evans. Given such a response, they had taken swift action to purchase a steed and hoped it would arrive in time for that evening's meeting, even though Evans was only programmed in the junior scratch event!

A break of seven days followed before Norwich returned to Bristol for a British Speedway Cup match. The Bulldogs put on a marvellous show for the 10,000 spectators, running out victors on the night by 50 points to 44. The homesters were boosted by the inclusion of Mike Beddoe, who notched 7 points in a steady if unspectacular return to track action. Roger Wise led the way with a 12-point tally, while Jack Mountford totalled 10. Paddy Mills picked up 14 points for the Stars but, with Bert Spencer missing, they lacked the necessary strength required to win the fixture. In the match programme, it was explained that the promoters had made tentative offers for the services of Odsal rider Fred Tuck. After the previous problems encountered when trying to sign riders, it was little surprise that the promoters doubted that they would be lucky enough to get their man, since Odsal promoter Johnnie Hoskins considered Tuck too valuable a member of his side. In spite of their lack of confidence, the move did go through and the incoming rider was to prove extremely popular with the Bristol fans. The programme also included a touching letter from Frank Evans, thanking those responsible for their generosity in supplying him with a brand new machine.

It was back to The Firs for the return British Speedway Cup tie v. Norwich on 21 June, when the Bristol boys capitulated, eventually going down to a 73-23 defeat. Bert Spencer was back for the Stars, reeling off five superb wins, with Sid Hipperson (11), Phil Clarke (11) and Roy Duke (10) offering great support. Meanwhile, for the battered Bulldogs, Mike Beddoe was the top scorer with just 6 points. It has to be said, however, that, due to call-ups for the British Riders' Championship round at Birmingham, the Bulldogs were without the services of key riders Billy Hole, Jack Mountford and Cyril Anderson.

Bristol were back in league action with a visit to Sheffield on 26 June but, despite showing an improvement on their previous visit to

Owlerton in May, they still slumped to a 60-24 reverse. For the rampant Tigers, both Jack Bibby and Bruce Semmens plundered 12-point maximums, while Jack White supplied superb backing with 11. As he had done at Norwich, Mike Beddoe again headed the Bristol scoring, albeit again with only 6 points.

One night later, Bristol entertained Sheffield at Knowle Stadium, gaining a rapid revenge with a brilliant 47-36 success. It was a wonderful meeting for the 11,000 supporters in attendance, with a solid team effort providing the basis for victory. Jack Mountford recorded 10 points to head the Bristol scoring, with Mike Beddoe grabbing 8. An item of interest from the programme was the introduction of a beauty contest to discover a Bristol Speedway Queen. Heats would be held on Friday nights in accordance with the number of entries, culminating in a grand final. The judges would be the Bristol riders themselves, with the eventual winner receiving a monumental £75 prize. In the meantime, the supporters' club were busy organising trips, including one to Exeter Speedway for a fare of 10s, one to Birmingham Speedway (fare 12s 6d), and one to a grass-track event at Farleigh Castle (fare 4s 6d).

On 4 July, a Best Pairs meeting was staged at Knowle and this gave Fred Tuck the ideal platform, following his transfer from Bradford. A gate of 9,000 witnessed a superb performance from the lanky new Bulldog as he took to the circuit superbly. Starting with a win in his opening ride, Tuck went on to record 13 points from five starts and, with partner Jack Moutford scoring 10, the duo were worthy winners of the event. Second place went to Eric Salmon and Billy Hole, while Mike Beddoe and Roger Wise were third. Full result: Tuck (13) and Mountford (10) 23; Salmon (12) and Hole (10) 22; Wise (8) and Beddoe (7) 15; Norman Evans (11) and Bonny Waddell (1) 12; Jack Hodgson (7) and Herbie King (4) 11; Roy Dook (4) and Stan Dell (3) 7. The meeting also included several other events, including an attempt by Jeff Lloyd on the one-lap (flying start) track record, in which he equalled the long-standing best time of 15.8 seconds, which had been clocked by both Jack and Cordy Milne before the Second World War. Lloyd's New Cross teammate Geoff Pymar made an attempt on the two-lap record, but his time of 32.8 seconds was 0.8 of a second outside Cordy Milne's previous best for the distance. Lloyd and Pymar also took part in a match-race series, and it was Lloyd who comfortably took the first two races, rendering the third heat unnecessary.

It was back to serious league business at Newcastle on 7 July, when the Bulldogs struggled to cope with the tricky 359-yard Brough Park circuit, slipping to a 53-31 defeat. The Bristol men could only produce three race winners on the night, one of those being Mike Beddoe's shock victory in heat two, when he headed Wilf Jay from start to finish. That was to be Jay's only dropped point of the evening on his way to 11 points, as he supplied solid support for maximum man Alec Grant (12), while Doug McLachlan also tallied 11 for the rampant Diamonds. Making his debut for Bristol, Fred Tuck topped the scoring with a steady 8 points, his total including a race win in heat twelve.

The match at Newcastle was the first part of a mini-tour, which concluded two nights later at Glasgow. It was a better showing from the Bulldogs, although they still went down to a 48-36 defeat at the well-appointed White City Stadium. 'Friar' Tuck, as he was referred to in the *Speedway News* match report, won three heats on his way to a superb 11-point tally, and he received good support from Mike Beddoe, who weighed in with 8. Meanwhile, the so-called 'Terrible Twins' headed the Tigers' scoring, with Will Lowther scorching to a four-ride maximum and Joe Crowther grabbing 10 points.

At Knowle on 11 July, the Bulldogs produced a powerhouse performance to thrash Birmingham by 62 points to 33 in a British Speedway Cup match. This was Bristol's most convincing performance of the season thus far and the Brummies simply didn't know what had hit them as they were sent packing back to Perry Barr. Fred Tuck's 12 points led the way, while Eric Salmon notched 11 in a superb personal display. To emphasise the Bulldogs' dominance of the match, not one Birmingham rider reached double figures, Bob Lovell being the best visitor with 9 points.

Bristol travelled up to Birmingham for the return match the following night buoyed by their success, but they found the Brummies' heat leaders determined to exact revenge. Indeed, Stan Dell rattled up 14 points, while Tiger Hart and the fit-again Roy Dook each scored 12 as the homesters eased to a 59-37 success. The only resistance Bristol could offer came from Fred Tuck (8) and Mike Beddoe (7), with the rest of the side mainly picking up the odd point on the receiving end of maximum heat advantages from the Birmingham boys. Billy Hole had an alarming crash with Tiger Hart during the proceedings and, although he was knocked unconscious at the time, he was back practising at Knowle the following Tuesday, thankfully none the worse for wear.

The supporters' club had made arrangements for five coaches to travel up to Birmingham but, in the event, only two were made available after one coach company gave just three days' notice that they were unable to provide the service. Miss Pomphrey, secretary of the supporters' club, spent hours on the telephone trying to arrange alternative transport, with some 120 fans eventually making the trip by train. The railway people were very understanding and allowed the fans to travel for 15s 8d each, rather than the usual charge of £1. However, the 15s 8d train fare was actually 3s 2d more than the coach fare, and it was decided that this was unfair to those fans that had to make the journey by rail through no fault of their own. All the travelling Bristol fans were therefore charged 12s 6d, with the train fares being made up from the supporters' club fund.

Back at Knowle Stadium on 18 July, Bristol entertained Wigan in another Speedway Cup encounter and eventually ran out 52-44 victors in a closely fought match. After their indifferent start to the season, this was the Bulldogs' sixth home win on the trot and was met with great approval by a healthy 12,000 gate. Mike Beddoe could only return a 5-point score from the match, having received a nasty wrench to his left shoulder in one of his rides. Meanwhile, with 14 points, Eric Salmon gave his best-ever display, dropping just a single point to Warriors' captain Jack Gordon in heat twelve. Gordon and Percy Brine were Wigan's most productive riders on the night, each notching 11 points. Talking of Brine, who was the brother of Wimbledon's rising star Cyril, the programme revealed that, away from the track, he was a stuntman, doubling for actors in car and motorcycle pile-ups. Percy and Wigan teammate Dick Geary were actually brothers-in-law and lived in the same house as Cyril, close to the film studios in Elstree. While on the subject of the film industry, part of the meeting against Wigan was attended by Stan Laurel and Oliver Hardy, who also brought their wives along and were introduced to the crowd from the centre green during the interval. The appearance of the legendary comedy duo could be regarded as a coup and was attributed to the efforts of hard-working press officer Bob Chapple. Briefly referring back to the meeting, prior to heat one, Billy Hole set a new one-lap (clutch start) record, when clocked at 18.4 seconds. Following that, Fred Tuck blitzed around the circuit in 32.0 seconds to equal Cordy Milne's best time over two laps (flying start). In the 'What's What' column, Reg Witcomb and Bob Steel stated: 'We are sorry that it has become quite obvious that Cyril Anderson, one of

174

the Bulldogs' acquisitions, will never settle down on such a small circuit as ours; therefore we have decided that it is only fair to both Cyril and the team that he should try his hand at another track. In consequence, we are arranging a transfer for Cyril to Norwich Speedway and wish him the best of luck with his new club.' The programme also included a full-page advert for a forthcoming grand boxing tournament, promoted by Bristol Speedway Ltd, which was to be held on Monday 21 July. The main event in the six-bout programme would see the featherweight Champion of Wales, Syd Worgan, come face-to-face with Jimmy Jury from Bournemouth. Other contests of intrigue included a heavyweight bout between Nick Fisher and Tommy Paddock, while Bristol's Young MacAvoy was set to tackle Bath's Len Dyer in a lightweight contest. Admission prices for the event ranged from a mere 2s 6d (standing) to £1 1s for the best seats in the house.

On 19 July, the Bulldogs, minus Mike Beddoe, made the trip to Lancashire for the return match v. Wigan. Heavy rain had fallen in the area during the afternoon and this obviously affected the attendance, with only 5,000 hardy folk braving the conditions. Having already appeared at the 321-yard circuit on two previous occasions earlier in the season, the Bulldogs acquitted themselves well, keeping the scores close until a disastrous heat eleven, when both Jack Mountford and Jack Cooley crashed out. Despite that, the Bristol boys still topped 40 points for the first time on their travels, finally going down 52-42. Dick Geary (14) and Jack Gordon (12) led the Warriors to victory, while Fred Tuck (13) and Roger Wise (10) doggedly kept Bristol in the hunt throughout.

The final track action of the month saw the seventeenth meeting of the year at Knowle, with Sheffield returning for their second National League visit on 25 July. It was actually Sheffield's third trip down, as they had also appeared at Bristol for a British Speedway Cup match on 23 May. The Bulldogs were severely handicapped after Fred Tuck's car had broken down on his journey from London. With Mike Beddoe also missing, the remaining Bristol lads showed great determination to win the match by 46 points to 38. There was no outstanding figure on the night, with the scorechart jointly headed by Jack Mountford and Roger Wise on 9 points apiece. For the Tigers, Tommy Bateman (12) and Jack Bibby (11) recorded a total of 23 points to emphasise a lack of depth in their line-up although, to be fair, they were without Jack White,

Bruce Semmens and Stan Williams. In their programme notes, Messrs Witcomb and Steel revealed an added attraction to the beauty competition, with local hair salon 'Barbara's' offering a free permanent wave to the winner and the two runners-up in the contest!

Bristol made a quick start to August, with a home match against Newcastle in the British Speedway Cup on the first day of the month. Extending their ever-impressive home run of winning performances, they collected another victory by 53 points to 42. Despite still missing Mike Beddoe, the remaining Bulldogs rallied, with Eric Salmon (13) and Billy Hole (10) being particularly impressive. Opposing skipper Norman Evans was the only visitor to reach double figures in scoring 11 points, while Doug McLachlan finished on 9. Meanwhile, Ken Le Breton had a very disappointing night for the Diamonds, scoring just 3 points. In the race-day programme, the always interesting 'What's What' page kicked off with this opening volley: 'First of all, we would like to call upon all young boys who pop around of an evening, and if the window of Jean's (Miss Pomphrey) office is open and everything in their favour, beg, borrow or steal the photograph of their favourite rider. We have now moved the photos along so that they are out of reach until you grow up, by which time we are quite certain you will be able to afford a shilling to purchase same.'

An extra home meeting was slotted in three days later on the Bank Holiday Monday, 4 August, when Bristol entertained 'The Rest'. The visiting composite side included the likes of Bob Lovell (Birmingham), Mick Mitchell (New Cross), Roy Dook (Birmingham) and Norman Lindsay (Glasgow), but the Bulldogs were undaunted by the opposition, storming to a 74-33 success. Eric Salmon blasted his way to 17 points, receiving great support from Fred Tuck (16), Jack Mountford (10) and Billy Hole (10). There was further good news for Bristol, with Mike Beddoe making a return to the cinders and, although understandably tentative, he still recorded a tally of 6 points. Lindsay was the pick of the visitors, notching 10 points, while Dook scored 8. Prior to the match, Roger Wise set a new best time for the one-lap (clutch start) record when recording 18.2 seconds. Jack Mountford then had a go at the two-lap (flying start) record, but his time of 32.8 seconds was outside the best time for the distance shared by Cordy Milne and Fred Tuck. Although not appearing in the main match, Jack Cooley was involved in a junior scratch race, but fell awkwardly, spraining his shoulder. Unfortunately he aggravated the injury that had bothered him prior to linking with Bristol and this would mean another lengthy spell on the sidelines.

The speedway supporters of Bristol were certainly getting plenty of racing, as the third meeting in eight days was held at Knowle Stadium on 8 August, with the visit of Norwich for a league encounter and the Bulldogs went to town, completely overwhelming the Stars by 62 points to 22. Billy Hole went through the card unbeaten with a 12-point maximum, while Fred Tuck further endeared himself to the fans with a hard-earned tally of 11. Phil Clarke was the best performer for the beleaguered visitors, but he was often out-ridden and could only muster a total of 7 points.

The Bulldogs were back on the road the following day, travelling east for the return league fixture v. Norwich. Having ridden four successive home matches at the tight 290-yard Knowle circuit, the Bristol boys had great difficulty in getting to grips with the pacy 425-yard Firs Stadium raceway and it was no surprise that they crashed to a 55-29 defeat. The homesters featured three men in double figures, namely Paddy Mills (11), Ted Bravery (11) and Phil Clarke (10), while Fred Tuck's 8 points were enough to top the Bristol score grid.

At their Knowle headquarters on 15 August, the Bulldogs recorded an eleventh successive home win, convincingly beating Glasgow 57-27 in a Second Division match. Both Fred Tuck and Eric Salmon romped to 12-point maximums, while Mike Beddoe proved he was back on-song with a well-taken 10 points. A Bristol rider crossed the line ahead in no fewer than thirteen of the heats, with Will Lowther providing the Scottish side's only race win on his way to 8 points. The Bristol management introduced a new interval attraction at the meeting, with a boxing exhibition between Carl Bradbury of Bristol and Roy Coles of Weston-super-Mare. However, the bout only lasted for a few seconds, due to a first-round knock-out. Hurried arrangements had to be made for another contest, which fortunately lasted the distance!

Three days' rest was followed by another mini northern tour that took in Newcastle and Glasgow in British Speedway Cup matches. First stop was Brough Park on 18 August, when the Bulldogs performed admirably before going down 54-42, with Wilf Jay (12), Alec Grant (11) and Norman Evans (10) leading the Diamonds' scoring. Meanwhile, Fred Tuck continued his impressive run of form, yielding 10 points for the battling Bristol boys. At Glasgow two nights later, the Bulldogs went down by an identical score in another fighting show. Led by Will Lowther (14) and Bat Byrnes (12), the Tigers only pulled away during the last five heats of the match. For Bristol, Fred Tuck and Mike Beddoe plugged away throughout, each netting 12 points for their efforts.

Sad news was reported in the *Speedway News* dated 21 August, when Bristol supporters learned of the tragic death of Cyril Anderson. The Bexley Heath-born rider had been participating in a Best Pairs meeting at Norwich on 16 August and had over-slid in heat five, with two closely following riders having no chance of avoiding the subsequent pile-up. Regrettably, Anderson died almost instantaneously, having suffered a broken neck. The irony was that he had only come into the race as a reserve replacement for Wilf Plant, who had been unable to get his machine started.

Back at Knowle on 22 August, Newcastle paid their second visit of the month, this time for a National League encounter. Remarkably showing little tiredness from all their travelling, the Bristol riders ripped into the Diamonds and amassed a huge 62-22 victory in front of 12,500 cheering spectators. Indeed, the Bulldogs were rampant, winning thirteen of the fourteen races and carding nine maximum advantages. Fred Tuck walloped home a four-ride maximum, receiving great backing from Mike Beddoe, who scampered to 11 points. Meanwhile, Newcastle skipper Norman Evans provided his side's only race winner in heat twelve, on his way to a 7-point total. Phyllis McQuillen, manageress at Brough Park was heard to remark: 'My word, it makes a difference riding away from home; these Bristol boys can certainly move on their own track.' At the meeting, a collection was organised for the Cyril Anderson Memorial Fund and this eventually realised a total of £203, which was subsequently passed on to Mrs Anderson and her two children. During the interval, the final of the beauty contest was held, with Miss Freda Dowson of St Anne's Park, Bristol emerging as the winner. It had been hoped to have Cary Grant at the stadium in order to present the prizes, but the actor apologised most profusely for his absence, as he had to be in Paris for another engagement. Standing in to present the prizes, however, was Edgar Allen, the director of the Knowle Stadium.

On 28 August, another excursion took Bristol up to Cleveland Park for a league meeting against table-topping Middlesbrough. The match started well enough for the Bulldogs, with Fred Tuck defeating the

Hodgson brothers in the opening heat, but things quickly deteriorated thereafter and they ended up suffering a 59-25 mauling. For the victors, Wilf Plant got the lot (12) and Kid Curtis scored 10 points, while Fred Tuck was Bristol's best, finishing on the 6-point mark. After the match it was a mad dash down to Bristol, as both teams were again in opposition the following evening at Knowle. The Bears certainly proved why they were the best side in the Second Division, as they won the match 45-38, becoming the first side to win at Bristol since 26 May, when New Cross had triumphed in a challenge match. A record league crowd of 14,000 was in attendance and saw the Bulldogs throw all they had at their opponents, but it was simply not to be. Curtis registered an unbeaten 12 points for the flying visitors, with Plant notching 10, while Mike Beddoe's tally of 10 was sufficient to make him the top Bulldog of the evening. Reg Witcomb was a very disappointed man for, not only did Bristol lose the match, he was also ill in bed and missed his first home match of the year as a result.

A big forthcoming attraction was arranged for 12 September, with First Division West Ham having accepted an invitation to race at Knowle in a challenge match. Despite their defeat at the hands of Middlesbrough, Bristol were confident of beating the Hammers, with co-promoter Bob Steel quoted as saying, 'Let 'em all come, we can beat the big boys on our own pitch.'

The Bristol lads were on their travels again on 4 September, when they journeyed up to Sheffield on league business. The home riders were right on the gas at their full-throttle 390-yard circuit and the Bulldogs were unable to mount a serious challenge, going down to a heavy 57-27 loss. Aside from heat four, which was won by Roger Wise, a member of the Sheffield side took the chequered flag in twelve of the first thirteen races. There was a shock for the homesters in the final heat though, when Fred Tuck sped away to win, beating Tommy Allott and Tommy Bateman, both of whom had taken victory in each of their previous three races. That left Allott on top of the Tigers' scorecard with 11 points, while Tuck totalled 7 to head the Bristol scoring.

Wigan were the visitors at Knowle the very next night, with a couple of league points up for grabs. Although the Bulldogs provided nine of the race winners, they were made to fight all the way for a 47-36 victory over a very determined Warriors outfit. Star man for the homesters was Billy Hole with 9 points, while Dick Geary was

Wigan's best, also with 9. The second half saw the track return of Jack Cooley, but this most unfortunate of riders was dogged by more bad luck in his comeback race and crashed, breaking a small bone in his foot. Before and during the interval, the St John's Ambulance Band played under the direction of Mr Yabsley and a collection was taken. The match programme contained the amazing statistic that, aside from injuries to riders during the season, the St John team had also attended to no fewer than 151 casualties among the crowd! Also in the programme, the supporters' club were offering tickets for the British Riders' Championship at Wembley on 11 September. Prices started at just 2s 6d and ranged all the way up to 21s for the prestigious event.

After much advance publicity, the night of 12 September arrived, when the mighty West Ham side were in town for a challenge match that was played out in front of a massive 16,000-strong crowd. The Hammers clearly meant business, fielding a full-strength side as follows: 1. Eric Chitty, 2. Aub Lawson, 3. Malcolm Craven, 4. Cliff Watson, 5. Tommy Croombs, 6. Bob Harrison, 7. Cliff Parkinson, 8. Danny King. Despite the awesome power contained in the visitors' line-up, the Bulldogs put in a spirited effort, finally going down 54-40. The undoubted highlights of the match were when Billy Hole defeated Canadian ace Eric Chitty in heat twelve, and a win by Eric Salmon over both Malcolm Craven and Chitty in heat sixteen. That was Craven's only loss on the way to a total of 14 points, with Salmon's tally of 11 leading the Bristol scoring.

A week later, on 19 September, Bristol completed their home fixtures in the British Speedway Cup, handsomely defeating Middlesbrough by 64 points to 32. This was some performance against the leading side in the Second Division, but the Bears simply had no answer to an on-song Bristol outfit. The 12,000 fans in attendance went wild with delight, roaring their heroes home throughout the match. On his way to a brilliant 14 points, Billy Hole lost out only to Wilf Plant in heat three, while Jack Mountford weighed in with a tally of 11. Frank Hodgson did his utmost to stem the tide and his 10-point return was the Bears' best on the night. The programme notes for the meeting revealed that 266 people had travelled from Bristol to Wembley for the British Riders' Championship on 11 September. A great time was had by all who witnessed legendary Belle Vue and England rider Jack Parker take victory in a run-off after finishing level on 14 points with Bill Kitchen. Also mentioned was the newly published *Speedway*

World Diary, containing twenty-four photographs, league tables and Test match details etc, which was available by post for a mere 4*s* 6*d*.

Rounding off the month, on 26 September, Newcastle paid their third visit to Knowle in an eight-week period. With league points at stake, a huge gate of 15,000 packed into the stadium to witness the Bulldogs triumph 51-32 in a thrill-packed encounter. Roger Wise was on top form, scoring 11 points, but in actual fact the only point he dropped was to teammate Eric Salmon in heat two, so technically he recorded a paid maximum, although such things went unrecognised in those days. For the Diamonds, the best performer was Doug McLachlan, whose efforts yielded 9 points. Meanwhile, Ken Le Breton again failed to get to grips with the tight track and only scored 2 points. An interval attraction saw the Royal Corps of Signals' trick cyclists go through their entertaining routine, having come over from their base in Northern Ireland. There were also some anti-aircraft guns displayed on the centre green in connection with a recruiting drive by the Territorial Army. Indeed, the inner green resembled a battlefield, with heavy lorries, trailers, motorcycle dispatch riders, artillery and gun crews all going through a brilliantly presented and slick demonstration.

The final month of a busy season began with Bristol's last match in the British Speedway Cup on 2 October. This entailed another long journey up to Middlesbrough, a track where the Bulldogs had twice previously been thrashed during the campaign. Despite putting in their best Cleveland Park performance of the year, the Bristol boys still went down to a heavy 61-35 reverse. Frank Hodgson and Wilf Plant topped the Bears' scoring with 12 points apiece, while Kid Curtis netted 10. Only Roger Wise (10) and Fred Tuck (9) offered any real challenge to the onslaught, with Eric Salmon's score restricted to 5 points due to a nasty knock on the ankle. The final table for the British Speedway Cup showed Sheffield in first position, with Middlesbrough occupying the runner-up slot. The Bulldogs had to be satisfied with sixth place, with Wigan finishing one position higher by virtue of a better race-points difference.

On 3 October, Knowle Stadium played host to an interesting affair that pitted Bristol against a composite Captains' and Vice-Captains' side made up from other teams in the Second Division. The 14,000 supporters in attendance yelled with excitement throughout the meeting, which was always close and eventually went down to a last-heat decider with the scores level at 45 points apiece. Frank Hodgson sped to victory in the final heat, but with Jack Mountford and Roger Wise packing the minor positions, Bristol secured a 48-48 draw. This really was some performance when you stop to take in the make-up of the opposition: 1. Norman Evans; 2. Tommy Allott; 3. Jack Gordon; 4. Dick Geary; 5. Frank Hodgson; 6. Stan Dell; 7. Roy Dook; 8. Norman Lindsay. For Bristol, Jack Mountford was a tower of strength with 12 points, while Roger Wise chipped in with a solid tally of 11. Although Eric Salmon only scored 4 points, the fact that he rode at all was amazing, considering the limp he was carrying after his smash at Middlesbrough the previous evening. Incredibly, Salmon then went on to win his heat in the second-half scratch race event, before going on to take the final ahead of fellow Bristol riders Fred Tuck, Jack Mountford and Cyril Quick. In the 'What's What' column, Reg Witcomb and Bob Steel were looking forward to the following week's match against Johnnie Hoskins' First Division Odsal (Bradford) side in a challenge. They went on to pose the question as to why they were arranging such stiff opposition for the Bulldogs to compete against? They answered this themselves by stating that if, as had been suggested, Bristol were to ride in the First Division in 1948, then they wished to gauge how their riders would measure up. On a completely different note, their piece closed with the following: 'Now to bring a little domestic matter to your attention. As you all know, the soap position is very crucial at the moment and we are unable to obtain an allocation for our boys. Some of you have been good enough to send along a tablet or two, and if there is any more about that you can spare, will you kindly hand it in to the speedway office so that it may be evenly distributed amongst the riders.'

So to the much-anticipated challenge match *v.* Odsal on 10 October, and one man who was particularly looking forward to the encounter was Fred Tuck, having joined Bristol from the Boomerangs earlier in the season. The meeting served up some fantastic racing and had a 12,000 audience on their toes for the duration. After three shared races, the Bulldogs took the lead in heat four, through maximum points from Jack Mountford and George Craig. Odsal hit back to draw level in heat nine, only for Bristol to immediately wallop in another 5-1, courtesy of Tuck and Mountford. The see-saw continued in heat eleven, thanks to another maximum for the visitors, which left the teams level at 33-33. A shared heat twelve was followed by a 3-0 to Odsal, when only Norman Price finished after George Craig, Eric Salmon and Ernie Price had all pulled up with motor problems. Heat fourteen was drawn before Cyril Quick and Craig secured a 5-1 to leave Bristol 44-43 ahead with just the final race remaining. The Bulldogs were on the cusp of a major victory as the riders were selected for the nominated heat sixteen, with Bristol electing Mountford and Roger Wise, while the Boomerangs chose Alec Statham to partner Price. It wasn't to be, however, as Statham took the flag from Mountford, while Price picked up the odd-point to secure a 47-46 victory for the visitors. With 10 points, Mountford was the leading Bulldog on the night, while Statham headed the Odsal figures on 14. In fact, Statham's only loss came at the hands of teammate Ron Mason in heat nine, so technically he recorded a paid maximum.

Birmingham were back in town for what was Bristol's final home league match of the campaign on 17 October. The Bulldogs signed off with a convincing win by 60 points to 24, with Fred Tuck romping to an undefeated 12 points, while Eric Salmon and Jack Mountford each plundered totals of 10. This was a dominant performance, emphasised by the fact that Stan Dell provided the beleaguered visitors with their only race winner in heat two, on his way to a 9-point tally. The second half of the meeting featured some new juniors who were each taking their introductory ride on the Knowle circuit, namely Dick Bradley, Bob Jones and Doug Lean. Also racing in the junior scratch event was a certain Stan 'Ginger' Nicholls, who would later go on and become the very first race winner at Swindon's opening meeting in 1949.

There was no rest for Bristol as they faced the long haul up to Wigan the following day in their penultimate Second Division match of the season. Somehow, the Bulldogs, who were struggling to avoid the wooden spoon, pulled off the shock of the season, winning 43-41. This was an amazing result, as they had lost each and every one of their previous twenty away matches in all competitions over the course of the campaign. To put the victory into context, Bristol were the first visitors to win at Poolstock Stadium since high-flying Middlesbrough had triumphed on 28 June. The vast majority of the 6,000 attendance watched in disbelief as Dick Geary (11) became the only home rider to reach double figures, while Bristol boasted two such scorers in Roger Wise (11) and Fred Tuck (10).

It was back to home cinders on 24 October for a star-studded Best Pairs event that featured each Bristol rider lining up alongside a top First Division ace. This saw Wimbledon's Lloyd 'Cowboy' Goffe making his one and only Knowle appearance of the season, while the other stars on show were brothers Jeff and Wally Lloyd (of New Cross and Belle Vue respectively), Eric French (New Cross), Jim Boyd (Belle Vue) and Les Wotton (Wimbledon). The prospect of seeing several high-fliers obviously whetted the appetite of the local fans, for an amazing gate of 20,000 was reported for the meeting. The spectacle was terrific, with the home lads faring well against their more renowned opponents. With a combined total of 22 points, Mike Beddoe formed a formidable partnership with Wotton as they swept all before them to take the title. On only one occasion did they fail to take maximum points from a race and that occurred in their first ride together (heat three), when Boyd took the flag ahead of Wotton, while Roger Wise hemmed Beddoe in at the rear. In a real festival night of action, a Junior Best Pairs event was also held and this saw Cyril Quick and Dick Bradley share top honours with Bill Clifton and Ginger Nicholls on combined totals of 11 points apiece. Full result: (senior event) Beddoe (11) and Wotton (11) 22; J. Lloyd (12) and Billy Hole (4) 16; Fred Tuck (8) and French (8) 16; Boyd (14) and Wise (1) 15; Jack Mountford (9) and Goffe (3) 12; Eric Salmon (5) and W. Lloyd (4) 9; (junior event) Quick (9) and Bradley (2) 11; Clifton (7) and Nicholls (4) 11; Bob Jones (6) and George Craig (1) 7; Graham Hole (5) and Johnny Hole (0) 5; Harry Hughes (reserve) 1.

Over the course of the season, the Bristol supporters had voted for their most valuable rider after each home meeting. The final result in this interesting contest revealed that Jack Mountford had come out at the head of the standings with a total of 32.5 points. The other scorers were: Billy Hole 19.5, Roger Wise 17, Eric Salmon 12.5, Fred Tuck 12, Mike Beddoe 10.5, Cyril Quick 3.5, George Craig 3 and Jack Cooley 3.

It was off to Birmingham for the last league match of the season at the Birchfield Harriers' plush Alexander Sports Stadium in Perry Barr on 25 October. Buoyed by their success at Wigan the previous week, the Bulldogs gave it everything before going down to a narrow 44-40 defeat. Stan Dell recorded 10 points and led the Brummies to victory with a last-heat win over Fred Tuck and Mike Beddoe. In totalling 11 points, it represented Tuck's only defeat of the night, while Beddoe gave great support, tallying 8. Both Tuck and Beddoe battled their way through to the Scratch Race final in the second half, with the latter going on to take a tremendous victory ahead of home riders Jimmy Wright and Geoff Bennett, while Tuck brought up the rear.

1947

The curtain came down on the season on 31 October, as Knowle staged its thirty-second meeting of the year. What a finish it was too, with the staging of the West of England Trophy. An attendance in excess of 12,000 witnessed sixteen of the finest Second Division men battle it out for the prestigious trophy and there was joy unbounded for the Bristol fans as Fred Tuck produced a masterly show to win all five of his rides and take the title. Middlesbrough's Frank Hodgson finished second on 14 points, having lost out to Tuck when they met in the all-important heat eleven. Full result: Tuck 15; Hodgson 14; Eric Salmon 11; Dick Geary 11; Mike Beddoe 9; Norman Evans 8; Jack Gordon 7; Cyril Quick 7; Jack Mountford 7; Roger Wise 7; Billy Hole 6; Will Lowther 6; Wilf Plant 5; Bill Clifton (reserve) 4; George Craig (reserve) 1; Tommy Allott 0. The final track action of the year saw a race for the 1947 Novices' Trophy, with victory going to Bob Jones ahead of Dick Bradley, Doug Lean and Ginger Nicholls. That was followed by the presentation of the trophies and community singing, led by the Bulldog Choir, directed by George Craig and Bob Chapple, with music by the Nolan Accordion Three.

A larger-than-usual programme was produced for the final meeting and the special edition allowed Bob Hatsell the extra space to review the season. The great friend of the sport went on to state: 'It's been another wonderful speedway year. Bigger crowds than ever, better riding and plenty of top-class cinders entertainment to keep the Bristol supporters on their toes. Two outstanding features of the season are: (1) the remarkable headway the Bulldogs made in the Second Division without starting the year with at least one well-seasoned star performer in the side; (2) the big attendances at the Bristol track, which have lasted throughout the season, and right through to the final meeting.' On the subject of gate figures, a grand total of some 370,000 people passed through the Knowle turnstiles for the thirty-two meetings, averaging over 11,560. As a matter of interest, the total attendance for speedway meetings throughout Britain in 1947 was a staggering 9,238,660.

Miss Jean Pomphrey revealed that membership of the supporters' club stood at 4,700 as the season drew to a close and all 1947 members would automatically remain so during 1948. This would also apply to anyone joining after the end of the season. In their final 'What's What' column, promoters Witcomb and Steel reviewed the year thus: 'We cast our minds back to the dark days of April when we lost our first six matches on the trot, three of them at home and three away. During this

185

period, many people said that, with a team of novices, we should never be able to hold our own, but on 2 May, they were disillusioned when we defeated Middlesbrough, the League Champions, inflicting their first defeat of the season.' The promotional duo went on to comment that the side's home record had been very good from that point onwards, although they conceded that away form had been poor. However, they were not unduly concerned about this due to the inexperience of their riders. That said, the riders had shown improved form virtually with each away match, culminating with the win at Wigan and the narrow loss at Birmingham. Witcomb and Steel concluded that away victories would be more frequent in the following season.

A last look at the season saw the Bulldogs occupying sixth position in the Second Division table, just 2 points ahead of Wigan and Glasgow; their victory at Wigan on 18 October making a huge difference to the final positions. Taking a look at the riders, Bristol had an astounding total of seven riders who each accumulated in excess of 200 points from all team matches. Jack Mountford headed the scoring with 325 points from forty-nine matches, while the other double-centurions finished in the following order, with their number of meetings shown in brackets: Mike Beddoe 296.5 (forty-one), Billy Hole 272 (forty-eight), Eric Salmon 266 (forty-nine), Roger Wise 262 (forty-four), Fred Tuck 246 (twenty-seven) and Cyril Quick 205 (fifty). Incidentally, Quick was the only rider to appear in a full quota of meetings (twenty-eight National League, two National Trophy, fourteen British Speedway Cup and six challenge).

1947 STATISTICS

(Bristol's score shown first unless otherwise stated)

NATIONAL LEAGUE SECOND DIVISION

Opponents	Home	Away
Birmingham	L35-49	L31-53
	W60-24	L40-44
Glasgow	W57.5-26.5	L36-48
	W57-27	L36-48
Middlesbrough	W47-35	L23-61
	L38-45	L25-59

1947

Newcastle	W62-22	L34-50
	W51-32	L31-53
Norwich	L39-44	L26-58
	W62-22	L29-55
Sheffield	W47-36	L24-60
	W46-38	L27-57
Wigan	L37-43	L35-49
	W47-36	W43-41

MATCH AVERAGES

Rider	Matches	Points	Average
Fred Tuck	14	131	9.36
Mike Beddoe	27	199.5	7.39
Jack Mountford	28	170	6.07
Billy Hole	28	166	5.93
Roger Wise	26	124	4.77
Eric Salmon	27	125	4.63
Jack Cooley	4	15	3.75
Cyril Quick	28	100	3.57
Cyril Anderson	2	7	3.50
Frank Evans	10	30	3.00
George Craig	25	52	2.08
Bill Clifton	2	3	1.50
Graham Hole	2	3	1.50
Charlie Bourdon	1	0	0.00

NATIONAL LEAGUE SECOND DIVISION TABLE

Team	Matches	Won	Drawn	Lost	For	Against	Pts
Middlesbrough	28	20	0	8	1,363	977	40
Sheffield	28	17	2	9	1,315	1,022	36
Norwich	28	16	0	12	1,182	1,142	32
Birmingham	28	14	0	14	1,118	1,222	28
Newcastle	28	12	2	14	1,128.5	1,200.5	26
Bristol	28	11	0	17	1,125.5	1,215.5	22
Wigan	28	9	2	17	1,068	1,266	20
Glasgow	28	10	0	18	1,044	1,299	20

SPEEDWAY IN BRISTOL 1928-1949

DAILY MAIL NATIONAL TROPHY

Opponents	Home	Away	Aggregate
Wigan	W62-45	L34-73	L96-118

MATCH AVERAGES

Rider	Matches	Points	Average
Roger Wise	2	27	13.50
Jack Mountford	2	13	6.50
George Craig	2	12	6.00
Cyril Anderson	2	11	5.50
Eric Salmon	2	11	5.50
Jack Cooley	1	5	5.00
Cyril Quick	2	9	4.50
Billy Hole	2	7	3.50
Frank Evans	1	1	1.00

BRITISH SPEEDWAY CUP (SECOND DIVISION)

Opponents	Home	Away
Birmingham	W62-33	L37-59
Glasgow	W59-37	L42-54
Middlesbrough	W64-32	L35-61
Newcastle	W53-42	L42-54
Norwich	W50-44	L23-73
Sheffield	L44-50	L20-76
Wigan	W52-44	L42-52

MATCH AVERAGES

Rider	Matches	Points	Average
Fred Tuck	9	83	9.22
Mike Beddoe	9	61	6.78
Jack Mountford	13	88	6.77
Roger Wise	12	80	6.67
Eric Salmon	14	87	6.21
Cyril Quick	14	74	5.29
Billy Hole	13	66	5.08
George Craig	11	45	4.09

Jack Cooley	7	22	3.14
Frank Evans	4	10	2.50
Cyril Anderson	3	7	2.33
Bill Clifton	3	2	0.67

BRITISH SPEEDWAY CUP (SECOND DIVISION) TABLE

Team	Matches	Won	Drawn	Lost	For	Against	Pts
Sheffield	14	11	0	3	771	569	26
Middlesbrough	14	9	0	5	750.5	587.5	21
Norwich	14	7	0	7	676.5	659.5	15
Newcastle	14	7	0	7	664	671	15
Wigan	14	6	0	8	627	708	12
Bristol	14	6	0	8	625	711	12
Glasgow	14	5	0	9	625	717	10
Birmingham	14	5	0	9	610	726	10

NOTE: 3 points were awarded for an away win.

CHALLENGE

Opponents	Home	Away
Birmingham	L49-57	–
Captains' & Vice-Captains' Team	D48-48	–
New Cross	L44-64	–
Odsal	L46-47	–
The Rest	W74-33	–
West Ham	L40-54	–

MATCH AVERAGES

Rider	Matches	Points	Average
Jack Mountford	6	54	9.00
Fred Tuck	4	32	8.00
Roger Wise	4	31	7.75
Mike Beddoe	5	36	7.20
Eric Salmon	6	43	7.17
Billy Hole	5	33	6.60
Cyril Quick	6	22	3.67
Frank Evans	2	6	3.00

George Craig	5	10	2.00
Ken Monks	1	1	1.00
Graham Hole	1	0	0.00

NOTE: The match *v.* New Cross featured a composite side made up of Bristol and West Ham riders, therefore only the points scored by Bristol riders are included in the above chart.

1948

After the long winter break, the speedway roar returned to Knowle Stadium on Friday 19 March, when Bristol faced a combined Southampton and Hastings side in a fourteen-heat challenge match. Apart from trying to sign pre-war Bulldog Bill Maddern, the management had resisted the temptation to recruit other riders, believing strongly in the men that had served them so well and improved considerably during the course of the previous year. The aforementioned Maddern was eventually allocated to the new Edinburgh team, the Control Board having decided that the Monarchs' needs were greater than Bristol's. In effect, the only real change on the personnel front saw Bob Steel move on to pastures new, with Reg Witcomb taking on the sole responsibility of managing the Bulldogs' affairs. A crowd of 15,000 were in place to see the tapes go up on the new campaign and the first action they witnessed was a match race between West Ham's Eric Chitty and Bill Kitchen of Wembley. Kitchen took the first race in a super-quick time of 67.2 seconds but, when the two aces resumed their contest after the main match, it was Chitty who took the second leg. The Wembley man wasn't to be denied though and scorched to victory in the deciding race, clocking 68.8 seconds. In their challenge fixture, Bristol showed their visitors no mercy whatsoever, providing the race winner in every heat and recording eleven maximum advantages in the process. Fred Tuck and Billy Hole sped to immaculate 12-point full-house scores, while Eric Salmon weighed in with a tally of 11 to start the season in grand style. With a meagre 4 points, Alf Bottoms topped the scoring for the opposition, picking up four third places on the wrong end of Bristol 5-1s. In the match programme, Reg Witcomb mentioned a comment at a recent supporters' club meeting suggesting that the BBC were not doing enough for speedway. He went on to say that with all the supporters the sport enjoyed, the broadcasting corporation could be persuaded to do something about their lack of coverage and announce the results of meetings during the ten o'clock news, along with the leading scorers. He encouraged fans to write to the sports editor at the BBC to see if they might take this idea on board.

On 25 March, Bristol appeared in their opening Second Division match of the year, with a trip to Owlerton Stadium in Sheffield. The Bulldogs turned in the most spirited of performances before going down to a narrow 43-40 defeat. Ex-Bristol rider Jack Bibby rode effortlessly to a four-ride maximum for the Tigers, while Len Williams provided fantastic support, notching 11 points. In what was a solid team performance, Fred Tuck and Billy Hole headed the Bristol scoring, tallying 9 and 8 points respectively.

One night later, Edinburgh were the visitors to Knowle for a Good Friday fixture, as the Bulldogs kicked off their home league programme. The Bristol boys were certainly pumped up for this one and blasted their way to a 64-20 success. Fred Tuck laid the foundation for the victory, blistering around the 290-yard circuit in just 66.6 seconds to win the opening heat. The beleaguered Monarchs, who were still to stage their first ever meeting at Old Meadowbank Stadium, had no answer to the onslaught and failed to win a single race. The vast majority in the huge 20,000 audience didn't mind, however, as they cheered their heroes home in every heat. Both Tuck and Billy Hole went through the card with maximum points to their names, while Eric Salmon clocked in with 11. Dick Campbell proved to be the leading performer for the Scottish side, yielding 6 points from his four starts. Pre-season Bristol target Bill Maddern captained the visitors, but the Australian could only manage a 5-point return.

Birmingham provided the next league opposition at Knowle Stadium on 2 April and, once again, the Bulldogs were in rampant mood. Run on a soaked track, with wind and rain swirling around throughout, a Bristol rider again took the chequered flag in every heat. Considering the weather, it was amazing that 12,000 folk turned out to watch the match, but those present were delighted to see their team run out victors by

65 points to 19. Fred Tuck was invincible, romping to another 12-point maximum, while Billy Hole (11) and Roger Wise (10) provided excellent backing. Charlie May did best for the Brummies but 6 points was all he could muster against the Bristol onslaught. The 'What's What' feature in the programme was as interesting as ever. Reg Witcomb mentioned that he had received a large amount of letters from supporters, with a number saying they didn't like seeing the team win by such big scores and suggesting that the side should be weakened! Not everyone was of the same opinion though and, in stark contrast, some fans had even put forward the idea that another heat leader should be signed as part of an all-out effort to win the league! Later in his piece, Mr Witcomb further urged the fans to bombard the BBC with letters about giving speedway the coverage it deserved.

The Bulldogs made the journey up to Birmingham for the return fixture on 3 April and, in what was a super performance, they rode to a brilliant 44-39 victory. An inspirational showing from Billy Hole saw him notch a maximum as the solid-scoring Bristolians won a ding-dong battle thanks to a last-heat 5-0, courtesy of Mike Beddoe and Fred Tuck. Former Bristol rider Roy Dook proved the best performer for the Brummies, scoring 9 points, while Stan Dell carded 8.

At Knowle on 9 April, the Bulldogs expected their toughest home test thus far, with League Champions Middlesbrough providing stiffer opposition in front of 14,000 expectant supporters. Although it was to prove a harder match, Bristol thoroughly deserved their 49-35 victory, the highlight being the team riding of Jack Mountford and Fred Tuck when they combined to defeat Frank Hodgson in the opening race. When Middlesbrough's Benny King took victory in heat two, he became the first visiting rider to win a race at Knowle in 1948! Jack Hodgson then won heat three before normal service was resumed with a Mountford victory in the next race. The Bulldogs went on to take the flag in eight of the remaining ten heats, with only Frank Hodgson bucking the trend in heats nine and fourteen, on his way to a 9-point haul. With four straight wins, Mountford went through the card unbeaten, further extending the sequence of home matches when at least one Bulldog recorded a maximum.

Next up at Knowle Stadium was a visit from Newcastle on 16 April when, in front of 13,000 spectators, the Bristol boys put together another powerful display to overwhelm the Diamonds by 57 points to 27. While both Billy Hole and Eric Salmon charged to 12-point maximums, the Bulldogs didn't have it all their own way, as Norman Evans won heat one in the fastest time of the night (67.6 seconds) and Wilf Jay collected a fine win in the final race of the match, thereby topping the Newcastle scoring on 8 points. Harking back to earlier comments about whether Bristol ought to de-strengthen when facing weaker opposition, promoter Reg Witcomb answered this with an emphatic 'No' in his programme notes, going on to state that it was his desire to strengthen the team still further.

In a break from league racing, Edinburgh returned to Knowle for an Anniversary Cup encounter on 23 April, but they met a Bristol side that ripped them to shreds. Having lost 64-20 on their previous visit, the Scottish outfit hoped to fare a little better, but the Bulldogs simply turned up the heat and blasted their way to a 71-25 success. Fred Tuck was the latest maximum scorer in the home camp, winning all five of his rides by a country mile. On the other hand, their opponents couldn't manage a single race win, with Bill Maddern's 6-point tally representing their best individual performance. A look at the programme revealed that Tuck had been chosen to contest the Silver Helmet Match-Race Championship against Fleetwood's Dick Geary. There was also a train trip planned for the Bulldogs' visit to Birmingham on 5 June, although it would only definitely run if there were over 200 bookings.

After three consecutive home meetings, Bristol got back on the road on 24 April, making the arduous journey up to Edinburgh on league business. The Scottish side had only run their opening home meeting the previous week and the public were obviously eager for more as 16,500 people turned up to watch as they squared up to the Bulldogs. A thrilling meeting ensued, but any hopes the Monarchs had of winning were dashed in the opening race when Dennis Parker crashed out and took no further part in the proceedings. Bill Maddern swept to a brilliant 12-point maximum for the homesters, but his team lacked the solidity of the Bulldogs, who secured an important 46-38 victory. With 10 points, Billy Hole led the Bristol scoring, while Jack Mountford ended the night as the track-record holder, having clocked 71.0 seconds in heat four.

On 29 April, Bristol faced a difficult Anniversary Cup encounter at Sheffield, having already lost at the South Yorkshire track in their first away match of the season. The Bulldogs were unable to live with the top-end power of the Tigers as they went on to triumph 56-40, led by double-figure returns from Tommy Bateman (15), Stan Williams (13) and Jack Bibby (10). On a disappointing night for Bristol, Fred Tuck ended up as top man, scoring 9 points.

Back at their home base the following evening, the Bulldogs ended the month with a comfortable 53-31 win over Glasgow. Prior to the fixture, Fred Tuck burned up the track to inflict a 2-0 defeat on Dick Geary in the Silver Helmet. Bristol then opened the match with a 5-1 advantage from Mike Beddoe and Billy Hole but, although they went on to win the Second Division encounter at leisure, visiting rider Joe Crowther proved to be a thorn in their side. The top Tiger won heat three, ahead of Roger Wise, before beating Beddoe as he took victory in heat seven. Crowther went on to finish the night with a 9-point score and, for the first time in 1948, no home rider recorded a maximum, with Beddoe's 11 points being the highest individual total for the Bulldogs.

Bristol's next league activity took them up to Brough Park to face Newcastle on 3 May. Making their intentions clear from the start, the Bulldogs began the meeting with maximum points from Mike Beddoe and Billy Hole, before Fred Tuck and Jack Mountford repeated the tonic in heat two. With Bristol threatening to run riot, Wilf Jay collected a good win for the homesters in heat three; however, the Bulldogs weren't about to ease up and Mountford immediately linked with Cyril Quick to hammer home another 'fiver' in the next race. With a tight grip on the match, the Bulldogs eventually cruised on to a 47-37 victory, with Tuck helping himself to a superlative 12-point maximum. Meanwhile, Jay topped the Diamonds' scorechart, notching a 10-point tally, but he fought a lone battle and lacked any real support from his teammates.

The match at Newcastle formed the first part of a sojourn that then took Bristol up to Glasgow on 5 May for a further league fixture. In between the two matches, Fred Tuck made the journey to Fleetwood for the second leg of the Silver Helmet against Dick Geary. The match-race series preceded the Flyers' Second Division match against Birmingham, and Tuck didn't disappoint his fans as he rode to another splendid 2-0 victory, making him the first holder of the coveted trophy. So to the fixture at Glasgow, and again the Bulldogs tore into the match from the start, gaining a 4-2 in the opening race and a 5-1 from heat two. They never looked back from there and went on to record an untroubled

48-36 victory, with that man Tuck blasting his way to another 12-point maximum. Meanwhile, the 'Terrible Twins' Joe Crowther and Will Lowther were Glasgow's leading lights, both notching 9-point tallies.

Returning to home territory, the Bulldogs faced Newcastle in an Anniversary Cup match on 7 May and, while they had little difficulty in stretching their unbeaten home record for the year, the Diamonds at least had the distinction of scoring more points than any other visiting side thus far. A gate of 12,000 witnessed Bristol collect a 58-38 success, with Eric Salmon's 13 points topping the scorecard. Meanwhile, Wilf Jay was the brightest of the Diamonds in carding three wins on his way to 11 points. In the second half there was an interesting junior scratch race that saw Lew Coffin take the winning flag ahead of Graham Hole and Bob Jones. Turning to the programme, in the 'What's What' column Reg Witcomb relayed some good news on the BBC front, having received a letter stating that commentary on part of the Sheffield *v.* Bristol match would be broadcast on the North of England Home Service from 8.00-8.30 p.m. on 27 May.

Off on their travels up country again, the Bulldogs faced league meetings at Fleetwood and Middlesbrough. First stop was the Highbury Avenue home of the Fleetwood Flyers on 11 May and, apart from Fred Tuck in his Silver Helmet success of the previous week, none of the other Bristol riders had previously appeared on the 325-yard circuit. The home side opened well and were leading by 6 points after heat four, but the Bulldogs gradually hauled themselves back into the match and, by heat eight, the scores were level at 24-24. A 4-2 from Billy Hole and Mike Beddoe put Bristol ahead in heat nine, only for Cyril Cooper and Dick Geary to inflict maximum points over Jack Mountford and Tuck in the very next race, giving the homesters a 2-point advantage. That lead was maintained until heat thirteen, when Fleetwood were the victims of rotten luck. With the race seemingly in the bag, Ron Hart's motor blew up yards from the finish, causing him to swerve over the inner white line and earn a disqualification. Having been some 30 yards adrift, Eric Salmon gleefully took the win from Percy Brine to give Bristol a 3-2 advantage and send them into the final heat just a single point behind. With everything resting on the last race, Beddoe and Roger Wise came to the line to face the Fleetwood duo of Jack Gordon and Cooper. A terrific tussle reached boiling point on the last corner, with Wise holding the lead from Gordon and Cooper, while Beddoe brought up the rear.

A sudden burst saw Beddoe edge past Cooper and he almost squeezed ahead of Gordon as they flashed across the line in a blur. There wasn't a lot of room and Beddoe careered into the corrugated safety fence, suffering a serious foot injury. The fact that his point had secured a 42-41 victory for the Bulldogs seemed unimportant, as mayhem erupted with arguments raging over who was to blame for the accident. Wise's heat-fourteen victory took his total for the night to 11 points, which was more than enough to head the Bristol scoring, while Dick Geary's 10-point haul saw him sit nicely on top of the Fleetwood pile. Regrettably for Beddoe, the subsequent diagnosis was that part of his right foot had to be amputated and the operation duly took place at the Blackpool Victoria Hospital the following day.

Two nights after the drama at Fleetwood, the Bulldogs took to the track at Middlesbrough's Cleveland Park raceway and came crashing back to reality with a thud in front of 9,000 spectators. Even allowing for the absence of Mike Beddoe, they were no match for the previous season's Second Division Champions and found themselves on the wrong end of a 50-33 scoreline. One man stood out like a beacon though, as Fred Tuck went through the card to record an unbeaten 12 points. Although not as fast as the home lads on the straights, Tuck was so quick on the bends that nobody could get near him. Meanwhile, in netting 9 points, skipper Frank Hodgson was the best performer for the victorious Bears.

Immediately after the loss at Cleveland Park, the Bristol riders travelled back through the night and made ready to entertain Sheffield in a potentially tough league match the following evening. Clearly smarting from their hefty defeat, the Bulldogs were in no mood for complacency and went on the rampage, walloping the Tigers by 61 points to 23. Played out in front of 13,000 patrons, one of the undoubted highlights was the heat-eight ride of Johnny Hole, who took victory over Bruce Semmens in the finest ride of his fledgling career to date. The Sheffield boys didn't know what had hit them and had to wait until heat eleven for what was their only race win of the night, courtesy of Tommy Bateman. Again Fred Tuck headed the Bristol scoring with another four-ride maximum, with Bateman's tally of 7 points topping the Tigers' chart.

The Bristol public didn't have long to wait for their next speedway fix, as First Division New Cross arrived in town for a special Whit Monday challenge match on 17 May. Parading all their star riders, it was no surprise that the Rangers strode to a 50–34 success and, despite the score, an audience of 17,000 thoroughly enjoyed the spectacle. Although the Bulldogs were bolstered by the inclusion of Eric Chitty, who top scored with 8 points, they didn't possess the depth to cope with the opposition who were led to victory by the solid efforts of Jeff Lloyd (10), Ron Johnson (9), Bill Longley (8) and Ray Moore (8).

For their third home match in a week, another 14,000 spectators turned up for the league visit of Norwich on 21 May, meaning an amazing total of 44,000 good folk had gone through the Knowle Stadium turnstiles for the three meetings! The Stars were expected to push Bristol hard but, with Bert Spencer and Syd Littlewood reportedly involved in a car accident on their way to the meeting, they were forced to borrow junior riders Graham Hole and Lew Coffin. As a result, the Norwich challenge fizzled out in another one-sided Bulldogs' triumph by 60 points to 24. Fred Tuck plundered another maximum and Billy Hole also joined in with a 12-point haul, while Eric Salmon notched 11. The Stars' scoring was headed by Phil Clarke, who did well to accumulate 7 points against the non-stop Bristol dominance. In Reg Witcomb's programme column, the Bulldogs' promoter explained that Mike Beddoe was doing fine despite the seriousness of his injury and was just itching to get back in the saddle! He suggested that people might like to write letters or send books that could be passed on. Indeed, one supporter had already sent a card with a £1 note attached, with the writer suggesting that Beddoe's parents bought him some grapes. The recuperating rider didn't think he was ill enough for grapes, however, commenting that he would prefer 'some nice fresh prawns' instead!

The next track action took Bristol back up to Sheffield for important league business on 27 May. It was the Bulldogs' third trip of the year to Owlerton and, as on their previous two visits, they were again defeated, going down by 51 points to 32. Fred Tuck won the opening heat, and the next race was drawn, before the Tigers took a grip on the match that they were not to relinquish. With a full 12 points, Bruce Semmens was Sheffield's leading light, while Tommy Bateman and Len Williams both notched tallies of 10 apiece. For Bristol, Tuck top scored with 11 points, suffering his only defeat to Semmens in heat five.

The riders wearily wended their way home after the drubbing but, thankfully, there was a break from important team matches, as Knowle Stadium hosted a Best Pairs event the following evening. A 10,000 gate was recorded for the meeting, which predominantly featured Bristol riders, although Dick Geary, brothers Frank and Jack Hodgson, Jack Gordon, Norman Evans and Wilf Plant also participated in the mix. The fans were treated to some great entertainment, with Frank Hodgson being particularly impressive as he took victory in each of his heats. Indeed, he certainly set the raceway alight in heat one, thundering around in 67.0 seconds to defeat Dick Geary, his time being just 1 second outside Jeff Lloyd's track record. Unfortunately for Hodgson, his partner Cyril Quick could only muster 3 points, giving the duo a combined total of 18. They therefore had to settle for second position behind Billy Hole and Geary, who totalled 19 points. Following the main event, brothers Johnny and Graham Hole took victory in a Junior Pairs contest, with Bob Jones and partner Lew Coffin finishing as runners-up. Full result: (senior event) B. Hole (11) and Geary (8) 19; F. Hodgson (15) and Quick (3) 18; Eric Salmon (10) and Plant (5) 15; Evans (9) and Jack Mountford (6) 15; J. Hodgson (6) and Roger Wise (6) 12; Fred Tuck (11) and Gordon (0) 11; (junior event) J. Hole (5) and G. Hole (5) 10; Jones (3) and Coffin (3) 6; Bill Downton (1) and Harry Widlake (1) 2. In the programme, Reg Witcomb mentioned a recent transfer that had seen Wilf Plant join Fleetwood from Middlesbrough. Understandably he was somewhat miffed about this, as he had previously made several attempts to lure the rider to Bristol, only to be informed that he wasn't for sale.

Still making progress, Mike Beddoe sent a message from the Victoria Hospital in Blackpool: 'Tell the folks I shall be home pretty soon and all set for action. I'm now using crutches and hobbling about the ward. My old foot gives me pins and needles, but that's a good sign, so I'm told, because the nerve is coming back to the ankle.'

Next on the agenda, the Bulldogs made the jaunt across country for a Second Division fixture at Norwich on 29 May. Unlike their visit to Knowle eight days previously, the Stars were at full strength and it showed, as Bristol found themselves on the receiving end of a battering, going down by 56 points to 28. This was after Fred Tuck had beaten Bert Spencer in the opening race, and Billy Hole had taken the victor's flag in heat two! The Bulldogs only gained three further race winners thereafter and ended the night a well-beaten side. Spencer headed the Norwich scoring with 11 points, while Ivor 'Ossie' Powell grabbed 10. For Bristol, Tuck and Hole fought a brave battle, recording 9 points apiece.

Although the team had completed their May programme, no fewer than seven of the Bulldogs travelled down to Poole on the final day of the month to compete in the Silver Trophy. What a night it was too, with all three rostrum positions being filled by a Bristol rider: first, Fred Tuck 15; second, Jack Mountford 14; third Roger Wise 12. On a fabulous evening for the Bulldogs' representatives, Mountford also broke the Wimborne Road track record when winning heat one in the time of 80.4 seconds. For the record, the other Bristol riders on show scored thus: Billy Hole 10; Eric Salmon 4; Johnny Hole 2; Graham Hole 1.

The date of 4 June saw the first-ever visit of Fleetwood to Bristol, when the Lancashire side came down for a league match and, although the Bulldogs raced to a 49-35 success, the Flyers acquitted themselves very well indeed. The win was well received by promoter Reg Witcomb, as it was good enough to establish Bristol at the head of the Second Division league table. Prior to the match, Newcastle's Wilf Jay sped to a surprise 2-0 success over Fred Tuck in the first leg of the Silver Helmet Match-Race Championship. Then, when the domestic fixture got underway, Cyril Cooper and Dick Geary linked up to score maximum points in heat one after Tuck had suffered a two-minute exclusion. The Bulldogs rallied and eventually got a grip on the match, which was run amid driving wind and rain; indeed, it was hardly surprising that only 8,000 spectators turned up, given the atrocious conditions. A look at the completed scorechart showed Billy Hole and Roger Wise on top of the homesters' pile, each with 10 points, while Wilf Plant was Fleetwood's best, tallying 9.

There was no rest for the Bristol boys, as they were at Birmingham the very next night for an Anniversary Cup match. Before 21,000 spectators, the Bulldogs were unable to contend with the all-round strength of the Brummies and slumped to a 59-37 defeat. With 14 points, Stan Dell topped the Birmingham scoring, while Fred Tuck's tally of 13 gave him top spot on Bristol's chart.

On 7 June, Fred Tuck travelled up to Newcastle for the second leg of his Silver Helmet challenge against Wilf Jay. Unfortunately he met a man in inspired form, for Jay stormed to a 2-0 success, equalling George Pepper's Brough Park track record of 74.0 seconds in the initial heat.

Making their second visit of the season, Sheffield were the next attraction at Knowle Stadium in another Anniversary Cup match on 11 June. Despite another avalanche victory for the Bulldogs, on this occasion by 66 points to 29, the racing was always interesting, particularly when Tommy Bateman was on the track. Bristol boasted three men in double figures, namely Billy Hole (12), Eric Salmon (11) and Jack Mountford (10), while Bateman notched 11 points for the Tigers.

Staying with the Anniversary Cup, the Bulldogs journeyed up to Fleetwood on 15 June and they arrived at Highbury Avenue in confident mood, having won on their previous visit to the 325-yard circuit on 11 May, although that success had of course been marred by the serious injury to Mike Beddoe. Things started well too, with Fred Tuck blasting to victory in heat one and setting a new track-record time of 64.8 seconds in the process. The meeting developed into a nip-and-tuck battle and, although the Flyers possessed only one man in double figures, their middle-order solidity gave them the edge over Bristol's longish tail. With 10 points, Norman Hargreaves led his side to a 51-45 victory, while the bulk of the Bulldogs' points came from Billy Hole (12), Roger Wise (11) and Fred Tuck (10).

Fleetwood were again Bristol's opponents in what was the fifteenth meeting of the season at Knowle Stadium on Friday 18 June. This time, the two sides met in an elimination round tie of the *Daily Mail*-sponsored National Trophy. The Flyers were in a determined mood and battled hard for every point. This was fully emphasised by the events of heat twelve, when Norman Hargreaves found himself disqualified by the ACU steward for boring into the Bristol riders. After the race had been stopped, the subsequent re-run saw visiting skipper Jack Gordon show gritty determination to take victory ahead of Eric Salmon and Cyril Quick. In the end, Bristol were only able to carve out a 65-43 victory and were left wondering if it would be a sufficient advantage to take up north for the return leg. Fred Tuck once again headed the Bulldogs' scoring with a magnificent 17 points, suffering his only loss to Dick Geary in heat ten. Roger Wise also gave a marvellous display to accumulate 15 points, while Gordon, Geary and Hargreaves jointly finished on top of the Flyers' scorecard, each notching 9 points. The second half of the meeting featured the usual array of scratch events, but one name caused quite a stir among the 9,000 fans, and that was the appearance of pre-war Bristol rider Bill Rogers in three of the races. Regrettably, he was a pale shadow of his former self, trundling home last in two heats and failing to finish the other. Reg Witcomb relayed an amusing story concerning Rogers in his programme notes, stating, 'Bill tried to get more kick out of his machine back in Australia by having rockets fixed to the model. He tried it out one Friday, which was also the thirteenth of the month. He pressed a control button to fire two of the rockets during the first lap, but nothing happened. He tried again the second time round, with the same lack of results. The third lap was sensational, for all the rockets went off together. When the clouds of smoke and dust had cleared, Bill was found upside down in the fence, unhurt, but I am told he used some entirely new words, which I am forbidden to repeat!'

Bristol returned to Fleetwood on 22 June, making it the third meeting in eight days against the Lancashire side. This latest match was the second leg of the National Trophy tie, with the Bulldogs defending a 22-point lead from the fixture at Knowle four days previously. Things didn't look too good before the start, with Jack Mountford missing, having nearly collapsed through exhaustion during the first leg. Bristol began well enough though, with Fred Tuck taking the chequered flag in heat one. However, that was followed by a Flyers 5-1, as Dick Geary and Jack Gordon defeated Billy Hole. Heats three and four were shared, before the Fleetwood lads gradually started to erode Bristol's overall lead. Several 5-1s brought the aggregate scores closer and, with the Bulldogs reeling, maximum heat advantages from Wilf Plant and Reg Lambourne in heat sixteen, and Dick Geary and Plant in heat eighteen gave Fleetwood a 69-39 victory on the night. Disappointingly from Bristol's perspective, it meant the Flyers progressed through by an 8-point margin on aggregate, 112-104. Geary took six rides and won the lot for a scintillating 18-point maximum, while Plant (15) and Cyril Cooper (10) provided superb backing in what was a marvellous team performance from the homesters. Meanwhile, although heavily laden with a bout of 'flu, Tuck battled his way to 13 points for the Bulldogs but unfortunately received little support.

At Knowle Stadium on 25 June, a challenge match pitched the Bulldogs against a composite side who went under the title of 'Kangaroos'. Needless to say, this was a team of Australian riders drawn from other Second Division tracks as follows: 1. Bill Maddern, 2. Bat Byrnes, 3. Doug McLachlan, 4. Graham Warren, 5. Ken Le Breton, 6. Charlie Spinks, 7. Arthur Payne, 8. Clem Mitchell. Despite the strong-looking opposition and the fact that Jack Mountford was again an absentee, not to mention Mike Beddoe, the Bulldogs cruised to a substantial 60-36 victory. No fewer than four home riders totted up double-figure scores, namely Roger Wise (13), Eric Salmon (12), Fred Tuck (11) and Billy Hole (11). For their opponents, Spinks, McLachlan and Payne jointly finished on top of the scorechart, each with a measly 6 points. Referring to the 'What's What' column in the match programme, Reg Witcomb revealed the contents of a letter he had received from Mr C. Robinson of 699 Muller Road, Eastville. Mr Robinson was concerned about the number of huge winning margins achieved by the Bulldogs and suggested a system that would entail teams gaining different points for the same finishing position, as follows: home team: first place = 3 points; second place = 2 points; third place = 1 point; away team: first place = 4.5 points; second place = 3 points; third place = 1 point.

On 2 July, the first action of the month brought Middlesbrough down to Knowle for an Anniversary Cup meeting. With Jack Mountford still resting, Exeter's Johnny Myson stepped into the Bristol side and, although he failed to score, the rest of the team pulled together to win 58-37. Billy Hole led by example, taking the flag in each of his five rides for a fantastic maximum, while Fred Tuck plugged away as ever, backing his captain with a solid tally of 12 points. Aside from the big two scorers, a special word of praise was due for Johnny Hole, whose impressive 7-point return included a race win over Geoff Godwin and Frank Bettis in heat thirteen. Reg Witcomb was as interesting as ever, writing in the programme: 'You will be sorry to learn Arthur Bush, who was down here on trial last Friday from Harringay, received two fractures when Lew Coffin collided with him, one fracture in the hand and the other in the shoulder. I thought he put up a most promising performance and hope to secure his transfer. It will, however, be five or six weeks before he is able to ride again.' Mr Witcomb closed his piece by once again stating that he wouldn't be happy until the BBC broadcast all speedway results during their 10 p.m. news bulletin.

Individual fare was on the agenda at Bristol on 9 July, with the staging of the first round of the British Riders' Championship. There was a top-quality field for this meeting, including Tommy Croombs (West Ham), Louis Lawson (Belle Vue), Freddie Williams (Wembley) and Dick Harris (Wimbledon). As expected, racing was tight throughout, providing plenty of thrills for the 12,000 fans in attendance. Lawson was particularly quick, winning heat six in 66.6 seconds, before going even faster to win heat nine in 66.4 seconds. However, in the final outcome, home favourite Fred Tuck came out on top with a 14-point tally to his name, landing a £50 cheque for his efforts. As a wonderful gesture, Tuck shared his winnings with the injured Mike Beddoe, clearly showing the excellent team spirit that existed within the Bristol camp. In netting 13 points, Jack Hodgson finished as runner-up, while the fast-riding Lawson was third with a 12-point haul to his name. Apart from Tuck's success, the Bristol supporters were also cheered by the track return of Jack Mountford, although he was only able to accrue 3 points. Full result: Tuck 14; Hodgson 13; Lawson 12; Williams 11; Harris 8; Doug McLachlan 8; Alec Grant 8; Billy Hole 7; Roger Wise 7; Norman Hargreaves 6; Bert Spencer 6; Croombs 4; Phil Clarke 3; Norman Evans 3; Mountford 3; Jock Grierson 3. Reg Witcomb explained in the programme that he was still trying to strengthen the side and had heard that Nobby Stock of Harringay was looking for a move. Having negotiated with the Harringay management, the Bristol promoter was pleased to reveal that an agreement had been reached that would see Stock help out the Bulldogs for the remainder of the season. Mr Witcomb also looked forward to the following Friday's intriguing challenge match that would see Bristol take on a team called 'Gayleydons'. The quirky name arose as the opposition was to be made up of riders from HarrinGAY, WembLEY and WimbleDON.

Prior to that, the Bulldogs faced another trip to Birmingham on 10 July, for what was their second National League match of the season at the Perry Barr venue. Unfortunately, before a huge crowd of 21,000 spectators, the under-strength Bristol team were completely outridden by the Brummies and went down to a mighty 62-22 hammering. The home side had two maximum scorers in Graham Warren and Arthur Payne, while Doug McLachlan also weighed in with 11 points. Billy Hole was the only Bulldog to make any impression, being Bristol's only race winner in heat two, on his way to a total of 7 points.

The next action was the previously mentioned challenge match *v.* the interestingly titled Gayleydons on 16 July, when Bristol ran out victors by 57 points to 39. Before the meeting, Fred Tuck made an attempt on Jeff Lloyd's four-lap track record and, amid a crescendo of noise from the 10,000 spectators, the popular lanky rider scorched around the 290-yard track, clocking a new best time of 65.8 seconds. In the main meeting Nobby Stock made his first appearance for the Bulldogs, adding much solidity to the side in netting 8 points, his performance including a race victory in heat seven. Meanwhile, Eric Salmon topped the Bristol scoring on 11 points, with Tuck supplying valuable support in tallying 10. Ex-Bristol rider Mike Erskine headed the composite team's attack, plundering 10 points, with Bob Wells collecting 9. Other members of the Gayleydons' line-up included Freddie Williams, Joe Bowkis and Dick Harris, although the late withdrawals of George Saunders, Jack Arnfield and Bill Gilbert somewhat took the edge off the meeting.

Next on the rollercoaster schedule was an Anniversary Cup match at the Old Meadowbank Stadium against Edinburgh on 17 July. With Roger Wise missing from the line-up after collapsing at home in the middle of the night, and Cyril Quick also absent after feeling unwell the previous evening, the Monarchs thundered to a 64-32 success. Due to their rider shortage, Bristol were forced to borrow Edinburgh junior Don Cuppleditch, who revealed great promise with a 4-point return. Providing only three race winners all night, the Bulldogs offered little resistance, with only Fred Tuck showing any true grit as he fought his way to an 11-point haul. For the rampant home side, Clem Mitchell (14) and Eddie Lack (13) certainly demonstrated the quickest route around the 368-yard circuit, receiving excellent backing from their teammates, with scoring all the way down the line.

There was great anticipation at Knowle on 23 July, when 15,000 folk were in place for a Best Pairs event that was packed with First Division track aces. The usual Bristol speedsters partook in the meeting, but riding alongside them were the likes of Wilbur Lamoreaux, Split Waterman, Eric Chitty and Norman Parker. The stars put on a marvellous exhibition of racing, with Chitty blazing a trail to win all five of his outings as he partnered Roger Wise to a 19-point total and first place on the rostrum. Full result: Chitty (15) and Wise (4) 19; Waterman (14) and Eric Salmon (2) 16; Fred Tuck (11) and Dent Oliver (5) 16; Lamoreaux (7) and Jack Mountford (6) 13; Billy Hole (9) and Les Wotton (4) 13; Parker (8) and Nobby Stock (5) 13. The up-to-date league table was reproduced in the programme, showing Bristol and Sheffield on top of the tree, both on 26 points, with the Bulldogs holding the edge by virtue of a slightly better race-points difference.

On 29 July, Billy Hole, Jack Mountford, Fred Tuck and Eric Salmon travelled further west for the Plymouth Trophy, which featured top riders from the Second and Third Divisions. Out of the Bristol contingent Tuck did the best, notching 12 points to finish joint-third with

Graham Warren, while Jack Mountford scored 8 points to finish seventh overall. As a matter of interest, Eric Salmon gleaned 7 points, with Billy Hole only mustering 5. The meeting winner was Geoff Bennett of Birmingham, while Exeter's Stan Hodson filled the runner-up spot.

More First Division aces appeared at Bristol on 30 July, when West Ham were the visitors for a grand challenge match. The Hammers had their star performers on show and Canadian Eric Chitty again showed a penchant for the Knowle circuit, blasting his way to a 12-point maximum. Backing him brilliantly, Malcolm Craven barnstormed his way to 11 points, suffering his only defeat at the hands of Fred Tuck in heat ten. With 8 points, Tuck was the leading Bristol performer on the night as they went down 48-36 to their more illustrious opponents. Tuck's superb heat-ten triumph wasn't the end of his exploits on the night for, in the second half, he took the chequered flag in his heat of the senior scratch event before defeating Chitty, Nobby Stock and Tommy Croombs in the final. In his programme notes, Reg Witcomb relayed an interesting story concerning the Best Pairs meeting that was staged the previous week. Wilbur Lamoreaux and Split Waterman had travelled down together from London but were troubled by misfortune when their car ran into a ditch, with the trailer that was carrying their bikes breaking away and running into a field on the opposite side of the road. Luckily both riders were only slightly shaken, while their machines only suffered minimal damage. Thankfully, they were quickly able to gather everything together and continued on their journey to Knowle without further incident.

Bringing the month to a close, Bristol travelled down to Third Division Exeter's sweeping 433-yard circuit at the County Ground Stadium for a challenge match on 31 July. However, the Bulldogs didn't take kindly to the steel safety fence that surrounded the track and suffered a 57-27 defeat. Both Norman Clay and Don Hardy knocked up 11-point scores, with Arthur Pilgrim yielding 10 for the victorious Falcons. On a disappointing night for Bristol, Roger Wise headed their scoring with just 7 points.

The next action involving Bristol saw them participate in a four-team tournament at Third Division Poole on 2 August. Run over just six heats, it was staged as a second-half event and followed a league fixture that had seen Poole defeat Hastings by 49 points to 35. In totalling 13 points, the Pirates also went on to take victory in the four-team event, with Bristol finishing second on 11. There was an interesting format for this, as Poole and Hastings were both represented by six riders, while Bristol and Southampton only had two riders apiece! Full result: Poole 13 (Alan Chambers 3; Fred Pawson 3; Joe Bowkis 3; George Butler 2; Sid Clark 1; Charlie Hayden 1); Bristol 11 (Billy Hole 6; Eric Salmon 5); Southampton 7 (Jimmy Squibb 6; Alf Kaines 1); Hastings 5 (Jock Grierson 3; Pete Mold 1; Ron Clark 1; Ken Tidbury 0; Wally Green 0; Frank Holcombe 0).

Returning to more serious matters, the Bulldogs journeyed up to Glasgow for another engagement in the Anniversary Cup on 4 August. Although the men in orange and black put in a more solid away performance than they had for some time, a 56-40 loss was still recorded. As ever, Will Lowther (13) and Joe Crowther (12) headed the Tigers' scoring, while Bristol's main men were Fred Tuck (14) and Nobby Stock (10). Looking further down the scorechart, Roger Wise came up with 8 points but, with the other five members of the side only contributing a tally of 8 between them, the Bulldogs' lack of depth on the road was fully emphasised.

Back home on 6 August, Bristol again faced Glasgow in the return fixture. Despite appalling weather conditions, the match went ahead, although with only a die-hard audience of 7,000 hardy souls present. Nobby Stock revelled in the wet, winning all four of his starts to record the first maximum in his new colours, as the Bulldogs ran out comfortable 55-39 victors. Backing the new recruit with 11 points each were Fred Tuck and Roger Wise, while Glasgow were best served by Will Lowther, who also notched 11. The programme took a look at the Anniversary Cup table, which showed Birmingham in pole position, with Bristol somewhat disappointingly lying in fifth place.

The very next day Bristol travelled across country to Norwich, again on Anniversary Cup duty. After Geoff Revett had flashed across the line to win the opening heat, the homesters hit top form and Bristol were quite literally wiped out as they succumbed to a 69-27 battering. To be fair though, the Bulldogs were shorn of the services of Fred Tuck due to illness but, even if their top man had been on board, the match would still have resulted in a hefty defeat. Revett went on to reel off another four wins on his way to a 15-point maximum, with teammates Ted Bravery and Phil Clarke giving full support as they raced to 10 points apiece. On a night to forget, Nobby Stock's 7 points were more than enough to head the Bristol scoring.

Bristol faced another daunting away match when they visited Middlesbrough in the Anniversary Cup on 12 August. With Fred Tuck still missing and the track wet from afternoon rain, the Bulldogs were up against it from the start and it was little surprise that they crashed to a 66-30 loss. Bears legend Frank Hodgson scorched to a fantastic five-ride maximum, while Derek Close and Benny King each recorded 12 points. For the under-fire Bristol side, Roger Wise was the only race winner (heat two) and his tally of 7 points was sufficient to top the scorecard.

The Bulldogs soon had the opportunity to atone for their dreadful display at Norwich, as the Stars were the visitors to Knowle Stadium for a league engagement on 13 August. Right from the opening heat, which was won in grand style by the returning Fred Tuck, Bristol set about their opponents with great gusto and rattled up an important 49-35 success. This was despite a point-less night for Billy Hole, whose machine was playing up and resulted in him being replaced by Cyril Quick in his last two scheduled outings. Following his recent illness, Tuck was back with a vengeance, scorching to another three wins after his heat one success and thereby laying the foundation for his team's victory. Eric Salmon dropped only 1 point all night, losing out to Phil Clarke in heat eight, while Nobby Stock netted 9 points in another useful performance. Turning to the visitors, Paddy Mills, on the 9-point mark, joined Clarke at the top of the Norwich score grid. Among other events in what was a full and varied programme for the 11,000 supporters to enjoy, the Novices' Knock-Out event saw Ginger Nicholls triumph over Dennis Matthews, Lew Coffin and Bill Bundy in an impressive time of 71.0 seconds. With Reg Witcomb away on holiday, the job of writing the notes for the 'What's What' page was taken over by supporters' club secretary Jean Pomphrey. The column revealed that Arthur Bush had joined the Bulldogs and would be making the odd appearance at reserve, as well as riding in the second half of home meetings. It was stressed, however, that Bush was only on loan from Harringay for the remainder of the season. The programme also had a look at the Second Division league table and showed Bristol in a neck-and-neck battle at the top with Sheffield, both having accumulated 26 points, with the Bulldogs enjoying a slightly better race-points difference.

Newcastle beckoned on 16 August, although Bristol stood little chance in the Anniversary Cup encounter as Fred Tuck was again an absentee. With Arthur Bush making his debut, the Bulldogs tried hard enough but were often caught out by the tricky shape of the Brough Park circuit and eventually went down to a 63-33 hiding. Star men for the Diamonds were Jack Hunt (13) and Ken Le Breton (11), with Jack Mountford's 8 points heading the Bristol scoring.

The twenty-fourth meeting of the year at Knowle saw Birmingham supply the opposition in the Anniversary Cup on 20 August. Fred Tuck was back on board and scorched to victory in heat one, before going on to total 9 points in another dominant home showing from the Bulldogs. Indeed, a Bristol rider crossed the finish line ahead in ten of the first thirteen heats, although a late rally from the Brummies saw them take victory in each of the last three races to bring a bit of respectability to their score. The Bulldogs had in fact been 53-24 ahead after heat thirteen, but a 5-1 and two 4-2s to the visitors gave a final result of 58-37. In an amazing solo performance, Brummies' reserve Buck Whitby won all four of his rides, thus denying any maximums in the home camp. As it was, a total of 12 points from five starts gave Roger Wise top spot in the Bristol attack, while Eric Salmon plundered 11. Second-half action saw Dick Bradley take the winner's flag in the Novices' Knock-Out race from Harry Hughes, Norman Meek and Dingo Davey.

Back from holiday, Reg Witcomb went to great lengths to explain the situation regarding Fred Tuck, stating in his programme notes, 'I understand a number of rumours have been floating around concerning Fred leaving Bristol. I would like you to know that he has not suggested such a move to me, and I am sure he will be with us till the end of the season, at least. What will happen next season I cannot say, as Fred had decided to retire from speedway racing during the last closed season, but finally agreed to have at least one more season in the saddle. He has been a sick man recently and has ridden against doctor's orders at Bristol, but has not been riding at our away matches, because of the travelling. You will be glad to know he is now feeling much better and he will be with the team when they ride at Edinburgh on Saturday next.' A final look at the programme saw an advert for the following week's home league match *v.* Sheffield, which would feature an appearance of 'The Thrill King and his Motoring Maniacs'. Thrills and spills were promised, with a sensational rodeo, variety and unlimited laughter from England's premier outdoor show.

The important top-of-the-table clash against Sheffield soon came around on 27 August and saw the Bulldogs take an early lead after walloping in 4-2 and 5-1 advantages. Although the Tigers managed to share five heats, the Bristol boys didn't ease off the gas, banging in three further maximums and another four 4-2s to claim a major 55-29 victory. Eric Salmon went through the card unbeaten for a fine 12-point maximum, receiving superb back-up from Fred Tuck (11) and Billy Hole (10). For the disappointing Sheffield outfit, only Tommy Bateman provided any resistance, riding well for a 9-point return. In the second half, the Novices' Knock-Out contest reached the semi-final stage, with Ginger Nicholls shooting to success over Bob Jones, Dick Bradley and Norman Meek in the first race. The second semi-final followed, with Lew Coffin racing home ahead of Harry Hughes, Colin Kite and Bill Downton. A further five junior and senior scratch races then took place, before The Motoring Maniacs gave an outstanding display to the delight of their 12,000 audience. Reg Witcomb's programme notes contained news that the following week's meeting *v.* Birmingham would be featured on the BBC's West of England Home Service, as well as the Midland Regional Service. Highly regarded Exeter team manager Frank Buckland would be the commentator, with ACU steward Cliff King adding expert analysis in between races.

Bristol traipsed up to Edinburgh for another important league encounter on 28 August, when the vast difference in home and away form was once again demonstrated as the Monarchs faced little in the way of resistance on their way to a 53-31 victory before 15,000 spectators. Fred Tuck and Billy Hole took one race win apiece, with an Edinburgh rider crossing the line ahead in each of the other twelve heats. With 11 points, Danny Lee was the Monarchs' main contributor, while Dick Campbell chalked up 10. For the battered Bulldogs, Billy Hole led the scoring with 9 points, while Tuck yielded 8.

On 3 September, Birmingham paid their second visit to Knowle in the space of just two weeks, on this occasion for league business. Despite torrential rain, the meeting went ahead as scheduled, with 10,000 hardy souls braving the elements. Prior to the start, Roger Wise clocked 32.8 seconds and only just failed in his attempt at a new two-lap (flying start) track record. Then, Eric Salmon was timed at 18.6 seconds as he had a go at Wise's one-lap (clutch start) best time of 18.2 seconds. Once the main match got under way, it was clear there was only going to be one result after Bristol had opened with a double 5-1 salvo. Aside from maximum points by Charlie May and Geoff Bennett in heat three, the Brummies' only other heat advantage occurred in heat twelve, when Stan Dell and Doug McLachlan gained a 4-2. The Bulldogs' 52-32 success was littered with six 5-1s, as Fred Tuck romped to a 12-point maximum, while Salmon tallied 10. Graham Warren proved to be Birmingham's best on the night, earning 9 points from his four starts. Immediately after the match, the Novices' Knock-Out final took place, with Ginger Nicholls emerging triumphant from Lew Coffin, Harry Hughes and Bob Jones. An ecstatic Nicholls was subsequently presented with the Wild West Trophy by Big Bill 'Mighty Fine' Campbell, who was taking an evening off from appearing at the Empire Theatre in Bristol.

The 'What's What' column revealed that Cyril Quick had asked to be released for personal reasons. The rider wished to point out that he had no problem with his riding colleagues or the management, but felt a Third Division track might be beneficial to his progress. In his place, Ginger Nicholls, who lived close to Knowle Stadium, would be given a run in the team, having been recalled from Poole. Mr Witcomb also voiced concern about the number of huge home victories that were being seen in the sport. He suggested that all track surfaces be standardised, with a rule laid down by the Speedway Control Board to this effect. Another of his ideas was that all league encounters should be decided on aggregate scores, similar to the system used in the National Trophy. The Bristol promoter proved to be well ahead of his time, for the British League eventually adopted the idea in 1985, with the side who won on aggregate earning an extra bonus point!

For their next match, the Bulldogs travelled up to Newcastle for a Second Division fixture on 6 September. Bristol's dismal run of away form continued, however, with a disappointing 51-33 loss. It really was a poor showing, with only Eric Salmon (8) and Fred Tuck (7) offering any resistance to the dominant Diamonds. The home team were brilliantly led on this occasion by Wilf Jay's 12-point maximum, with Jack Hunt (11) and Norman Evans (10) lending great support. Two nights later, the Bulldogs were on parade at Glasgow, searching for the elusive away victory that would enhance their bid for the Second Division Championship. Looking at Bristol's record over the year, it was incredible to think they had won five of their first seven away matches but since the last victory at Fleetwood on 11 May they had actually lost fifteen successive fixtures on the road! The string of away defeats soon became sixteen as the Bulldogs slipped to a 46-38 reverse at the hands of the White City-based Tigers. The Bristol lads battled hard, but had no answer to the combination of Bat Byrnes (10), Junior Bainbridge (8) and Joe Crowther (8), who rode well throughout and always seemed to have the knack of picking up points in vital races. Indeed, it was Byrnes who produced the match-winning ride in heat thirteen, when he allowed colleague Buck Ryan to take the win, while he gave a tremendous exhibition of team riding behind. With 11 points, Fred Tuck again headed the Bristol scoring as he had done for much of the season.

Returning home, Edinburgh were the latest side to face the steam-roller on 10 September, when the Bulldogs raced to a 64-19 success. Before a crowd of 10,000, the Monarchs were well and truly mauled as both Jack Mountford and Eric Salmon blitzed their way to 12-point maximums. Dick Campbell was the Scottish outfit's only race winner, and the 3 points he gained from heat eight proved to be the only time he troubled the scorers all night. Of Bristol's thirteen race victories, ten were turned into maximums, while two others resulted in 4-2 advantages. Visiting skipper Bill Maddern was Edinburgh's best performer on the night, but even the ex-Bristol rider could only register 6 points. Later in the evening's schedule, a special match race series was held, which saw Odsal's Oliver Hart defeat Norman Parker of Wimbledon by two races to one. The 'What's What' column gave Reg Witcomb the room to explain a little more about the Cyril Quick situation. He stated: 'Arrangements had all been made last week for Cyril to go on loan until the end of the season, to Yarmouth. This, however, was not sanctioned by the Control Board, as the ACU ruling is that no transfers shall take place after 31 August. This week Poole Speedway, who have been very hard hit by injuries, applied for Quick, and the Control Board have now made a special exception to the ruling, and have consented to his transfer on loan to Poole for the remainder of the season.'

The quest for league points continued on 14 September, when the Bulldogs once again made the trek up to the Highbury Avenue home of Fleetwood. Bristol were hampered before the start, as they arrived minus the services of Jack Mountford, who was confined to bed with 'flu. Once again, Fred Tuck proved to be the mainstay of the side, scoring 10 points as they slumped to a 51-33 defeat. Meanwhile, for the Flyers, Wilf Plant was in sensational form, romping to an unstoppable 12-point maximum.

Three nights on and Fleetwood made the journey down to Knowle for an Anniversary Cup meeting. Although Bristol had little difficulty in racking up a 56-40 win, the Flyers possessed the undoubted star of the evening in Wilf Plant. After winning the opening heat, Plant romped to 14 points from five starts, suffering his only defeat to Nobby Stock in heat twelve. The on-song Fleetwood rider received great support via Dick Geary's hard-fought 12 points, while the Bulldogs featured three men in double figures: Billy Hole (11), Fred Tuck (10) and Roger Wise (10). Having received approval from the SCB, Bristol welcomed Jack Gordon to the club, the rider having joined on loan from Fleetwood until the end of the season, when a decision would be made whether to secure his services on a permanent basis. Gordon did well in his debut match, notching 5 points, but his performance also included one alarming moment. This occurred when Johnny Hole's handlebars got caught up in the rear guard of Gordon's machine, but thankfully all ended well, with both riders making it safely to the inner edge of the track despite being locked together. In the match programme, Reg Witcomb made something of a rash prediction regarding Ginger Nicholls. Commenting on the previous week's match against Edinburgh, he expressed the opinion that the youngster had ridden well, particularly when he had borrowed a bike from Roger Wise. In fact, Nicholls was on the verge of buying a new machine and Mr Witcomb believed he had a great future ahead, stating that he wouldn't be surprised if he turned out to be Bristol's Split Waterman! The Bristol boss also made mention of the exciting battle at the top of the league table, especially after a recent away victory for Birmingham at Norwich, which had been a body blow to Dick Wise's team. That result and their subsequent victory at Middlesbrough had brought the Brummies into the running, and Bristol would have to guard against losing a match at home.

It was somewhat ironic that the Bulldogs were the next visitors to Middlesbrough on 23 September and, following the example set by Birmingham, they ended any lingering title hopes that the Bears held courtesy of a stunning 45-38 victory. Fred Tuck led from the front, scampering to a faultless 12-point maximum, while receiving tremendous back-up from Nobby Stock (11) and club skipper Billy Hole (9). Roger Wise also did extremely well, notching 8 points from his first three rides, before falling after a robust challenge from Frank Hodgson in his final outing. The only downside of the win was an injury sustained by Jack Gordon in his only ride of the night, but at least he was able to make the journey back to his home in Bolton, where he could recuperate.

Hodgson topped the Bears' scorechart with 9 points but, with Derek Close next in line on 7, the homesters' title tilt melted into the night air at Cleveland Park.

The curtain came down on September the following night, when Glasgow made the long and tiring journey down to Knowle Stadium for more league action. Before the meeting, there was a performance by the Band of the 9th Queen's Royal Lancers, conducted by bandmaster H. Boyson Clarke. Then the riders took to the track and the Bulldogs' merciless machine swung into action, blitzing to nine 5-1s, three 4-2s and even a 5-0 on their way to a season's best 65-18 victory. The only respite for the Tigers came in heat thirteen, when Norman Lindsay and Nobby Downham managed to gain a share of the points behind maximum man Eric Salmon. Joining Salmon on a full-house total of 12 points was Jack Mountford, while Billy Hole chipped in with 10. Meanwhile, the visiting duo of Lindsay and Downham headed the Glasgow scoring with a meagre 4 points apiece. Following the second half, there was some wonderfully varied entertainment for the 15,000 spectators from the Royal Signals Olympia Display Team who, for thirty-five minutes, went through a spectacular routine. The machines they used included the standard civilian Triumph 349cc, as well as the 498cc speed twin, with the riders doing solo tricks, jumps, ladder rides, sidecar antics, multiple combinations, fire jumps, chariot riding and a whole host of other stunts. Reg Witcomb again used the programme to launch an attack on the BBC, reproducing a letter that staunch Bristol supporter Mr W.E. Ridler of 9 Friendship Road, Knowle, had sent to the famous broadcasting company. The writer protested strongly about the recent coverage of the British Riders' Championship from Wembley. It had been announced that the broadcast would last from 9.30-10 p.m. yet, at 9.55 p.m., listeners were returned to the studio, thereby missing the run-off for second position. Although it was subsequently promised that the result would be given during the 10 p.m. news, it wasn't. Mr Witcomb stressed that folk should continue to protest to the BBC and in the end they would surely properly recognise speedway. Other news from the Bulldogs' camp was that Arthur Bush had been released following a few disappointing displays. The rider quickly linked with Third Division Yarmouth and made a great start, scoring 5 points on his debut v. Hull.

With September done and dusted, Bristol's next match was a home league fixture against the Diamonds from Newcastle on 1 October.

Spurred on by their success over Glasgow, the men in orange and black rode like demons and fairly battered their North-Eastern visitors by 67 points to 17, in the process improving on their season's best of the previous week. Right from the start the Bulldogs ripped into the opposition with maximum points courtesy of Fred Tuck and Jack Mountford. A further six 5-1s followed before Ken Le Breton and Maurice Stobart forced a share of the points in heat eight. However, the final six heats featured five maximum advantages plus a 4-2 as Bristol relentlessly pounded their opponents into oblivion. Needless to say the score grid was impressive, with six men going through the card unbeaten by an opponent. Billy Hole led the way with 12 points, while Roger Wise (11), Tuck (10), Mountford (10), Eric Salmon (9) and Nobby Stock (9) provided exceptional support. They didn't recognise them in those days, but all five of Hole's supporting cast would have been credited with a paid maximum today. Alec Grant topped the Newcastle chart, but 4 points was all he could yield against such a powerful combination. The second half of the meeting featured a five-heat junior mini-match between Bristol and Exeter. The youngsters failed to repeat the dominance of their senior counterparts, though, and went down to a 17-13 defeat with Norman Clay collecting 8 points from his three rides as he led Exeter to victory. With 7 points, Johnny Hole headed the Bristol scoring, while Dick Bradley, Graham Hole and Ginger Nicholls all chipped in with 2 points each.

The programme notes for the match *v.* Newcastle were of a very serious nature as Reg Witcomb made several points regarding a behind-closed-doors meeting that had taken place with the riders. He was angered by various misleading reports in certain evening newspapers, with the exception of the *Evening World*, which had given an accurate account of the talks. Going on, he explained that it had actually been a friendly meeting, with Fred Tuck acting as the riders' spokesman. The talks had been brought about when Jack Mountford was to be programmed at reserve in the previous month's away match at Middlesbrough, with Jack Gordon taking his place in the main body of the side. The riders felt that Mountford should be retained in his usual position as he was regarded as one of the old school, and they wished to keep the side together in their bid for the League Championship. The management understood the riders' point of view in the end and agreed, with Mountford subsequently taking his place, as usual, in the top six of the side at Cleveland Park.

On 2 October, Bristol completed their away league fixtures with a potentially difficult match at Norwich. Fired up for the occasion though, the Bulldogs raced to a fantastic 50-34 victory and, with the exception of Phil Clarke, who scored 10 points, the Stars offered little in the way of resistance. For the brilliant Bristol side, watched by 125 loyal supporters who had made the journey cross-country, Billy Hole gave a true captain's performance, sweeping to a four-ride maximum, while Fred Tuck, Roger Wise and Nobby Stock all finished with 8 points apiece. The win meant that all Bristol had to do was triumph in one of their remaining two home matches and the Championship was theirs!

So to the momentous date of 8 October, when the Bulldogs took on Middlesbrough with the title firmly on everyone's mind. Frank Hodgson opened with a stylish win for the visitors, before Eric Salmon and Roger Wise calmed the nerves with maximum points in heat two. There was no looking back from there on, aside from a share of the points in heats four and nine, with the Bristol men piling up the points to lead 49-23 after twelve races. That meant the Kemsley Trophy for the Second Division Championship, with medals and a cheque for £400, was in the bag. A drawn heat thirteen followed, before Jack Mountford and Billy Hole wrapped things up with a 4-2 to complete a 56-28 rout. The celebrations had long since begun, but the 12,000 crowd yelled and sung their approval even more, no doubt spurred on by Reg Witcomb's closing salvo in the race-day programme, written in block capitals on the 'What's What' page: 'LATE NEWS – WE HAVE MADE AN APPLICATION TO THE SPEEDWAY CONTROL BOARD FOR PERMISSION TO RACE IN THE FIRST DIVISION OF THE NATIONAL LEAGUE NEXT SEASON.' Looking at the completed programme, Bristol possessed three men on the 10-point mark, namely Mountford, Wise and Salmon, while Frank Hodgson led the Bears' scoring, also with 10 points. The second half of the meeting included a match-race challenge between Eric Chitty and Les Wotton but, with the former seizing a motor, Wotton sped to victory in the first encounter. With no machine, Chitty was subsequently replaced by Jack Mountford in the second race, and Eric Salmon in the third, with both Bristol men taking super victories over Wotton.

On 11 October, four Bristol men travelled down to Poole for a six-heat three-team tournament against the home side and Wombwell. The Bulldogs stamped their authority over the contest, scoring 19 points to take victory, while Poole scored 9 and Wombwell 8. Billy Hole and Eric Salmon recorded 6 points apiece, while Jack Mountford notched 4 and Roger Wise gleaned 3. As a matter of interest, the Poole team included Sid Clark, Dick Howard and George Butler, with Wombwell's side featuring Harwood Pike, Harry Welch and Son Mitchell.

Moving deep into the West Country, the Bulldogs took part in a five-heat challenge match at Plymouth on 14 October. The mini-match was included in the second half of a Third Division fixture that had seen the home side thrash Wombwell by 65 points to 19. However, Bristol then brought the Devils down to size as they sped to a 19-11 success, with skipper Billy Hole charging to 8 points, while Fred Tuck scored 7. Having dipped into a lower sphere of racing, it is interesting to note the riders on show and, as such, the Plymouth quartet for the match was made up of Peter Robinson, Len Read, Alex Gray and Pete Lansdale.

Returning to Knowle Stadium on 15 October, Bristol took on Fleetwood in their final league match of the campaign. Even though they had already secured the Championship, the Bulldogs thundered to a 57-27 win on a rain-soaked track. With a combination of poor weather and the result being academic, it was hardly surprising that only 9,000 people were in attendance. Billy Hole continued his brilliant end to the season with a maximum, and Roger Wise grabbed 11, while Wilf Plant's 7 points were sufficient to head the Flyers' scorecard. The final league table saw Bristol on top, having won twenty-three of their thirty-two matches. That gave them a total of 46 points, with Birmingham filling second place on 41. In the programme, Reg Witcomb revealed that the First Division promoters had met in London the previous Friday, and had agreed to recommend to the Control Board that Birmingham should be promoted, and not Bristol. The promoter went on: 'Why the First Division promoters do not want Bristol promoted, I don't know, but our application was sent to the Control Board and this will be considered at their next meeting, together with the recommendation from the promoters that Birmingham should go up. Some say that our stadium is not large enough for First Division crowds, but we have already had over 20,000 at a speedway meeting, since when the banking has been considerably extended and, by next season, 25,000 could attend. If this was not sufficient, further stands could be erected and we should then be able to accommodate 30,000 or more. Whether our application will be successful or not, I cannot say, but it is our ambition to have the Bulldogs race in the First Division, and we shall continue to press on with our claim if necessary year after year. If we have to remain in Division Two next season, you can rest assured that Bristol Speedway meetings will still be well worth your coming to see.'

Norwich were the visitors as Bristol completed their Anniversary Cup fixtures on 22 October and, after starting the match with a maximum from Fred Tuck and Jack Mountford, the Bulldogs ran riot once more, eventually hammering the Stars by 62 points to 32. Billy Hole scorched to a brilliant 15-point maximum, with Roger Wise plundering 13 points, but the most pleasing factor from the match was the fantastic form of junior riders Johnny Hole and Dick Bradley. The younger Hole rode well to collect 5 points, while Bradley's tally of 7 included his first race win for the Bulldogs in heat fifteen. Norwich were a poor outfit, with Wal Morton and Phil Clarke collecting one race win each on their way to 8-point totals. A look at the final Anniversary Cup table showed that it wasn't a particularly good tournament for the Bulldogs, with a seventh-place finish out of the nine competing teams. They had won all eight of their home matches, but there was no benefit from this, as they failed to do anything on their travels when 3 points were available for a win and 2 for a draw.

A special challenge match was staged between the Bulldogs and an all-star side entitled 'Split Waterman's Team' on 29 October. The opposition were a powerful outfit too, lining up as follows: 1. Split Waterman; 2. Jeff Lloyd; 3. Oliver Hart; 4. Eddie Rigg; 5. Kid Curtis; 6. Jim Boyd; 7. Howdy Byford; 8. Louis Lawson. A superb souvenir programme was issued for the meeting, giving the management and each of the Bulldogs the space to air his thoughts on the season, as well as the opportunity to thank the fans for their support. There were also the facts and figures on the season, as well as a brilliant match-by-match rundown of every meeting, along with results and scorers. Prior to the main event, Lawson clocked 66.2 seconds in an attempt on the track record, before Byford screamed around in 65.8 seconds, equalling Fred Tuck's best time for the circuit. Heat one of the match saw Waterman surge to the chequered flag in a shared race, before Roger Wise and Billy Hole sandwiched Hart to give the Bulldogs a 4-2. A tight tussle ensued with Bristol holding a 32-28 advantage when the interval was reached after heat ten. A special match-race challenge was then held, which saw Lawson defeat Byford in a time of 69.4 seconds. When the team match resumed, Rigg and

Lloyd combined to register a 5-1, restoring parity to the scores at 33-33. Two maximums in heats fourteen and sixteen gave Waterman's side a 53-49 advantage going into the final race, but some fantastic team riding saw Jack Mountford and Tuck combine to inflict a 5-1 over Byford and Boyd, leaving a final result of 54-54. Bristol could count themselves unfortunate though, for a second-race fall ruled Billy Hole out of the remainder of the meeting, with the reserves having to take his subsequent rides. Despite this, it had been a fantastic spectacle for the 12,000 supporters in attendance, with Tuck (15) and Mountford (13) heading a brilliant effort from the Bulldogs. Meanwhile, Waterman led his side superbly, notching 14 points although, somewhat surprisingly, no other member of his side reached double figures.

It transpired that Bristol did not get their wish regarding First Division racing and, according to the *Speedway News* dated 4 November, a petition was signed by hundreds of supporters in protest about the team's non-promotion, with a trip to London planned. One loyal fan was quoted as saying, 'We want about 1,000 followers to make the trip and we can let the London teams know exactly how strongly Bristol feel about the whole business. After all, we can understand the board suggesting improvements are needed at the Knowle track before First Division racing is permitted, but why, in the name of fortune, do such a stupid thing as to put Birmingham up? It's an insult to the West Countrymen and gives the impression Bristol are not wanted. We want fair play at Bristol – let the Control Board send a representative down to tell a supporters' club meeting just why the promotion bid of the Bulldogs was defeated. After all, we deserve to know.'

The final action of the season saw Bristol stage a charity meeting in aid of the Riders' Benevolent Fund on 5 November, with fifty per cent of the proceeds going to their own injured star Mike Beddoe. The thirty-fifth home meeting of the year, a Best Pairs event, was run in wintry conditions and saw the legendary Jack Parker link with Eric Salmon to form a potent duo. In front of an 11,000 gate Parker began the meeting in devastating style, clocking a new track-record time of 65.2 seconds as he cantered to victory in heat one. Among the other stars on show were Split Waterman, Oliver Hart, Frank Lawrence and Frank Hodgson. Nobody could live with Parker, however, and the Belle Vue star was untroubled on his way to a 15-point maximum. Salmon's contribution of 6 points was sufficient to partner Parker to victory, while

Waterman and Roger Wise filled the runner-up spot. Full result: Parker (15) and Salmon (6) 21; Waterman (11) and Wise (8) 19; Jack Mountford (10) and Hart (7) 17; Nobby Stock (8) and Hodgson (7) 15; Fred Tuck (10) and Ray Moore (1) 11; Lawrence (5) and Bill Pitcher (3) 8. In the programme, Reg Witcomb brought the curtain down on the season by reproducing a statement issued following the meeting of the Speedway Control Board on Wednesday 3 November. In its entirety, the statement read, 'As the result of our appeal, Mr George Allen and Mr Edgar Allen (the Knowle Stadium directors) attended a meeting of the Speedway Control Board yesterday, to state Bristol's case for promotion to the First Division. The board was sympathetic in their hearing, but made it quite clear that a system of automatic promotion and relegation is not their policy at present, and this year, having given consideration to all factors, they decided that only one additional team could be admitted to the First Division. Their choice of Birmingham was, we understand, based on accommodation, geographical situation and attendances. The board therefore, regretted their inability to promote Bristol this year, but said that all things being equal there is a good chance of our promotion next year.'

Reviewing the year, a total of 411,000 spectators clicked through the Knowle Stadium turnstiles for the thirty-five meetings, giving a fantastic average of 11,742. The overall attendance figure at British tracks in 1948 was 10,694,361, which brought a total income of £1,013,938 and earned the taxman £484,626. In total the Bulldogs appeared in fifty-seven fixtures (thirty-two National League, two National Trophy, sixteen Anniversary Cup and seven challenge) and, running through the riders, Fred Tuck was the Bristol master, scoring a total of 535 points from fifty-four matches. Exactly 300 of those points were attained in league matches alone, making the mighty Friar top points-man in the entire Second Division. Meanwhile, Billy Hole produced a captain's innings, remaining ever-present throughout the entire programme to net 457 points. Providing outstanding backing, Roger Wise ended the campaign with 429 points from fifty-six matches, while Eric Salmon notched 361 points and, like Wise, he missed just one match all season.

1948 STATISTICS

(Bristol's score shown first unless otherwise stated)

NATIONAL LEAGUE SECOND DIVISION

Opponents	Home	Away
Birmingham	W65-19	W44-39
	W52-32	L22-62
Edinburgh	W64-20	W46-38
	W64-19	L31-53
Fleetwood	W49-35	W42-41
	W57-27	L33-51
Glasgow	W53-31	W48-36
	W65-18	L38-46
Middlesbrough	W49-35	L33-50
	W56-28	W45-38
Newcastle	W57-27	W47-37
	W67-17	L33-51
Norwich	W60-24	L28-56
	W49-35	W50-34
Sheffield	W61-23	L40-43
	W55-29	L32-51

MATCH AVERAGES

Rider	Matches	Points	Average
Fred Tuck	32	300	9.38
Billy Hole	32	266	8.31
Nobby Stock	15	109	7.27
Roger Wise	32	229	7.16
Mike Beddoe	11	77	7.00
Eric Salmon	32	213	6.66
Jack Mountford	30	196	6.53
Cyril Quick	22	69	3.14
Johnny Hole	26	53	2.04
Ginger Nicholls	8	12	1.50
Dick Bradley	3	3	1.00
Arthur Bush	2	2	1.00
Johnny Myson	1	1	1.00
Graham Hole	6	5	0.83
Bill Clifton	1	0	0.00

Jack Gordon	2	0	0.00
Bob Jones	1	0	0.00

NATIONAL LEAGUE SECOND DIVISION TABLE

Team	Matches	Won	Drawn	Lost	For	Against	Pts
Bristol	32	23	0	9	1,535	1,145	46
Birmingham	32	20	1	11	1,489	1,195	41
Middlesbrough	32	18	2	12	1,445	1,237	38
Sheffield	32	17	1	14	1,355	1,324	35
Norwich	32	17	0	15	1,371	1,312	34
Glasgow	32	14	3	15	1,289	1,390	31
Newcastle	32	11	0	21	1,214	1,468	22
Fleetwood	32	10	1	21	1,254	1,425	21
Edinburgh	32	10	0	22	1,112	1,568	20

DAILY MAIL NATIONAL TROPHY

Opponents	Home	Away	Aggregate
Fleetwood	W65-43	L39-69	L104-112

MATCH AVERAGES

Rider	Matches	Points	Average
Fred Tuck	2	30	15.00
Roger Wise	2	22	11.00
Billy Hole	2	15	7.50
Eric Salmon	2	13	6.50
Johnny Hole	2	11	5.50
Jack Mountford	1	4	4.00
Cyril Quick	2	6	3.00
Lew Coffin	1	1	1.00
Graham Hole	2	2	1.00

ANNIVERSARY CUP (SECOND DIVISION)

Opponents	Home	Away
Birmingham	W58-37	L37-59
Edinburgh	W71-25	L32-64
Fleetwood	W56-40	L45-51
Glasgow	W55-39	L40-56

Middlesbrough	W58-37	L30-66
Newcastle	W58-38	L33-63
Norwich	W62-32	L27-69
Sheffield	W66-29	L40-56

MATCH AVERAGES

Rider	Matches	Points	Average
Fred Tuck	13	139	10.69
Billy Hole	16	135	8.44
Roger Wise	15	125	8.33
Nobby Stock	8	59	7.38
Mike Beddoe	3	22	7.33
Dick Bradley	1	7	7.00
Eric Salmon	16	87	5.44
Jack Gordon	1	5	5.00
Cyril Quick	13	62	4.77
Jack Mountford	15	71	4.73
Don Cuppleditch	1	4	4.00
Ginger Nicholls	2	8	4.00
Graham Hole	6	13	2.17
Johnny Hole	14	30	2.14
Arthur Bush	2	1	0.50
Johnny Myson	2	0	0.00

ANNIVERSARY CUP (SECOND DIVISION) TABLE

Team	Matches	Won	Drawn	Lost	For	Against	Pts
Birmingham	16	12	0	4	851	681	29
Sheffield	16	9	0	7	807	725	19
Glasgow	16	8	0	8	750	781	17
Middlesbrough	16	8	0	8	735	798	17
Norwich	16	7	1	8	792	733	16
Fleetwood	16	7	1	8	779	755	16
Bristol	16	8	0	8	768	761	16
Newcastle	16	6	0	10	728	784	12
Edinburgh	16	6	0	10	663	855	12

NOTE: 3 points were awarded for an away win and 2 points for an away draw.

1948

CHALLENGE

Opponents	Home	Away
Exeter	–	L27-57
Gayledons	W57-39	–
Kangaroos	W60-36	–
New Cross	L34-50	–
Southampton/Hastings	W66-18	–
Split Waterman's Team	D54-54	–
West Ham	L36-48	–

MATCH AVERAGES

Rider	Matches	Points	Average
Fred Tuck	7	66	9.43
Mike Beddoe	1	8	8.00
Eric Chitty	1	8	8.00
Eric Salmon	6	48	8.00
Roger Wise	7	53	7.57
Jack Mountford	6	39	6.50
Kid Curtis	1	6	6.00
Billy Hole	7	41	5.86
Nobby Stock	4	23	5.75
Cyril Quick	6	22	3.67
Dick Bradley	1	3	3.00
Graham Hole	1	2	2.00
Johnny Hole	6	12	2.00
Johnny Myson	2	3	1.50

MINI-MATCHES

(Staged at Poole)	Poole 13, Hastings 5, Southampton 7, Bristol 11
(Staged at Bristol)	Bristol 13 Exeter 17
(Staged at Poole)	Poole 9, Wombwell 8, Bristol 19
(Staged at Plymouth)	Plymouth 11 Bristol 19

MATCH AVERAGES

Rider	Matches	Points	Average
Johnny Hole	1	7	7.00

Fred Tuck	1	7	7.00
Billy Hole	3	20	6.67
Eric Salmon	2	11	5.50
Jack Mountford	1	4	4.00
Roger Wise	2	5	2.50
Dick Bradley	1	2	2.00
Graham Hole	1	2	2.00
Ginger Nicholls	1	2	2.00
Nobby Stock	1	2	2.00

1949

A new season dawned with Bristol somewhat begrudgingly facing another year of Second Division racing. Five new teams boosted their particular sphere of domestic racing, however, with Cradley Heath, Southampton, Ashfield (Glasgow), Coventry and Walthamstow coming on board, although that number was offset slightly as Middlesbrough had closed down and Birmingham had been promoted. The Bulldogs kicked off on Friday 25 March, ironically with a challenge match *v.* Birmingham, and Reg Witcomb welcomed everyone to the new season with the question: 'Shall we win the League Championship again, or will Walthamstow?' Certainly, in his opinion, these were the only two teams in with a shout. The Bristol side that faced Birmingham was very similar to the one that had finished 1948, with the only exception being the return of Mike Beddoe. That he rode again was down to sheer courage and determination, for the accident at Fleetwood had left him with such a terrible foot injury that many folk thought he would never come to terms with it. A total of 18,000 speedway-starved spectators were in attendance for the match and Bristol swept to a convincing 68-39 victory, with Billy Hole and Eric Salmon notching 14 points apiece, while Jack Mountford scored 10. Meanwhile, Fred Tuck won all three rides that he took part in, withdrawing from the rest of the meeting due to a bout of influenza. Meanwhile, the brave Beddoe took five rides and collected three third places in a steady if unspectacular return to the saddle. For the Brummies, Graham Warren fought a lone battle, gleaning a 13-point tally. Salmon produced the ride of the night in heat fourteen, defeating Warren and clocking a time of 65.4 seconds, just a fifth of a second outside Jack Parker's track record.

The Bulldogs opened their league campaign a week later on 1 April, with the visit of Fleetwood. The men in orange and black started where they had left off the previous year, hammering their opponents by 61 points to 22 before an audience of 15,000. A Bristol rider won every one of the fourteen heats, with seven 5-1s thrown in for good measure. Jack Mountford and Billy Hole completed wonderful 12-point maximums and, having got close to the track record the week before, Eric Salmon smashed in a new best time of 65.0 seconds when winning heat three, on his way to a superb 11-point haul. For the Flyers, Wilf Plant's 7-point return was sufficient to head the scorechart. In his 'What's What' column in the programme, Reg Witcomb was as candid as ever, stating: 'I am ending this article on a personal note. Most of you will know by now that I have resigned my position at this stadium, as director of Bristol Speedway and racing manager of Knowle Greyhound Stadium. The decision to do this after twelve years with the company was made after much careful thought. I have been appointed managing director of Abbey Stadium Ltd, Blunsdon, Swindon, and I intend to have my own speedway team in the near future. It will not be possible to enter a league this year, but I am hoping to stage friendly matches from about the end of May, so that in 1950, Swindon can have a team in the league.' He went on to thank all the people who had written or telephoned with good wishes and explained that stadium director George Allen would be taking over the running of Bristol Speedway. It was subsequently revealed that Harold Windows would be installed as the new manager of greyhound racing at Knowle.

Next on the agenda was a trip to Sheffield on 7 April, when the homesters sped to a 49-35 success on a wet and blustery night. Despite three days of continuous rain, the circuit was in a remarkably good condition, borne out by the fact that the track record was broken in each of the first three heats, with Bruce Semmens clocking the best time of 71.6 seconds. Semmens went on to take the flag in all four of his outings, before also winning the final of the second-half scratch event. Stan Williams supplied wonderful support to Semmens with 11 points, while Eric Salmon (11) and Billy Hole (10) headed the Bulldogs' scoring.

The following night it was back at Knowle for another thrashing, with Newcastle being the recipients of the Bulldogs' stampede. It might have been a bitterly cold evening, but that didn't stop 12,000 fans from turning up to witness their heroes romp to a 60-24 victory. Eric Salmon was again in superb form, landing a 12-point full-house, while Fred Tuck netted 11 points and Billy Hole 10. There was great joy too when Mike Beddoe won his first race since coming back, heat two, and went on to also win heat thirteen, finishing the night with a 7-point total. Having moved from Middlesbrough, Jack Hodgson topped the newly nicknamed Magpies' scoring with 8 points, while brother Frank notched 7. Among other events in the second half, a junior scratch race saw Graham Hole take victory from Ginger Nicholls, Ernie Brecknell and Don Lawson. The programme cover was changed for the meeting, with a fierce-looking bulldog replacing the previously used illustration of two riders going at full pelt.

Another week passed before Sheffield journeyed down to Bristol for a league engagement on 15 April. The Bulldogs again demonstrated their strength in depth around their own patch with a solid 55-29 success, witnessed by a huge 20,000 Good Friday attendance. Jack Mountford and Fred Tuck opened the proceedings with maximum points, before Billy Hole and Mike Beddoe repeated the dose in heat two. Although Sheffield provided three race winners, they failed to gain a single heat advantage as Hole completed an unbeaten 12-point maximum while Roger Wise grabbed 11. Meanwhile, Len Williams proved to be top man for the Tigers with 8 points. The second half of the meeting proved very interesting, with Bristol taking on Tiger Stevenson's Hanley side in a junior mini-match. The Potteries team rode well too, earning a 17-12 success, courtesy of the following riders: Gil Blake (6), Ken Adams (5), Les Jenkins (4) and Dave Anderson (2). For the Bristol side, Johnny Hole headed the scoring with 5 points, while Dick Bradley and Ginger Nicholls netted 3 apiece and Graham Hole scored 1.

One night later, Bristol were in action at Coventry and a gate of 23,000 turned up to watch the 1948 Second Division Champions on their first ever visit to Brandon Stadium. Although Bob Fletcher took the opening race for the Bees and Jack White subsequently won heat two, the Bulldogs quickly got to grips with the 375-yard circuit and cruised to a 48-35 victory. Fletcher went on to head the Coventry scoring with a 10-point tally, while Bristol were best served by a Roger Wise maximum and 10 points from Billy Hole.

To conclude a busy few days, the Bulldogs travelled to Cradley Heath for an Easter Monday encounter on 18 April, when they put on a magnificent show to thump the Heathens by 50 points to 34. Time and again the Bristol riders were faster from the gate, with Billy Hole and Jack Mountford both blasting to 12-point maximums. Alan Hunt did his best to stem the onslaught, winning two races in a fighting 9-point return, while Les Beaumont was Cradley's only other race winner, the 3 points gained in the process being his only contribution to the Heathens' score.

Back at Knowle on 22 April, Edinburgh made the long trip south, only to be sent packing as the Bulldogs screamed to a 68-16 victory. Showing no let-up, the Bristol boys piled up twelve maximum heat advantages while securing 4-2s from the other two races. No less than six home riders went through the card unbeaten by a visitor, with Billy Hole and Eric Salmon weighing in with maximums, while Fred Tuck (10), Jack Mountford (10) and Roger Wise (9) played major supporting roles. The other unbeaten Bristol man was reserve Johnny Hole, who partnered Tuck home in heat four, prior to taking victory in heat thirteen. Meanwhile, 5 points apiece from Dick Campbell and Eddie Lack headed the Monarchs' meagre total. In the match programme, George Allen praised the Bristol Tramways officials and drivers for the very efficient manner in which they had got the spectators away after the previous week's match *v.* Sheffield. He went on, 'The final bus-load pulled out of the car park within thirty minutes of the last race, pretty good going, when you come to think of it, with a hundred and seventy motor coaches also leaving through the same entrance!'

On 28 April, the last away action of the month took Bristol down to Plymouth for a challenge match against a composite side named 'Devon', which mainly comprised of Plymouth and Exeter riders. The Devon side offered no resistance to the Bristol machine, which simply let rip and thundered to a 56-28 success on the 400-yard racing strip. Fred Tuck got the lot (12), with Billy Hole and Eric Salmon bagging 11 points each, while Don Hardy headed the Devon scorecard on 6. Amazingly, Salmon continued to get faster and faster, equalling the track record at Pennycross Stadium when clocking 76.8 seconds in heat eleven, and this despite appalling weather conditions, which had set in by that stage of the match.

Coventry were the visitors to Knowle on 29 April. However, it didn't appear to matter who the opposition were and the Bees were dispatched by 67.5 points to 16.5. Maybe the big wins were becoming monotonous, but a reduced crowd of 9,000 was recorded for the meeting. The Bulldogs collected eleven maximum race advantages and it would have been twelve had John Yates not dead-heated with Eric Salmon for second place behind Roger Wise in heat six, giving a 4.5-1.5 result. The only other glints of light in the Bees' performance were second places for former Bulldog Jack Gordon, in heat eight, and Bob Fletcher, in heat twelve. Fred Tuck and Billy Hole nonchalantly strode to maximums, with Wise netting 10 points, while Fletcher was Coventry's best on 5. After the encounter, Bristol beat Plymouth 16-14 in a junior mini-match, with Ginger Nicholls scoring 5 points from his three starts. Meanwhile, with a 7-point haul, Len Read topped the Plymouth scorers.

The Bulldogs had a week off before Fleetwood travelled down for their second visit in five weeks on 6 May. Having beaten the Flyers 61-22 on their previous visit, it came as no surprise that Bristol rattled up another mammoth 67-17 win before a 10,000 gate. Fred Tuck opened the match in a devastating manner, equalling Eric Salmon's track record time of 65.0 seconds as he and teammate Jack Mountford romped to a 5-1. Not to be outdone, Salmon subsequently zipped around the 290-yard circuit in a new record time of 64.4 seconds as he took victory in heat three. For the second successive home match, a race resulted in a dead-heat when, in heat seven, Tuck and Mountford flashed across the line in unison, gaining 2.5 points apiece. Salmon and skipper Billy Hole went on to complete full maximums, while Tuck ended the night with 11.5 points to his name. Meanwhile, the best Fleetwood representatives were Wilf Plant, Norman Hargreaves and Ernie Appleby, each of whom could only manage 4 points. The Knowle Handicap was held in the second half, with some riders going from as far back as fifty yards. The flying Salmon was the only rider able to win his heat from so far adrift, and he went on also to take the final from Dick Bradley, Cyril Cooper and Ginger Nicholls.

The agenda then took the Bulldogs up to Lancashire for a Second Division fixture against Fleetwood on 11 May. Still seething from their two wallopings at Knowle, the Flyers set about the meeting with great determination as Norman Hargreaves joined forces with Cyril Cooper for maximum points in heat two, before Frank Malouf linked with Ernie Appleby to repeat the dose two races later. The home side went on to record a thoroughly deserved 46-38 victory, with Hargreaves topping their scoring on the 10-point mark. Having won his first three races, Fleetwood's George Newton had his maximum hopes dashed in heat fourteen when he suffered an engine failure with the race seemingly in the bag. For the Bristol side, which had suffered only its second loss of the year, Jack Mountford headed the scoring with 11 points. A special word of praise is due to Mike Beddoe, as he returned to the scene of his horrifying crash and rode steadily to net 4 points.

Back on home territory, Ashfield were the next lambs to the slaughter as the league leaders rushed to a 63-21 victory on 13 May. The landslide began in heat one, as Jack Mountford and Fred Tuck galloped to a maximum advantage, and a further eight races resulted in 5-1s for Bristol. Topping the scoring were Billy Hole and Roger Wise with unbeaten 12-point tallies, while Mountford totalled 11. For the battered Giants, Norman Evans managed a couple of second-place finishes on his way to a 6-point tally, with Ken Le Breton notching 5. The evening's events were spiced up a little in the second half, with Split Waterman and Freddie Williams appearing in some challenge races against Bristol's best. The First Division aces didn't have everything their own way though, as Eric Salmon and Wise charged to victory over Waterman in the first contest, while Williams brought up the rear. Mike Beddoe won heat two from Waterman and Hole, before Mountford took heat three from Williams, with Tuck in third spot. Waterman finally got his act together in the final though, taking the chequered flag ahead of Salmon, while Williams beat Wise for third position.

The Firs Stadium at Norwich beckoned on 14 May and a crowd of 20,003 witnessed the Stars defeat Bristol by 52 points to 32. This was after Fred Tuck and Jack Mountford had got the Bulldogs off to a good start with a 4-2 in heat one. Norwich got into a smooth groove thereafter, and a 20-point loss was a real shock for the men in orange and black. The homesters were best served by a Paddy Mills maximum, while Fred Rogers and Jack Freeman both chipped in with 10 points apiece. On a disappointing night for Bristol, Billy Hole's 9 points were enough to top the score grid.

On 19 May, the Bristol lads travelled to Oxford, where they joined forces with the home side for a challenge match *v.* Southampton. The meeting had a topsy-turvy start, with the lead changing hands four times in the first six heats, before the combined Oxford/Bristol side pulled away to win 47-36. Jack Mountford was in sensational form, establishing a new track record of 73.2 seconds in heat one, before going on to complete a superlative maximum. Billy Hole scored 10 points, while the other representatives for the combined side were: Bert Croucher (8), Dennis Gray (7), Alf Viccary (6), Alf Elliott (4), Ernie Rawlins (0) and Bill Downton (0). Meanwhile, Tom Oakley headed the Saints' scoring with 9 points, while Jimmy Squibb notched 8.

It was a big night at Knowle on 20 May, when Bristol took on the mighty Belle Vue in a challenge match, and a record crowd of 22,000 was present to view the action. Once again, Fred Tuck and Jack Mountford linked together for maximum points in the opening race, amazingly leaving Jack Parker trailing in their wake. A lapse of concentration was later blamed for Parker's failure in this race, as he had actually forgotten to turn on his fuel tap! Three of the next four heats were shared, with Belle Vue gaining a 4-2 in the other, before Dent Oliver and Pee Wee Cullum combined to give the Aces a 5-1 in heat six, and with it the lead. The Bulldogs immediately hit back through a Mountford and Tuck maximum, followed by a 3-2 advantage. Five heats in a row were then drawn, before Belle Vue broke the Bristol hearts with successive 5-1s, courtesy of Louis Lawson and Parker, followed by Jim Boyd and George Smith in heats fourteen and fifteen respectively. With the final heat being shared, the world-famous Manchester club took a narrow victory by 50 points to 45 and boasted three men in double figures, namely Dent Oliver (12), Jack Parker (11) and Louis Lawson (10). Both Oliver and Parker gleaned their points from five rides apiece, while Lawson's score was achieved from four starts. Meanwhile, for the battling Bulldogs who fought all the way, Tuck and Billy Hole were joint top scorers with 10 points each. Among many highlights, Parker twice equalled the track record of 64.4 seconds, in heats nine and sixteen, while Louis Lawson also attained the exact same time in heat fourteen. In his programme notes, George Allen mentioned the critics who had groused about the facilities, or lack of them, at Knowle Stadium. The promoter explained, 'I wonder if they realise that our main stand and clubroom were blitzed and until such time as the War Damage Commission decide that we can rebuild, there is nothing we can do about it. Don't think it is for want of trying on our part. We are always worrying the Ministry for licences, but they, possibly rightly, say that there are far too many other jobs of higher priority to be done before we can go ahead.'

Another week of rest followed before Walthamstow visited Knowle on 27 May, as the Bulldogs embarked on a busy spell of five league matches in six days. For the seventh time in eight home Second Division matches, Bristol reached 60 points in another one-sided affair, and perhaps the public were showing what they felt about this as only 7,500 turned up, compared with the 22,000 of the previous week for the match *v.* Belle Vue! Billy Hole and Fred Tuck led the onslaught with a dozen points each as the Bulldogs scampered to a 60-24 success. The Wolves' riders didn't know what had hit them, and Jim Boyd was their only race winner, in heat six, on his way to a 7-point tally. A series of challenge races saw Odsal stars Oliver Hart and Ron Clarke take on the Bulldogs in the second half of the programme. However, in the three qualifying heats, Clarke won only one race, while Hart ran a last in each. Hole went on to win the final from Eric Salmon, while Hart pipped Clarke for third place.

Bristol then set off up north, with the first stop being Old Meadowbank Stadium in Edinburgh on 28 May. A crowd of 23,000 saw a tense battle, which only swung the Bulldogs' way thanks to three 4-2s and a 5-1 from Billy Hole and Mike Beddoe in heat nine. The Monarchs came back with maximum points from Clem Mitchell and Eddie Lack in heat ten, but Bristol managed to hang on for a narrow 44-40 victory. The main scorers of the meeting were Clem Mitchell (11) for Edinburgh, while Billy Hole (12) and Jack Mountford (10) did the business for Bristol.

On 30 May, the Bulldogs were in action at Newcastle and, after a quiet start with two shared heats, Jack Mountford and Fred Tuck fired in a 5-1, the former equalling Frank Hodgson's Brough Park track-record time of 73.6 seconds in the process. Bristol opened up after that and went on a scoring spree to win by 55 points to 29. Mountford completed a four-ride maximum, with Roger Wise lending great support on the 10-point mark. With 8 points, Jack Hodgson was the Magpies' best performer on what was a very unhappy night for the home team.

Next it was up to Glasgow on 31 May, and the Saracen Park home of the Ashfield Giants. Although the Bulldogs fell behind in the early stages they gradually hauled themselves back into the match as they became more accustomed to the 355-yard raceway. The telling races both featured Dick Bradley, who linked with Eric Salmon, in heat eight, and Jack Mountford, in heat thirteen, for maximum advantages that gave Bristol the edge, before they finally ran out 46-38 winners. Maximum man Ken Le Breton did his best to keep the Giants in contention, but his side lacked any real strength in depth. For the Bulldogs, it was a welcome return to the top of the scorecard for Mike Beddoe with 9 points.

Bristol's riders remained in the Scottish city overnight and completed their whistle-stop tour on the first day of June with a meeting against Glasgow Tigers at White City Stadium. The Bulldogs were on a roll and they made it an incredible four wins out of four on the northern tour, smashing their way to a 57-27 success. There was no early sign of such a result, but the visitors really clicked into gear after Johnny Hole and Roger Wise had charged to maximum points over Nobby Downham in heat four. The Tigers didn't know what day it was after that and Bristol's relentless charge left them reeling. Eric Salmon finished on top of the pile, scoring 10 points, while Bat Byrnes was the most productive rider for the home side in notching a tally of 9.

There wasn't much time to recover from such an arduous tour, with a home meeting *v.* Norwich just two nights later on 3 June. As had become the usual start to a match at Knowle, Fred Tuck and Jack Mountford flew to maximum points in heat one. A further six 5-1s followed before Ted Bravery managed to split Billy Hole and Dick Bradley in heat eight for 2 points. The steamroller carried on unabated, however, with Bristol eventually cantering to a 66-18 success before a crowd of 8,000. Four riders reached double figures for the brilliant Bulldogs, namely Billy Hole (12), Mountford (11), Eric Salmon (11) and Tuck (10), while Phil Clarke's lowly 5-point return headed the Stars' scoring. George Allen's programme notes explained that Ginger Nicholls had asked for a transfer to a Third Division track. The lad was keen and full of enthusiasm, but felt that he needed a move in order to get more rides and further his experience. The promoter also quashed rumours suggesting that Bristol were considering transferring some of their riders elsewhere.

Bristol fans didn't have long to wait until their next fix, with First Division Harringay arriving for a grand challenge match on Whit Monday, 6 June. The fixture obviously created increased interest among the supporters, as a 20,000 audience was in place to see former Bristol rider Vic Duggan skipper a Racers side that also included Geoff Pymar, Nobby Stock (who had rejoined the London side following his spell with Bristol the previous season), Ray Duggan, Danny Dunton and Lloyd Goffe. The match was tight throughout, with the sides level at 30 points apiece after heat ten. However, the Bulldogs managed to break the deadlock, recording two successive 4-2 advantages, before heat thirteen was shared. Billy Hole then took the flag in the final race, defeating Goffe, while Fred Tuck mopped up the odd point to secure an outstanding

Bristol victory by 45 points to 39. Both Hole and Roger Wise demonstrated they could mix it with the top boys, notching 11 points each. For the illustrious visitors, Stock showed he hadn't forgotten the quickest route around the Knowle circuit, topping the Harringay scoring with 10 points, while Geoff Pymar finished with a tally of 9.

The third home meeting in a week was a qualifying round of the World Championship on 10 June when, somewhat strangely, Fred Tuck was the only Bristol representative in the field. An attendance of 11,000 viewed the action and Tuck didn't disappoint them, blasting his way to five straight victories and taking the winner's cheque of £30. With 13 points, Poole's Alan Chambers claimed the runner-up position, while Ken Adams of Hanley was third on the 12-point mark. Full result: Tuck 15; Chambers 13; Adams 12; Ray Harris 11; Olle Nygren 10; Peter Robinson 9.5; Norman Hargreaves 9; Alex Gray 7.5; Herbie King 7; Fred Rogers 6; Ken Middleditch 6; Gil Blake 5; Buddy Fuller 3; Jack Freeman 3; Graham Hole (reserve) 3; Johnny Myson 0; Percy Brine 0.

Back on their travels again, the table-topping Bulldogs visited the well-appointed Banister Court home of Southampton on 14 June. Surprisingly, Bristol came up against an inspired Saints side that refused to buckle and, although the match was finely balanced throughout, the home side just held sway to record a fine 45-39 victory. Bristol captain Billy Hole gave another superb performance with maximum points but, unfortunately, the rest of his side appeared to have difficulty adjusting to the 333-yard raceway. On a night of great celebration in the home camp, Jimmy Squibb weighed in with 11 points and Bob Oakley netted 9.

In a break from league action on 16 June, the Bulldogs travelled to Sheffield for an elimination round of the *Daily Mail*-sponsored National Trophy. After their shock reverse at Southampton, Bristol were fired up for the tie and, although the Tigers fought hard, the Bulldogs always seemed to have matters under control. Going into the last heat, Bristol led 53-49, meaning Sheffield needed a maximum to force a draw. Tommy Allott and Len Williams looked set to get the result the homesters required, but a fantastic last-lap effort saw Billy Hole snatch second place from Williams on the line, giving the Bulldogs a 55-53 victory. Allott was brilliant for Sheffield on the night, finishing with a 17-point tally, while Len Williams plundered 16. Turning to the other half of the scorecard and Bristol's success was engineered mainly by Hole (14) and Fred Tuck (11).

The return match against Sheffield was held at Knowle Stadium the following evening, when the Bulldogs cruised through to the second eliminating round courtesy of a convincing 73-35 win. Indeed, they never looked back after Messrs Mountford and Tuck had walloped in their usual maximum start to the match. Seven more 5-1s were recorded during the meeting, although Stan Williams proved to be a real thorn in Bristol's side, thwarting any hopes of a home rider notching maximum points. The nearest anyone got was Roger Wise, but that man Williams took the chequered flag in heat seventeen, leaving the Swindon-born racer with 14 points to his name. Billy Hole and Eric Salmon each registered 10 points for the Bulldogs, while the battling Williams topped the Tigers' scoring on 13. Interestingly, with the passage to the next round sewn up, Bristol elected to nominate reserves Johnny Hole and Dick Bradley for heat eighteen. Unsurprisingly, Williams collected the win, but Bradley rode well to finish second, while the younger Hole beat Tommy Bateman for third place.

The date of 18 June was a momentous one in the history of Bristol Speedway, for the Bulldogs (minus Fred Tuck) made the journey up to Manchester in order to face the mighty Belle Vue in a challenge match. Despite the Aces being without heat-leaders Jack Parker, Louis Lawson and Dent Oliver, they completely outclassed the Bulldogs, blasting to a 66-18 victory. The first eight races resulted in maximum advantages for the home side and the pattern was only broken when George Smith fell in heat nine, allowing Billy Hole and Mike Beddoe to gain an even split of the points behind Ken Sharples. The Aces then hammered in four more 5-1s before another fall from Smith gave Bristol a shared heat fourteen. Looking through the scorechart, Belle Vue were spearheaded by Ron Mason and Sharples with 12 points apiece, while Bruce Semmens scored 11 and Wally Lloyd 10. Incidentally, the meeting marked Semmens' debut meeting for the Manchester outfit, the Cornishman having joined them from Sheffield earlier in the week. Skipper Billy Hole was Bristol's best representative on what turned into a disappointing night, recording just 6 points.

On 20 June, Billy Hole and Jack Mountford represented Bristol in a three-heat challenge match at Exeter. This formed part of the second half after the Falcons had defeated Hull 48-36 in a National League Third Division fixture. All of the heats featured Hole and Mountford and, although Exeter used three different pairings, it was the Bulldogs' duo that comfortably came out on top to register a 14-4 success.

Back home on 24 June the Bulldogs took out their frustration at the Belle Vue debacle on a Coventry side who were visiting on *Daily Mail* National Trophy business. The Bees certainly felt the backlash as Bristol smashed their way to an 80-28 triumph. Thirteen of the eighteen races resulted in 5-1 successes for the Bulldogs in another points avalanche, witnessed by 9,000 supporters. Billy Hole collected five wins and a second place behind Fred Tuck on his way to a 17-point tally, while Friar himself notched 16 points, his dropped points being behind teammates Jack Mountford, in heat one, and Hole, in heat nine. Aside from that, Roger Wise and Jack Mountford both finished on totals of 11, while Eric Salmon scored 10. For the battered Bees, 6 points apiece from Bob Fletcher and Bert Lacey was sufficient to jointly top their scorecard. In the second half, some interesting names appeared in the junior scratch event, with Crusty Pye taking the victor's spoils ahead of Jack White, Chris Boss and Norman Meek. In the match programme, Edgar Allen made his first attempt at journalism as brother George was lying in bed recovering from an operation. Although he didn't specify the reason for the surgery, he did mention that it had been successful and also hoped his sibling would be back on the scene at Knowle very shortly. Mr Allen went on to explain about Fred Tuck's absence from the away match at Belle Vue. Apparently, in heat fifteen of the National Trophy encounter with Sheffield at Knowle, the lanky rider somehow managed to get his leg twisted underneath himself and dislocated a kneecap. It sounded bad enough but, thankfully, it didn't keep the resiliant rider out of the saddle for long as he of course returned to the fold that night against Coventry.

For their final meeting of the month, Bristol travelled to Coventry for the second leg of their National Trophy tie on 25 June, with the meeting being nothing more than academic following the mauling they had dished out twenty-four hours previously. As things turned out, it was a complete stroll for the Bulldogs, who provided fifteen race winners. Only Derrick Tailby offered any resistance when taking the flag in heats eleven, fifteen and seventeen on his way to a 12-point tally. Aside from Tailby, everything went Bristol's way and they comfortably recorded a 66-42 victory, with the main players being Billy Hole (17), Eric Salmon (16) and Jack Mountford (10).

Returning to the cut and thrust of Second Division racing, Bristol entertained Cradley Heath on 2 July and, in a change from normal, the meeting took place on a Saturday evening. The Black Country outfit brought some noisy and enthusiastic support with them – some forty-five coach loads in fact! Unfortunately for them, the Heathens came and went as all previous league challengers had done since the season began, on the back of a thrashing. Ripping into the opposition from the opening heat, the Bulldogs walloped in five consecutive 5-1s before they were restricted to a 4-2 in heat six. The onslaught soon got back on track, however, with the final result being 62-22. Billy Hole was untroubled on his way to a maximum, receiving solid support from Fred Tuck (11), Roger Wise (10) and Jack Mountford (10). Meanwhile, Gil Craven's 5 points were sufficient for him to top Cradley Heath's scoring. Special guests Frank Lawrence and Jeff Lloyd appeared in the second half, but they were outgunned, with neither managing to win a single race against the on-song home riders. Despite this, the two aces were programmed directly through to the final of the scratch event, when they were again defeated, Tuck claiming an emphatic victory over Lawrence while Eric Salmon pipped Lloyd for third position. Edgar Allen revealed in his notes that it was something of an experimental move to try a Saturday night meeting in an effort to see what would be most popular with the fans. With 9,500 good folk turning up, the result was inconclusive though, as the Bristol management could well have expected a similar figure had they stuck to their usual Friday race night.

Back to their regular Friday night slot on 8 July, Bristol faced Fleetwood in the National Trophy semi-final elimination competition as it was called. A gate of 10,000 was in attendance for this one as the Bulldogs again went on the rampage, winning by 73 points to 35. Half of the eighteen heats resulted in 5-1s to Bristol, although the Flyers did provide six race winners in the other eight heats. The Bulldogs' main men on the night were Roger Wise (15), Billy Hole (12), Eric Salmon (11) and Fred Tuck (11), while Fleetwood's best was Wilf Plant with an outstanding 17-point tally. Plant's only defeat of the match occurred in heat one, when he had to settle for second place behind Hole. The Fleetwood representative gained revenge in heat twelve, however, for not only did he defeat Hole, but he also equalled the track record of 64.4 seconds. The Second Division table was reproduced in the programme and it showed that Sheffield had taken over top spot, having gleaned 33 points from twenty-two matches, while the Bulldogs occupied second place with 32 points from twenty meetings. Some way back in third position stood Norwich, the Norfolk outfit having gained 24 points from eighteen fixtures.

On 13 July, Bristol appeared in the return leg of the National Trophy tie at the Highbury Avenue home of Fleetwood. Although the 336-yard track was waterlogged following heavy rain, the meeting still went ahead as scheduled with the Bulldogs riding to a superb 60-46 success and a place in the final of the elimination competition. Skipper Billy Hole led the scoring with 14 points, while Eric Salmon came up with 13. As expected, Wilf Plant was the Flyers' best performer, weighing in with 16 points.

Returning to league activity, Southampton were the next visitors to Knowle on 15 July, but they weren't disgraced as the Bulldogs scampered to a 56-27 victory. Indeed, the Saints restricted Bristol to just six maximum scores, while gaining one of their own through brothers Bob and Tom Oakley in heat nine. The highlight of the meeting was the sight of super-fast Eric Salmon twice equalling his own track record of 64.4 seconds in heats eight and eleven, and this was after only finishing third in his opening ride. Billy Hole swept to another maximum, while Salmon recovered from his first-race blip to register 10 points. Turning to the other side of the programme, Bob Oakley was Southampton's top performer, notching a 7-point tally. The league encounter was followed by a five-heat junior mini-match between Bristol and Poole, which saw another home win, by 19 points to 10. Mike Beddoe headed the Bristol scorecard with 8 points, while Poole were best represented by Alan Chambers, who scored 6.

Home meeting number nineteen brought Walthamstow to Bristol for the second time in the season on 22 July and, having had 60 points knocked past them the first time, the visitors did reasonably well, pegging the Bulldogs to a 51-33 success. Bristol were never really troubled during the match, although the Wolves' lads did provide three race winners in the first six heats. This included a victory for Charlie May in heat three, although this could be attributed to Fred Tuck taking a nasty looking tumble while mounted on a new frame, fracturing his jaw in the process. There was nothing anybody could do in heat five other than sit back and watch in awe as Eric Salmon stormed around in 63.8 seconds to establish yet another new track record. Top of the pile for the Bulldogs were Roger Wise (11), Jack Mountford (10) and Salmon (10), while May was the best performer for the Londoners with 9 points. After the match, Bill Kitchen and Split Waterman appeared in a series of challenge races against the Bristol riders, but this was marred when Billy Hole and the two Wembley men had a coming together in heat three, resulting in Waterman suffering internal injuries and a damaged shoulder. It wasn't all bad news in the second half, however, as Mountford twice blitzed around the circuit in 63.8 seconds to equal the track record, which Salmon had earlier set in the main match.

Bristol engaged in combat with Norwich on 29 July in the first leg of the elimination round final of the National Trophy. This was a potentially difficult encounter but, as usual, the Bulldogs tore into the match, recording three successive maximums. It soon became obvious that the meeting would turn into another rout and Bristol roared on to win by a staggering 50-point margin, 79-29 – and that was without the injured Fred Tuck! The gate of 11,000 saw Jack Mountford thump in a scintillating 18-point maximum, while Billy Hole (16), Eric Salmon (12), Roger Wise (11) and Johnny Hole (10) provided powerful support. Phil Clarke sparkled brightest for the beleaguered Stars in scoring 8 points, while Jack Freeman was their only race winner in heat four.

The second leg of the National Trophy tie v. Norwich took place at The Firs Stadium the very next night. Bristol were under attack right from the start as the Stars raced to a heat-one maximum prior to notching up another five 5-1s in the next seven races. The Bulldogs rallied a little and managed to split heats ten, eleven and thirteen, before Jack Mountford became their only race winner of the night in heat sixteen. By the end, Bristol were only just hanging on, with Norwich adding a final-heat maximum to end up 76-32 victors. However, the Bulldogs had just done enough to gain an aggregate success courtesy of a 111-105 scoreline, with 7 points from Roger Wise being their highest contribution on the night. For the Stars, who dominated on their own raceway, Phil Clarke rode magnificently to an 18-point maximum, receiving terrific back-up from Bob Leverenz (14), Ted Bravery (12) and Bert Spencer (11). While Bristol were in action at The Firs, there was plenty going on at Knowle Stadium, as Reg Kavanagh's Hollywood Hell Drivers went through a breathtaking routine of death-defying stunts, crashes through walls of flame, high-speed reverse driving and car leaping as part of a busy and varied programme. George Allen later admitted he had been more than a little concerned when Mr Kavanagh had made several attempts to turn a car over. Worried that the track surface had been ripped up, Mr Allen returned with trepidation the following morning, only to happily find the circuit in fine condition, with no damage to speak of.

Bristol's next action took them to Chingford Road in London for a league encounter with Walthamstow on 1 August. This was actually the Bulldogs' first-ever visit to the 282-yard circuit and a number of the side had difficulty in adapting. The match was close throughout despite that, but a Wolves 5-1 in heat thirteen, courtesy of Harry Edwards and Archie Windmill, wrapped up victory for the homesters, with the final result eventually being 46-37. The victorious east London side were led by Jim Boyd's 8 points, while Benny King, Edwards, Reg Reeves and Charlie May were all solid contributors with tallies of 7 apiece. On a low night for Bristol, Roger Wise shone like a beacon with a maximum, while Jack Mountford scored 10 but, unfortunately, the remaining six members of the side only yielded a further 15 points between them. Bristol's cause wasn't helped by the absence of Mike Beddoe, although he had the perfect reason for missing the match, instead being present at wife Marion's bedside for the birth of their first child, a daughter named Suzanne.

Eager to atone for the loss at Walthamstow, the Bulldogs made the journey down to Southampton on 2 August. Despite 5-1s from Eric Salmon and Roger Wise in heats two and six, the Saints dug deep and refused to capitulate, and it wasn't until Johnny Hole and Chris Boss secured a 4-2 in heat twelve that Bristol pulled 7 points clear. Even then Southampton came back with a 4-2, as Phil Bishop won from Boss and Alf Kaines in the penultimate race, before Tom Oakley and Roy Craighead recorded a 5-1 in heat fourteen. The Bulldogs had just hung on to win 42-41 and only at the end did they realise how crucial the second-place finish from Boss had been in heat thirteen. The leading points scorers on the night were Bob Oakley with 11 for Southampton, while Salmon netted 10 for Bristol.

Newcastle were the next visitors to Knowle on 5 August, with a couple of important league points at stake. Normal home service was quickly resumed as the combinations of Mike Beddoe and Billy Hole, in heat one, and Eric Salmon and Roger Wise, in heat two, swept Bristol into a 10-2 lead. Although the Bulldogs finally ran out winners by 60 points to 24, the Newcastle riders restricted them to just four further 5-1s over the other twelve heats. Bristol's best performers on the night were Salmon and Jack Mountford with full-house dozens to their name, while Hole gleaned 10 points. Not for the first time, the Hodgson brothers proved to be the leading visitors, both jointly heading the Magpies' scoring on 7 points. After the main event, a special junior mini-match was held against a Halifax side featuring Arthur Forrest, Jack Dawson, Dick Seers and Al Allison. Bristol raced to a 22-8 victory, with their points coming from Johnny Hole (9), Dick Bradley (7), Chris Boss (4) and Graham Hole (2). Meanwhile, Forrest and Seers proved to be the top men for Halifax, although each could only yield 3 points. A quick glance at the Second Division table after the Bulldogs' match against Newcastle showed Sheffield on top with 43 points from thirty matches, while Bristol were lying second, having attained 40 points from only twenty-five meetings.

Still on their travels, Bristol journeyed to Fleetwood for the final time of the year on 8 August as the quest for league points continued. The Flyers were already hampered by injuries to Ron Hart and Wilf Plant, which prevented both from riding, and they then lost Ernie Appleby with a broken thigh early in the match. Despite this, the Lancashire side were no pushovers and the Bulldogs had to strain every sinew to eke out a 44-39 success. In notching 11 points, Norman Hargreaves gave a great display for the home side, while Billy Hole also registered 11 to top the Bristol scoring.

The league schedule meant a difficult match at table-topping Sheffield on 11 August, when the Bulldogs came across an in-form Tigers outfit, who swept to a 56-28 success. Billy Hole, in heat five, and Johnny Hole, in heat twelve, were Bristol's only race winners, while Roger Wise's 7 points headed a disastrous-looking scorecard. Jack Chignell recorded a four-ride maximum for the rampant home team, while Tommy Allott scored 11 points and former Bulldog Jack Bibby tallied 10.

Needing a rapid recovery, the Bristol lads looked forward to the visit of Glasgow at Knowle the following evening. The match report that appeared in *Speedway News* perfectly summed up their runaway 62-22 victory: 'The Bulldogs attacked from the start and there was no mercy. Billy Hole collected his fourteenth league maximum, Eric Salmon smashed the track record (63.4 seconds) and three Glasgow men (Bat Byrnes, Gordon McGregor and Alf McIntosh) travelled 394 miles to Bristol from Glasgow without getting a point between them!' Bristol's other leading scorers on the night were Salmon (11) and Jack Mountford (10), while the tamed Tigers were headed by Joe Crowther's meagre 6-point return. After setting his latest track record in heat five, Salmon went on to equal his new best time as he took the chequered flag ahead of Billy Hole, Junior Bainbridge and Norman Lindsay in the second-half scratch event final.

In a break from the league programme, Bristol journeyed to the Old Kent Road for an encounter with First Division New Cross in the second round proper of the *Daily Mail* National Trophy on 17 August. Played out in front of 25,000 spectators, the Bulldogs, still minus Fred Tuck, gave an outstanding showing, as they brilliantly took to the mini 262-yard track and most certainly worried their more illustrious opponents, before gallantly going down to a narrow 55-53 defeat. Considering that the Rangers' line-up included Bill Longley, Jeff Lloyd, Frank Lawrence, Don Gray and the Roger brothers (Cyril and Bert), this was a monumental result. Top of the scorecharts were Longley (12) and Lloyd (11) for the homesters, while Roger Wise and Jack Mountford performed heroically with 14 points apiece for the battling Bulldogs.

The return match *v.* New Cross was held at Knowle on 19 August and any thoughts of a fairytale aggregate success were quickly dashed when Bert Roger and Bill Longley sped to a 5-1 in heat one, with Jeff Lloyd and Frank Lawrence following suit in heat two. Unfortunately for the majority in the 22,000 audience, the Bulldogs were never able to get back into contention and the match slipped from their grasp, with a 60-47 defeat resulting. That meant an aggregate loss by 115 points to 100, but the Bristol riders could hold their heads up for extending one of British speedway's foremost teams with such vigour. The best performers on the night for Bristol were Billy Hole (13) and Roger Wise (10), with the leading Rangers being Longley (16), Lloyd (11) and Ray Moore (11). In the 'What's What' column, George Allen heaped praise on Eric Salmon for again breaking the track record the previous week. He went on, 'It is becoming a habit with him and, as I said to him after the race, it is mighty clever how he manages to clip off just one-fifth of a second every time. He gets a £6 bonus for each new record he sets up and somehow he makes quite sure that he does it by just enough and no more.'

The Bulldogs had little time to draw breath for, the night after facing New Cross, they were back in league action at Coventry's Brandon Stadium. An attendance of 21,000 folk witnessed the Bees push Bristol all the way on their super 375-yard circuit. After heat eleven, the Bulldogs held a slender 34-32 advantage and it was Johnny Hole who produced the match-winning rides, first linking brilliantly with Dick Bradley in heat twelve, and then brother Billy in heat fourteen to ensure victory by 46 points to 38. The last-heat success for Billy Hole completed yet another full maximum for the skipper, while Roger Wise and Jack Mountford lent solid support with 9 points each. Coventry possessed no outstanding rider, with Les Wotton and Roy Moreton jointly finishing on top of the pile having secured 7 points each.

There was a unusual occurrence on 22 August when Jack Mountford and Eric Salmon decided to make their way down to St Austell in readiness for a challenge match the following day featuring two composite sides. On the evening in question Exeter easily defeated Leicester 57-27 in a National League Third Division encounter. In the second half, a combined Exeter and Leicester side were scheduled to face a Swedish outfit, including Olle Nygren, in a four-heat challenge. However, the boat carrying the tourists was late in docking, so the Exeter management turned their attentions to Bristol and firstly tried to get hold of Billy Hole. Unfortunately the Bulldogs' skipper wasn't available as he was on his way to Glasgow to challenge Ken Le Breton for the Silver Helmet. Instead, it was arranged for one of the motoring organisations to intercept Mountford and Salmon on the Exeter bypass and the duo duly appeared that evening in a hastily rearranged four-heat challenge against the Falcons. The Bristol pair raced together in every heat to total 10 points, while Exeter used eight different riders on their way to victory with a 14-point haul.

On 23 August, Billy Hole arrived at Ashfield for his head-to-head Silver Helmet showdown with Ken Le Breton and the effort to get there proved worthwhile too, as the Bristol representative scorched to successive victories on a well-prepared raceway. To complete a night of misery for the Giants supporters, in the league match that followed, Norwich scampered away to an untroubled 50-34 success.

Southampton again travelled to Knowle on 26 August and a glimpse at the league table prior to the meeting revealed that Sheffield were still sat on top, having gleaned 49 points from thirty-three matches, while Bristol were still handily placed in second position on 46 points, with the added luxury of having four fixtures in hand. Before the match, Billy Hole secured the Silver Helmet with another 2-0 success over Ken Le Breton, taking both heats in 64.0 seconds flat. Before a gate of 12,000, the Bulldogs then raced to their twenty-fourth league victory of the season, whipping the Saints by 55 points to 26. The result was remarkable given that Fred Tuck was still missing and Mike Beddoe was also a non-starter due to a family bereavement. Ever-reliable Jack Mountford sped to a maximum, with Eric Salmon tallying 11, while Bob Oakley's 7 points were sufficient for him to secure top spot on the Southampton scorechart. Australian ace Ken Le Breton later gained some consolation for his Silver Helmet defeat in the second half of the meeting, thundering to victory in the scratch race final ahead of Billy Hole, Roger Wise and Jimmy Squibb.

On 29 August, Bristol sent a four-man team down to Poole for a mini-match that formed the second half of a meeting that had earlier seen the Pirates defeat Oxford 58-26 in a Third Division fixture. The mini challenge resulted in a 20-16 win for Poole, with the Bristol points coming from Billy Hole (6), Jack Mountford (6), Johnny Hole (2) and Mike Beddoe (2). This was an oddly organised event for, although the Bristol side comprised of the four named riders, Poole actually tracked an eight-man team as follows: Fred Pawson (9), Cyril Quick (7), Ticker James (3), Dave Anderson (1), Dick Howard (0), Charlie Hayden (0), Frank Holcombe (0) and Terry Small (0).

The next track action for the Bulldogs saw them entertain Edinburgh on 3 September, when Fred Tuck at last made his return to the saddle as the push for the Championship gathered momentum. Another hammering ensued as Bristol racked up nine maximum heat advantages on their way to a 60-24 win. Skipper Billy Hole secured yet another four-ride maximum, while Eric Salmon and the returning Tuck raced to 11 points each. Meanwhile, Dick Campbell collected both of the Monarchs' race wins on his way to an 8-point haul. The return match took place at Edinburgh the following evening, with the Scottish side in a determined mood. Dick Campbell and Danny Lee scored a big 5-1 in heat two, but it was immediately countered by a maximum advantage from Jack Mountford and Fred Tuck. The home side showed great resolve though and blocked all of Bristol's attempts to impose themselves, before taking a grip on the match courtesy of a 5-1 from Clem Mitchell and Eddie Lack in heat ten. Three shared races followed, before Edinburgh gained a last-heat 4-2 to secure a deserved 44-40 success. With a thrilling maximum, Mitchell led the Monarchs' charge, while Billy Hole and Tuck each netted 10 points for the Bulldogs.

The meeting at Edinburgh signalled the start of an arduous tour that would take Bristol to four different venues in a hectic five-day period. The next stop was Brough Park, Newcastle on 5 September and the Bulldogs were back on top form as they blasted in a couple of 5-1s in the first four races. The Magpies quickly became disillusioned following that and eventually succumbed to a 56-28 defeat. Newcastle's main man was Derek Close, but his score was restricted to 8 points, while Bristol were brilliantly led by tallies of 11 apiece from Roger Wise and Fred Tuck.

The tour continued with a trip to Ashfield on 6 September and, in a tense tussle, neither side gave an inch, with a 42-42 draw giving a fair reflection of the match. The Bulldogs did hold a slender 2-point lead going into heat fourteen, but Keith Gurtner and Alec Grant claimed a 4-2 over Jack Mountford to gain a share of the league points. Top of the pile for Ashfield was Merv Harding, courtesy of a brilliant unbeaten 12 points, while Billy Hole and Eric Salmon proved to be Bristol's highest scorers with tallies of 8 apiece. As they had done earlier in the season, the Bristol lads stayed in the Scottish city overnight, prior to appearing at Glasgow's famous White City Stadium the following day, as they brought their strenuous tour to a close. Will Lowther and Norman Lindsay gave the Tigers an opening race 4-2, but a heat-three 5-1 from Fred Tuck and Jack Mountford put the Bulldogs in the ascendancy and it was a lead they would increase to finally take the match by 49 points to 35. Junior Bainbridge produced a superb solo effort for Glasgow, thundering to a brilliant maximum, with Bristol being best served by Mountford's 10 points. Although the riders then faced the long journey home, it was made slightly more bearable by the fact that the win had taken Bristol to the top of the Second Division standings.

Ashfield made their second visit of the year to Knowle on 9 September, and they went home on the end of a hiding. As they had done on 13 May, Bristol ran out winners by an identical 63-21 scoreline. The Giants were never in the hunt, with the Bulldogs racking up nine maximum heat advantages on their way to a mammoth victory. Billy Hole cruised to another four-ride maximum, with Eric Salmon, Roger Wise and Mike Beddoe all totalling 10 points. Meanwhile, with a mere 5 points, Ken Le Breton was the top Ashfield performer. Prior to the match, the first leg of the Silver Helmet was staged, which saw Billy Hole take an untroubled 2-0 victory over challenger Phil Clarke. In the first race, Hole really let rip, screaming around the Knowle circuit in 63.4 seconds to equal Salmon's track record.

Billy Hole was back in action the following evening in the second leg of the Silver Helmet at Norwich. Having won the first leg, the Bristol skipper travelled in confident mood, but he was in for a shock when Phil Clarke raced to a 2-1 victory. That necessitated a decider and this was subsequently scheduled to take place at Glasgow on 21 September. Following the excitement of the Silver Helmet, Norwich maintained their top-four position in the league table with a 58-26 success, ironically against Glasgow.

On 16 September, the Bulldogs took to their Knowle circuit for a league encounter *v.* Cradley Heath. The visitors put up a good show and became only the second opposing team to reach 30 points in a league fixture all season. Running out 53-31 victors in the end, Bristol were led once again by the magnificent Billy Hole, who cruised to his eighteenth full-house of the campaign. For the Heathens, Gil Craven and Eric Williams never gave up on their way to 9 points apiece. In his programme notes, George Allen mentioned that the Bulldogs had taken a stand at the Bristol Ideal Home Exhibition. The event, held at Brislington, would see the riders displaying their machines and equipment etc. Fashion parades and a variety of entertainment were also on the agenda, including wonder musician Musaire, mind-reader Rayanne and hypnotist David Wolf. Major Moloney, who ran the show, very kindly presented Bristol Speedway with a number of free passes, which were made available to members of the supporters' club upon production of membership cards at the kiosks.

Billy Hole made the long journey to Glasgow for the deciding leg of the Silver Helmet on 21 September, but he was out of luck on the 430-yard track, losing 2-0 to Phil Clarke. The victor was not so fortunate in the match that followed, however, with Gordon McGregor's maximum leading Glasgow to a 47-36 victory over Clarke's Norwich side.

Somewhat disappointingly, a gate of only 11,000 was in place for the all-important top-of-the-table clash at Knowle on 23 September, when the Bulldogs took on Sheffield. The meeting was soon all but over as Bristol swept to seven successive 5-1s before Tommy Bateman broke the run by splitting Eric Salmon and Dick Bradley in heat eight. A further three maximums followed as the Bulldogs finally racked up a crushing 65-19 success. With his sixth maximum of the year, Jack Mountford headed the Bristol scoring, while Eric Salmon (11), Billy Hole (11) and Roger Wise (10) all made telling contributions to the thrashing. Turning to the opposition, Stan Williams (7) and Tommy Bateman (5) recorded 12 points out of a paltry total of 19 for a Sheffield side that surrendered all hope of taking the Championship. Wembley legends George Wilks and Bill Kitchen raced against the Bulldogs in the second half, with Kitchen taking two wins out of four, while Wilks ran a second place and three lasts.

With the Championship in the bag, the Bulldogs rounded off the month with a trip to Dudley Wood Sports Stadium for a league encounter against Cradley Heath on 30 September. Perhaps it was a reaction to the season's success, but the Bristol boys never really got going in the match, whereas the Heathens appeared to be highly motivated. As such, the meeting eventually resulted in a 54-30 win for the home side, with Gil Craven scoring a superlative maximum, while Alan Hunt recorded 11 points. On a poor night for the Bulldogs, 7 points was the most anyone could manage, with both Billy Hole and Jack Mountford sharing the dubious distinction.

A total of 14,000 spectators poured into Knowle Stadium on 1 October, as First Division New Cross returned for a challenge match on a rare Saturday race night. After their poor performance at Cradley Heath, the Bulldogs set about the meeting as if their lives depended on it. Indeed, a Bristol rider took the flag in eleven of the fourteen heats, with only Ray Moore, Cyril Roger and Bill Longley breaking the monotony for the Rangers as they collected a solitary race win apiece. Billy Hole led his side to a 53-30 success with yet another maximum, while Roger Wise and Eric Salmon provided solid backing on 10 points each. The New Cross scorecard made for shock reading, with every one of their established stars failing to reach double figures, thus: Cyril Roger 8; Bill Longley 7; Ray Moore 6; Eric French 3; Frank Lawrence 3; Jeff Lloyd 2; Bob Baker 1; Bert Roger 0. George Allen used the programme to praise his side for taking the league title, before stating, 'Now of course you will all be asking "what about promotion?" Well, beyond saying that I have made the necessary application to the Control Board, which, I understand will be considered at the end of the season, I do not want to make any premature statement. So, for the time being, we will just have to say that your guess is as good as mine, but believe me when I assure you that we are doing everything possible to bring you First Division league racing at Knowle next year.'

Back in their usual Friday night slot, Bristol entertained Glasgow on 7 October and the 8,000 folk who turned up for the meeting witnessed history being made before their eyes as the Bulldogs roared to an overwhelming victory. Billy Hole and Mike Beddoe set the ball rolling with maximum points in heat one and, incredibly, 5-1 followed 5-1 as

246

Bristol ran riot. After recording ten on the trot, everyone wondered if they could go through the entire card in the same manner. Heat eleven was no problem, with Roger Wise and Eric Salmon thundering home ahead of Norman Lindsay. Then Fred Tuck and Johnny Hole dismissed the challenge of Gordon McGregor in heat twelve. Amid mounting tension, Wise and Dick Bradley held everything together to defeat the demoralised Lindsay in heat thirteen, leaving just one race to go. Could they do it? Billy Hole and Jack Mountford were the men facing the task, with Ken McKinlay and Alf McIntosh standing in their way. There was no denying the Bulldogs a piece of history, however, as Mountford swept to victory, while Hole kept McKinlay at bay, to record the fourteenth 5-1 of the evening, giving an incredible 70-14 result. It is only right and fitting to record the riders' names for posterity, along with the points they scored on that memorable night: Wise 12; Tuck 12; Billy Hole 10; Beddoe 9; Mountford 9; Salmon 8; Bradley 5; Johnny Hole 5. On what was a truly dreadful evening for the Tigers, Jack Hodgson and Lindsay each recorded four third places to head a dismal scorechart. Following the excitement of the huge win over Glasgow, Cyril Brine and Mike Erskine appeared in a series of challenge races against the Bristol lads. Each took four rides, but neither managed a single victory, Brine running a couple of second-place finishes and two in third position, while Erskine could only manage a third-place finish and three lasts.

The evening after bashing Glasgow, the Bulldogs travelled up to the well-appointed Brandon Stadium for a challenge match *v.* Coventry. Pumped full of confidence, Bristol raced to a resounding 60-23 success, with Dick Bradley joining Billy Hole on maximum points. That was the skipper's twentieth maximum of the season in all competitive team matches, but for Bradley it was a wonderful achievement, being his first-ever unbeaten return. Backing up the top-scoring duo, Roger Wise also hit double figures with 10 points. Meanwhile, for the beleaguered Bees, Bob Fletcher was the leading scorer on 7 points.

The Second Division Champions then made the trip to Walthamstow on 10 October and, having previously lost at the Chingford Road venue on 1 August, they were eager to make amends. After opening with a 5-1 from brothers Billy and Johnny Hole, Bristol never looked back and oozed class as they strode to a 49-35 win. Roger Wise showed exceptional form, blasting from the start in each of his four rides to record a fine maximum. In the face of another wonderful display from the

Bulldogs, Harry Edwards fared best for the Wolves, notching a 9-point tally.

At Knowle on 14 October, Norwich were the next victims as the Bulldogs went on another points spree. Continuing where they had left off the previous week against Glasgow, 5-1 followed 5-1, with Bristol totting up a 65-13 lead after heat thirteen. Could they win 70-14 again? Well, you would have thought so. However, although Jack Mountford got away from the gate, teammate Fred Tuck was pushed wide on the first turn by Jack Freeman and Phil Clarke, and was unable to recover the lost ground. So, Bristol had to settle for thirteen 5-1s and a 3-3, giving a result of 68-16. To the fore on the score grid, Mountford recorded maximum points and it was great that battling Mike Beddoe joined him on the 12-point mark, while Billy Hole weighed in with 11. For the Stars, Paddy Mills and Bob Leverenz topped the scoring, each with just 4 points. Incidentally, the second-place finish for Freeman in the final heat gave him his only 2 points of the night! Aub Lawson and Malcolm Craven added plenty of interest to the second half, taking on the Bulldogs in four challenge races. Lawson rode brilliantly, collecting three wins and a third, while Craven didn't fare quite so well with four last places. In the race-day programme, apart from raving about the annihilation of Glasgow, George Allen also mentioned the number of requests that Bob Chapple, in his guise as disc jockey, had received over the course of the season. Amazingly, there had been 15,712 postcards and letters up to and including 7 October, and Mr Chapple had managed to play 4,215 tunes. Requests had come in from all over the world, including such far-flung places as Japan, Canada, India and America, and if the record existed, the music maestro would somehow obtain a copy and play it with the appropriate message. For the following week's meeting v. Coventry, he planned to run a 'cavalcade of turntable', when he would be playing all the top tunes of the season.

The Bulldogs appeared at Third Division Halifax in a challenge match on 19 October, when an attendance of 10,000 saw the visitors struggle to adapt to the steeply banked 402-yard sweeping circuit – so much so in fact that they went down to a 54-29 defeat. Arthur Forrest ripped to a maximum for the Dukes, while Billy Hole gathered 8 points to head the Bulldogs' scoring.

Bristol completed their home league programme on 21 October with a rain-affected match against Coventry. Prior to the meeting, the Duke of

Beaufort presented the Kemsley Cup, along with a cheque for £400 and individual medals, to the Bulldogs in recognition of their Championship success. Despite the presentation, the wet conditions understandably dampened the enthusiasm of the supporters, with only 7,000 in attendance as a result. Although Bristol had little difficulty in constructing a 52-29 success, it was the Bees who possessed the undoubted star in Bob Fletcher. The visiting number one showed no fear as he skated through the water to record a brilliant 12-point maximum. Mike Beddoe led the Bulldogs to victory with 11 points and had to be satisfied with second place when he met the flying Fletcher in heat five. Two more aces of the track entertained those present in the second half as Jack Parker and Louis Lawson engaged in a series of races against the Bulldogs. After beginning with a second-place finish behind Roger Wise, the legendary Parker took the winning flag in each of his next three races, while Lawson collected a couple of second places along with a third and a fourth.

Before the tapes went up on the final meeting of the year at Knowle, Jack Mountford and Roger Wise journeyed to Oxford and linked with the home side in a challenge match *v.* Walthamstow on 27 October. The home team were further bolstered by the inclusion of Cradley Heath riders Alan Hunt and Gil Craven, but it didn't stop them from going down to a narrow 43-41 defeat. Mountford registered 10 points, with Roger Wise netting just 2, while the rest of the composite side scored thus: Alan Hunt 11; Gil Craven 7; Dennis Gray 5; Bert Croucher 3; Alf Viccary 2; Bill Kemp 1. Meanwhile, for the triumphant Wolves team, Jim Boyd and Harry Edwards topped the points chart with 10 apiece.

The Knowle fixture list was completed the following evening, with an interesting Best Pairs event. Top stars Ray Moore, Louis Lawson, Nobby Stock, Bert Roger, Split Waterman, Ernie Price, Eddie Rigg and Cyril Brine were each paired with a Bristol rider. However, the format for the competition was unique as neither the riders nor the supporters knew who was partnering who. All the riders met over a twenty-heat format, after which the ACU steward opened a sealed envelope and the pair with the highest aggregate score shared the £15 bonus. An 11,000 crowd saw Billy Hole romp to a 15-point maximum and the Bristol captain was later to find that this was sufficient to win the meeting after his total was added to the 5 points of Brine. Full result: B. Hole (15) and Brine (5) 20; Dick Bradley (12) and Stock (6) 18; Mike Beddoe (8) and Moore

(8) 16; Lawson (11) and Chris Boss (4) 15; Jack Mountford (8) and Rigg (6) 14; Roger Wise (9) and Price (5) 14; Waterman (6) and Johnny Hole (4) 10; Roger (7) and Jimmy Grant (2) 9. The final home race of the year was for the Godfrey Novices' Trophy and saw Danny Malone take victory from Ken Wiggins, Bill Hurn and John Waterman in a time of 68.8 seconds.

Bristol's last track action of the season took them back to The Firs Stadium at Norwich for their one remaining league encounter on 29 October. Having been beaten on their previous two visits to the 425-yard raceway, it was no surprise that they again went down, but only by a 6-point margin, 45-39. A gate of 23,000 saw Syd Littlewood and Ted Bravery collect 10 points apiece for the Stars, while Roger Wise led the Bulldogs' scoring with 9.

Briefly reviewing the riders that represented Bristol over the season, skipper Billy Hole was outstanding, remaining ever-present to tot up 550 points from fifty-four offical meetings (forty-four National League and ten National Trophy). Jack Mountford also completed all fifty-four meetings to yield 476.5 points, while Roger Wise had a 100 per cent attendance record too, recording 460 points. Backing the top three was the speedy Eric Salmon, who accrued 424.5 points from fifty meetings. A special mention is also due to Mike Beddoe, who bravely came back from his horrific injuries to post 282 points from fifty-one matches. With the inclusion of challenge matches, the Bulldogs were able to boast three riders who netted in excess of 500 points: Hole (644); Mountford (551.5) and Wise (518).

A total of thirty-three meetings were held at Knowle Stadium during the year, with 388,500 supporters passing through the turnstiles for an average of 11,772. That completed four seasons of racing since 1946, without a single meeting being postponed, and a quite staggering total of 1,329,500 people had attended the 115 meetings staged at Bristol since the Second World War, averaging 11,560. Another interesting statistic regarding the year was that the supporters' club ran nineteen trips during the season, covering nearly 6,000 miles at a cost of £2,170.

After the season's end, it wasn't until 8 December that the *Speedway News* revealed just what everyone had been waiting to hear, stating: 'Bristol have been promoted from the Second Division to the First Division of the National League. The Speedway Control Board have pointed out to Mr G.A. Allen, Bristol managing director, that the board, which has no riders now for allocation, will not strengthen his team. If Bristol next season find that they need new riders, then they themselves must get them. Mr Allen gave his assurance that Bristol intended to stand on their own feet.'

1949 STATISTICS

(Bristol's score shown first unless otherwise stated)

NATIONAL LEAGUE SECOND DIVISION

Opponents	Home	Away
Ashfield	W63-21	W46-38
	W63-21	D42-42
Coventry	W67.5-16.5	W48-35
	W52-29	W46-38
Cradley Heath	W62-22	W50-34
	W53-31	L30-54
Edinburgh	W68-16	W44-40
	W60-24	L40-44
Fleetwood	W61-22	L38-46
	W67-17	W44-39
Glasgow	W62-22	W57-27
	W70-14	W49-35
Newcastle	W60-24	W55-29
	W60-24	W56-28
Norwich	W66-18	L32-52
	W68-16	L39-45
Sheffield	W55-29	L35-49
	W65-19	L28-56
Southampton	W56-27	L39-45
	W55-26	W42-41
Walthamstow	W60-24	L37-46
	W51-33	W49-35

MATCH AVERAGES

Rider	Matches	Points	Average
Billy Hole	44	429	9.75
Jack Mountford	44	382.5	8.69

Eric Salmon	40	329.5	8.24
Roger Wise	44	359	8.16
Fred Tuck	33	247.5	7.50
Mike Beddoe	41	232	5.66
Johnny Hole	43	149	3.47
Dick Bradley	44	129	2.93
Chris Boss	13	26	2.00
Graham Hole	5	7	1.40
Ginger Nicholls	1	0	0.00

NATIONAL LEAGUE SECOND DIVISION TABLE

Team	Matches	Won	Drawn	Lost	For	Against	Pts
Bristol	44	34	1	9	2,290.5	1,393.5	69
Sheffield	44	29	1	14	2,015.5	1,667.5	59
Norwich	44	27	0	17	2,031	1,649	54
Cradley Heath	44	25	0	19	1,908.5	1,772.5	50
Edinburgh	44	24	0	20	1,804	1,877	48
Walthamstow	44	21	3	20	1,841.5	1,833.5	45
Southampton	44	21	3	20	1,741.5	1,924.5	45
Glasgow	44	20	0	24	1,757.5	1,924.5	40
Fleetwood	44	18	1	25	1,765	1,916	37
Newcastle	44	17	1	26	1,735	1,949	35
Ashfield	44	12	1	31	1,645	2,034	25
Coventry	44	10	1	33	1,540	2,134	21

DAILY MAIL NATIONAL TROPHY

Opponents	Home	Away	Aggregate
Sheffield	W73-35	W55-53	W128-88
Coventry	W80-28	W66-42	W146-70
Fleetwood	W73-35	W60-46	W133-81
Norwich	W79-29	L32-76	W111-105
New Cross	L47-60	L53-55	L100-115

MATCH AVERAGES

Rider	Matches	Points	Average
Billy Hole	10	121	12.10
Roger Wise	10	101	10.10

1949

Eric Salmon	10	95	9.50
Jack Mountford	10	94	9.40
Fred Tuck	6	51	8.50
Dick Bradley	10	53	5.30
Mike Beddoe	10	50	5.00
Johnny Hole	10	50	5.00
Chris Boss	3	3	1.00
Graham Hole	1	0	0.00

CHALLENGE

Opponents	Home	Away
Belle Vue	L45-50	L18-66
Birmingham	W68-39	–
Coventry	–	W60-23
Devon	–	W56-28
Halifax	–	L29-54
Harringay	W45-39	–
New Cross	W53-30	–
Southampton	–	W47-36
Walthamstow	–	L41-43

MATCH AVERAGES

Rider	Matches	Points	Average
Billy Hole	9	94	10.44
Jack Mountford	9	75	8.33
Fred Tuck	6	48	8.00
Eric Salmon	7	50	7.14
Roger Wise	9	58	6.44
Chris Boss	2	7	3.50
Dick Bradley	8	27	3.38
Johnny Hole	7	22	3.14
Mike Beddoe	8	25	3.13
Phil Clarke	1	2	2.00
Graham Hole	1	0	0.00
Ginger Nicholls	1	0	0.00

SPEEDWAY IN BRISTOL 1928-1949

MINI-MATCHES

Opponents	Home	Away
Exeter	–	(1) W14-4
Exeter	–	(2) L10-14
Halifax	W22-8	–
Hanley	L12-17	–
Plymouth	W16-14	–
Poole	W19-10	L16-20

MATCH AVERAGES

Rider	Matches	Points	Average
Billy Hole	2	14	7.00
Jack Mountford	3	17	5.67
Dick Bradley	4	21	5.25
Mike Beddoe	2	10	5.00
Eric Salmon	1	5	5.00
Johnny Hole	5	23	4.60
Ginger Nicholls	2	8	4.00
Chris Boss	2	5	2.50
Graham Hole	3	6	2.00

Other Speedway titles published by Tempus

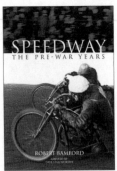

Speedway The Pre-War Years
ROBERT BAMFORD

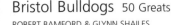

Following its arrival on these shores in 1928, speedway was an almost instant success. Great personalities came to the fore, including Sprouts Elder, Lionel Van Praag, Vic Duggan and Max Grosskreutz, capturing the hearts of the public. Furnished with photographs, programme covers and statistics, this evocative book will call to mind a bygone age of racing. It is the definitive history of the shale sport in its heyday.

0 7524 2749 0

Bristol Bulldogs 50 Greats
ROBERT BAMFORD & GLYNN SHAILES

Although they only rode as a team throughout eighteen seasons, Bristol Bulldogs enjoyed some of the best attendances in the country and some truly fantastic riders sported their famous colours. This fascinating publication looks at fifty such men, some world class like Cordy Milne and Phil Crump, some honest-to-goodness loyal club men like Billy Hole and Eric Salmon. Each of the chosen fifty has been afforded a detailed profile, along with relevant statistics and photographs.

0 7524 2865 9

Speedway's Classic Meetings
NORMAN JACOBS & CHRIS BROADBENT

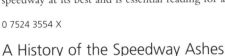

In this book, well-known speedway authors Norman Jacobs and Chris Broadbent focus on twenty of the meetings that have become part of the sport's folklore, looking in detail at what happened and the reasons why they are regarded as classics. Featuring the first ever meeting at High Beech, West Ham's victory over Wimbledon in the 1965 Knock-Out Cup, the 2004 World Cup and many others, this book celebrates the sheer excitement of speedway at its best and is essential reading for all fans of the sport.

0 7524 3554 X

A History of the Speedway Ashes
PETER FOSTER

In 1930 the first official Test series between England and Australia was staged. It was hugely successful and these 'Ashes' series quickly became a regular feature of the speedway calendar. Tests were suspended between 1939 and 1947, and Australia were replaced by an Australasian side in the 1950s after the original promoters pulled the plug, but this hugely popular event kept coming back. In this superb illustrated history, author Peter Foster recalls the glory days of the speedway ashes.

0 7524 3468 3

If you are interested in purchasing other books published by Tempus, or in case you have difficulty finding any Tempus books in your local bookshop, you can also place orders directly through our website

www.tempus-publishing.com